Diary of a Redneck Vampire

Diary of a Redneck Vampire

✦

The True Story of a Rock and Roll Girl in a Boy's World

Flo

iUniverse, Inc.

New York Lincoln Shanghai

Diary of a Redneck Vampire
The True Story of a Rock and Roll Girl in a Boy's World

iUniverse, Inc.

For information address:
iUniverse, Inc.
2021 Pine Lake Road, Suite 100
Lincoln, NE 68512
www.iuniverse.com

The story you are about to read is based on actual events. The names of people and events have been changed to protect the innocent.

ISBN: 0-595-29554-1

Printed in the United States of America

This book is dedicated to the unique breed of humans who not only dare to dream, but dare to wake up…

Contents

The author would like to thank: God (who I do not understand), Joanna Graves, the woman in Chicago who fed the band that Thanksgiving, Chris Fitzgerald-for being my muse, Amy Lee-you sang-I typed, Bonnie-for listening and not bitching about my chain smoking, the hookers-for loving me-rock star or not, Elizabeth Blocker Carlin for her legal advice, Dr. Smith, Mr. Wilson, Jimmy K., and all yawl peeps, my sisters in Avalon for encouragement, and **most** importantly, *my boys*. *"Am I the only one who remembers that summer?"*

Back cover photo of Flo is courtesy of Rick Dacus. Front cover photo insert of *The Redneck Vampires* also by Rick Dacus. Clockwise from the left is Jesse, Max, Ian, Ruger, and Flo.

Prologue

Until the summer of 2003, the story you are about to read existed only in memory and fourteen shitty notebooks bought at gas stations on various stretches of interstate highway. It is on such highways that much of what falls on these pages was originally written. Years after these events, the notebooks had found their home in a backpack, and have slept rather unsoundly in the tops of closets over the years. Much like the cat that curls up on the book you are trying to read, the journals demanded my attention and were never far from my mind. On a fall day several years ago, I took the dusty backpack to a park and began thumbing through the entries. I laughed and cried and laughed some more. It seemed they had a life of their own and had survived for some certain purpose. I began toying with the idea of publishing them. Years later, in the spring of 2003 while backpacking alone in Europe, I had dinner with three women I met in a youth hostel. Over the course of our meal, we spoke of our personal dreams. They asked me what my dream job would be. My response to them was "I have already done it." Curious, they inquired what I meant, and I began telling them the tales you are about to read. I left Europe with the conviction and determination to write this book—yet, in a way, the book had already been written. My job was just to transfer it to type.

My career in music started with a hideous mess of pressboard; a drum kit, courtesy of Sears catalog and my mothers desire to end my incessant whining for one. I was fifteen, with big rock-star dreams. The middle child of a middle class family, I went to suburban schools where all the other kids were rich—rich *and* mean, and I developed a serious contempt for society. Lost somewhere between my working parents, mean rich kids, and an even meaner older brother, I committed myself to becoming something that could simultaneously piss everybody off and make me important at the same time. Fueled with determination and an AC/DC tape, I taught myself how to play the drums. No one took me seriously. After graduating, I went to cosmetology school by day and played in various garage bands by night. I found a boyfriend that was just as mean as my brother, lost sight of my priorities, and quit playing. It is a miracle I escaped his wrath. Upon leaving him, I started practicing again. I found a band and re-dedicated myself to the dream. By now, the goal was in my blood and nothing would ever

1

again tear me away. This was early 1993. It was not long after this that my life would take an exciting turn that no one could have predicted. Amazingly, I documented most of it in what now lies in your hands.

The journal begins shortly after I auditioned for the alternative metal band *The Redneck Vampires* in late 1993. I was the only girl in the band. Having a female on drums was quite unusual for the metal music scene, especially in the early nineties. At the time of the first entry, I had just moved from my home in Memphis TN, to be with the band in Jackson TN, a town of about 100,000, seventy miles east of Memphis.

I had seen The Redneck Vampires perform, but knew *none* of them personally, before my audition. After being accepted into the band, I suddenly found myself in a new town, with a new job, and living with two of my band members-guys I barely knew. My whole world had just changed, and I took to writing as a means of dealing with it. To stay integral to the diary format in which the journal was written, I have not altered its form. The entries are not made on a daily basis, however many of them summarize events that were not logged at the time of their occurrence. In some cases there are several entries made in the same day. The word "later" appears next to the date in these cases. The book is very much *a diary*. My heart and soul are poured across these pages. It is full of my *very* personal thoughts and experiences. In no way do I wish to criticize, humiliate, embarrass, or otherwise condemn any person or persons as a result of publishing this book. The names of all people, bands, and band associates have been changed out of respect to all people involved.

The dairy logs the band's climb up the ladder of success in the music industry. The bulk of the story occurs while we are on the road, where the boys gave me the nickname "Flo". In late 1994, the band started touring on a consistent basis. The endless trail of asphalt made me think, and those thoughts are in the journal. At times, I am writing from the stream of my consciousness, and at other times, I am simply documenting events. The story is not always easy to follow, but it is always the truth. The story deserves to be told as it is.

Successful musicians are glorified; worshipped, in a way, by society. Not enough has been shared, however, of the determination, the countless risks, and the blind fury required of a human being to achieve this goal. When the muse of music enters a life, she never leaves. You are bound to her and she to you. Music propels you forward, becoming not just what you *do*, but what you *are*. Musicians reach a place where the *music drives them*; they are no longer driven by it. Somewhere on the narrow path, musicians lose their ability to *choose*.

It is easy to forget, in blind pursuit of the goal, that in real life, there is not always a handsome prince, and you don't always live happily ever after. It's true what they say…about life not being about the destination…but about the *journey*. This is one of many lessons I learn in the three years of my life that you are about to read. As the pages turn, it is very apparent that the band means *everything* to me, and I am willing to risk it **all** to make it happen.

Flo, 2003

"To have a soul, is to have a story"

—*David Patterson*

"See you all from time to time
Isn't it so strange
how far away we all are now
Am I the only one who remembers that summer…
Oh, I remember
Everyday each time the place was saved
the music that we made
The wind has carried all of that away…"

—Lane Staley, Mike Mc Cready 1994

1

It's Set in Stone

12.20.93

All around the stage was an impenetrable wall of bodies…clad in mostly black…bouncing in unison to the crushing wail of guitar and the thunderous drums. About halfway through the first song, I felt something hit me, hard, on my left side. I smelled the beer before I felt it seep into my clothes. It was New Years Eve 1993, and we were headlining a shitty club in Jackson TN. It was my first gig ever with them, and the packed club was dark except for the flashes from the hot lights behind my head. When the lights flashed on, I searched for clues, trying to figure out how I had been impaled with a flying beer. I was *beating the shit* out of my drums, trying to prove myself; fearing at any moment my sticks would slide out of my hands or I would fall off my drum throne and be the laughing stock of the place. The new drummer…the *girl* drummer who couldn't cut it, they would say. A flash of light. Bouncing bodies…illumined…and a cup flying through the air. My eyes followed its descent as it crashed into my snare drum and released its alcoholic contents in a mighty deluge. I kept playing. Beer was now *all over me*. Beer was *all over my kit*. I tried to keep my composure, as this was the most important gig of my career, yet before I made it to the second chorus, *another* one struck me, this time from the front of the crowd, the crumbled plastic slicing into my face as it hit. I felt a sick lump form in my throat as I realized what was happening. More cups. More beer. The raged fans were throwing their *beer* at me. They *hated* me. Through my sweaty, beer-soaked hair, I could see the disgust…the *outrage* in their faces. The next thing I knew, the stage-light tiers came crashing down…the guitars went quiet as the raging crowd had pulled the plug…my band members surrounded me and I fell off my throne to the ground. They began screaming at me to get the fuck up…get the fuck up…*get the fuck up*. The next thing I knew, I heard my alarm clock buzzing, and in my sleepy vision, I could see a face leaning over me saying, "Get the fuck up."

It's no wonder I keep having that fucking dream. Maybe its pot that makes me so paranoid. New Years Eve is getting closer and I am **so** fucking nervous. I just feel **so** damn unprepared. It's our *first* show—their 'back from the dead' gig after losing their old drummer and my *initiation* in front of their whole fucking crowd. My whole fucking future-hell, the *bands* future rides on this show. I've had that dream at least *three* fucking times in the past week. I think the look in my eyes scared the shit out of Ruger when he woke me up this morning. It just seemed so damn *real*. I put my hand to my forehead where the cup hit me in the dream and then I felt my hair to see if it was wet! It freaks me out when dreams are that real. If we could fucking rehearse then maybe I wouldn't have so much to worry about. I practiced by myself yesterday for the first time since I've been in the band…and that's been…two months? I have *never* gone that long without practicing before. I guess the move, getting a job, renting the house, and Max and Ruger moving in has thrown everything off schedule. The living situation kicks ass so far. This would be a lot scarier if Justine had not come with me. Since her boyfriend Jody is on the road with his band, Bone Squad, she didn't have any-thing else to do. Not everyone who takes a risk gets to have their best friend with them. I am really grateful for that, although I feel like I am cheating a little bit. God, I haven't written in a journal in a long ass time. It feels good just to chill on this old couch and collect my thoughts. I can't fucking *believe* I did this. How did **I** get **here**?

I remember seeing Redneck Vampires play at 616 probably a year and a half ago. I escaped from the evil boyfriend for a night and my little sister Savannah and I had gotten high and decided to go to the club. She had gotten married to this asshole she met through the personals. After being married for three weeks, he threw a box of cookies at her. She left him immediately. I guess she learned from me and Sam that she better get out of that shit fast. Mom is keeping it a secret from the family. Anyway, she took the husband's ATM card, withdrew all his money, and bought us a sack. I had no idea who would be playin. It was some sort of battle of the bands or some shit where a lot of bands were doing like three songs each. When Redneck Vampires took the stage, I was blown away. That sounds so cliché, but it's true. The singer was *amazing*, and he and the bass player, who stole the show, did this cool harmony stuff unlike anything I had ever heard. There was something **very** powerful about them. I knew when I saw them that night they were going somewhere, I just had no idea it was going to be with me.

A few weeks later, I drug the asshole boyfriend to Jackson, TN to see the Vampires. I could not *believe* how packed the club was. This band was more like a *movement*—they had **so** many dedicated friends. Everyone in there seemed to know everyone else. I felt this strange feeling of familiarity in the faces of the people there…I knew it was ridiculous…but I still felt it. We didn't stay long. I was enjoying it too much.

A year and a break up later I had started playin again. After practicing with my band one night, I went out with Justine and Jody. As we were leaving a club, I saw some guys that looked familiar walking down the street. As we got closer, I saw their leather jackets—they all had the same patches on them…and then I saw their faces…just for a moment…but it was long enough. It was them, The Redneck Vampires. I asked Jody what had happened to them. He told me they had lost their drummer six months ago and they were looking for a new one. My body began to shake. My heart began thundering the unfamiliar chorus of destiny. I have never felt anything like it. I saw my future like the headlights of an oncoming car on a country road at midnight…it is rare to have a moment where you absolutely, without question, know *exactly* the next course to take…I was convinced. Their new drummer was me.

My friend Tim had their number and I called and spoke to the bass player people called "Ruger". I thought that was the weirdest name. I was like "Rooger"? And Tim was like, "Yeah, you know, like the gun. People call him that cuz he fired his gun out of a car window showin' off one night…and the bullet flew into an old folks home and like almost killed this old lady." I didn't quite know what to think about that. Anyway, I asked him if they were lookin' for a drummer. He said yes. Then I asked him if they would have a problem jammin' with a chick. He said they didn't discriminate…like I was applying for a job at some company…anyway, I got his address and mailed them a tape of me playin'. They called a few days later and said I should come jam and we set up an audition. I snuck into my own bands practice room everyday for a week and played along to their tape. I listened to it *constantly*. While I played I thought about the time I saw them play live. It was Ruger that had impressed me the most. His stage presence was so impressive—he was a natural. For an entire week, their tape was all I listened to so I could memorize the songs. I snuck into the band room the day I was to go audition and packed up my gear. I bought a quarter ounce from the guy next-door, stashed half of it in my panties for the trip, and I was off in my faithful truck to Jackson. The drive was nerve racking. I will *never* forget the way that felt. I could almost feel the rest of my life lying before me…alongside every mile marker…engraved in the asphalt…written in codes in the license plates of the cars in front of me. I listened to that damn tape over and over…the hour drive felt like it took twenty minutes.

I can remember the rest like a video I have watched over and over. Max met me at a gas station off the highway inside town. I remembered him as being the perfect heavy metal band singer dude, with the great hair and a great smile. I followed him to their place and I met Ruger, who was just **scary**. He made some phone calls and we headed out for the practice space, which was a room in a storage facility. I had to make myself a trail through beer cans to get to where their old drummers gear was. I nervously put my kit together and waited on them to tune up. Erik, the rhythm guitarist, and Ian, lead, showed up about fifteen minutes later. I watched them all intently as they set up their stuff. Big, tattooed, burly grunge dudes. They joked among themselves and I felt like a total outsider. I wondered if they had **planned** to intimidate me! Like they had all talked before hand and said, "Let's scare the fucking *shit* out of her". I felt like such an amateur. I felt like a wannabe. I decided this was all a *huge* mistake. I kept my eyes on my snare so they wouldn't think I was a freak for staring at them, and on my snare head, I had written out the time changes of their songs…it was my cheat sheet. I thought about how excited I had been when I heard their demo for the first time…And how *desperately* I wanted this…and how brave I felt for traveling all this way to jam with a band of complete strangers…and how I had to at least try. I decided I was going to rock their fuckin' world. They practically ignored me as they set up. Ian was the dorky one—he seemed real nice and kind of aloof and goofy. Erik was the silent type…with long, jet black hair and piercing eyes. Ruger seemed to be the control freak of the band with his tattoos and long blond hair, yet he somehow reminded me of the Cowardly Lion on the Wizard of Oz. "What song do you want to play first?" Max asked me. He was the only one of them who had really even spoken to me at this point. I picked one, counted off, and we started playin'. I just started doing it. It wasn't the tape! It was **me**—*me* with **this** band. I know it's not really even been two months since we've been together, but from that first moment, I *felt* something with them. I don't know if it's just because I'd never played with such a great band…if it was created all in my head…if it was the powerful songs…Ruger's bass sound…or what. I guess it's the "chemistry" you hear about from time to time…I guess I've actually experienced it now. After we jammed about five songs,…we took a break. I sat on the old couch next to Ian and Max. Ruger started pacing. We started joking around and shit and the next thing I remember was Ruger saying something about how cool it would be to have a girl on drums…and they all started talking about how wild and unusual it would be…and how it was just what they needed. At that point, they were talking like I was in, but they hadn't **said** it. They were talking about how much they all missed playin', and how cool it would be to come back…to life. So, I just blurted it out. "Am I in or what?" I said. They each looked at each other and they were like fuck yeah, man…aw *fuck* yeah…it's set in stone…

12.21.93

We just got the news that Erik is "resigning" from the band. He has kids and a wife and they just had their second child about three weeks ago. I'm sure he is getting a lot of shit from his family about being a 'rock star'. I hope he sticks out through the 31st show. We have too much going for this band to have to slow down to the crawl of auditions and teaching someone the shit. I don't know what we are gonna do. It's shit like this I was hoping to get away from. Unorganized—uncommitted shit. Hell, I just quit the job I'd had for two years, packed up all my shit, and moved up here. I feel closer to Ian, Ruger, and Max on a personal level, but only cause Erik is not around much at all. I think I saw this coming. Luckily, we are continuing to practice without Erik so we don't sound like shit without him. Oh, get *this*…Ruger told me that Geoff, one of his best friends who is always hangin' around, (who I have a serious crush on) told every member of the band when he heard about the new drummer bein' a chick, that he was gonna fuck me. He had not even *met* me! He just told them that to piss them off! However, I do love the way he stares at me across the room. We've gotten to be buds…smokin out together every night…playin' dice and cards…he's funny and he has been friends with the guys for years. He gives me what he calls "the real story". I don't know the guys well enough to read them yet, but Geoff does so he fills me in. That song "Wicked Garden" reminds me of him…I play it when we hang out and I'm sure he thinks nothing of it. I love my room here. We are so lucky to have this big ass house. It practically has a parking lot in the front yard. My room is the original living room to the house. It doesn't look like one now! I painted it purple and hung up posters and put up my altar and all my cool shit. It's big enough for my grandma's old full size couch, two desks, and a twin mattress on the floor. We smoke pot and hang out in here more than any other room in the house. It's great to have Justine here with me. She is such a great friend. It was so fuckin' cool of her to move here. Jody was on the road with his band…she was lonely…we were hangin out a lot…then I was movin…so I asked her if she wanted to move with me. I couldn't believe she did! I am SO glad! I'd lose it without her. She got a job at a bar as a waitress…my job is going good, even though it is one of those slave-driver salons. It's nothing like the marble floors and champagne brunches at the salon I was in at home. But that's the thing about bein' a hairstylist…you can get a job anywhere. Even if you play in a band and need a lot of weekends off! We are supposed to take band pictures tonight at 6:00pm for the article in the paper due to print for next Monday. Some dude from Polygram called last week and wants us to go in the studio in Memphis in January. We've got Dallas, TX booked with Bone Squad on the 25th of February and some shows lined up for Memphis in January, but it's not definite yet. I am SO excited. I've never had things move so fast in a band before. Especially after just jumping in. *I cannot believe this is happening.*

12.22.93

We took pics for the newspaper article about seven the other night. Then we fucked off practice and caught a buzz. Jody and the rest of the guys in Bone Squad were in town hangin' out. We played cards and got fucked up smoking bowl after bowl. Max talked to Erik, who wasn't here for the shoot, and he said he's pretty much out for good. *Damn.* He said he'd call tomorrow about New Years Eve and shit. We can't agree on a future guitarist situation. It's not surprising, though, that we can't agree. Ruger wants to try being four piece. Ian and Max want to try to work someone else in. I dunno where I stand. Both arguments make sense.

Hope called from Los Angeles. She and I met in high school. We put a shitty band together over Christmas break my senior year. I was seventeen and she was fourteen. We played in numerous bands together after that…cover bands, original bands…we were best friends and blood sisters. We were determined to get signed, and do it together. At seventeen, she moved to Los Angeles to join a signed band. It pissed me off the way she did it…we were in a band together and she snuck behind my back to the audition. It was a year before I would speak to her again. She was jealous of the time I spent with my asshole boyfriend Sam, and she thought I wasn't serious about music anymore. I was serious, I was just up his ass and he was jealous as hell of any musical success anyone had, especially me. The thing with Hope fucked me real bad, though. I couldn't play after that. I'd never played with any other bass player. The sight of my drums made me cry. I hid out with Sam and avoided the music scene altogether. Of course, I was jealous that she was signed…but what hurt me so bad was the WAY she went about it. I also was hurt cuz I wanted us to get signed together. Hope came home for Thanksgiving one year and called me and we patched things up. I woke up from my miserable sleep and joined a band again, during which time Sam cheated on me and I found the strength to leave his dumb ass. He slammed me up against my truck one night at Stage Stop and one of my friends saw him. It wasn't until she SAW him doing it that I even took that shit seriously. I mean we fought…we *physically* fought…all the time…but it was my dirty little secret until then. Man. If I hadn't left him, I would *not* be here. I'd be like fat and pregnant and barefoot with three screaming kids and a sink full of dirty dishes with an absent father. I can just see it. I am so grateful that I am here. Hope is, too! She knew he was bad news from the very beginning. She demands tapes and pics and shit. Maybe she could hook us up with her Los Angeles connections. She said she sent me a cool X-mas present.

12.22.93

Geoff came by and I read Tarot for him. I've had that deck of Tarot since I was fifteen. Every time I smell a new waterbed or hear the Doors, I think of my cards. I bought them for myself for X-mas that year. I got a new waterbed and a Doors tape for X-mas too, so I jammed the Doors, while sittin on my new waterbed, playin' with my tarot deck. I feel pretty good about the readings. If I could just learn to trust what comes to mind when I read and have the guts to say out loud what I am thinking…a buzz really helps. I'm a lot more relaxed. A whole lot of weird shit happened to me that year. I guess that was when I realized that I was 'pagan'. At first, it was just a way to scare Mom and Dad and the preppy girls in high school, but it has kind of grown on me. Mom used to *freak* on my Tarot. I kept them, I still do, under my pillow. She used to come in my room and freak on them. She thinks I worship the devil. Sigh.

Well, its "Pool night" tonight, so no practice. It seems like we always have some excuse. I stayed stoned all day today. It was cool. I did the first edition of the Redneck Vampires newsletter and got it completed and mailed out. Jody was here and Ruger and all of us played dice and got stoned. No one has heard from Erik. I suppose he won't be doin' the show. That *really* sucks. We need him. We sound so much better with him. Geoff brought me some old Redneck Vampires flyers with great artwork on them. He is so cool. I'm diggin' him a lot, but I don't want the guys to know. It's like my big secret. I don't want to be all fallin' for their friends and shit. Geoff *seems* to dig me…or that's the way he makes me feel. But the fact that he said to the guys **before** he even met me that he was gonna fuck me makes me wonder if this is just all part of the "plan"…His plan to fuck the girl drummer…just like he said he would do. Sigh. I really want to believe he digs me the way I dig him—but I can't get that fear out of my head. The "fear" that he is just using me to prove a point or make a deep notch in his bedpost. The "fear" of looking like an ass for falling for him, when he was just trying to get in my panties.

We have all been playin' with my Ouija board tryin to contact the spirits in the graveyard on our fuckin property. Funny how the landlord forgot to mention it when we first looked at the place. Justine spotted it as we were pulling into the driveway one night. We couldn't believe it. One of the headstones is like six feet high. I know it sounds crazy but we really didn't even see it. Its all-overgrown and nasty dead leaves are piled up like three feet thick. It's got a small iron fence around it that is barely detectable through the brush. The oldest person buried there was born in the late 1700's! There are three smaller graves, and then six tiny ones…babies, we think. Justine and I are planning to go to the library and do some genealogical research on the site. Playin' on the Ouija has become a sort of nightly ritual for us…we get stoned and try to contact our dead neighbors. Christmas is this weekend. I haven't bought shit! Max is sick. It sucks. I hope he knocks it before our first show. Maybe he should hold off on practice, seeing how it is twenty-five degrees outside and feels five degrees below that in our outdoor practice room. Someday, this will all pay off.

12.26.93

Hangin with Geoff. Been high all day. Maybe he just hangs out with me because I have buds. Oh, who the hell cares. I'd like to say you can't fake looking at a person the way he looks at me…I guess I just don't want to get too far up his ass—only to find out it was all about pissing off the boys and scoring some free buds.

12.27.93

This SUCKS. My car is going to cost $571.43 to get fixed. The head gasket is blown. If it's cracked, it will cost me $300 more. Where am I gonna get this money? Maybe I still have credit with the company that loaned me the money for equipment a while back. I'm sick as hell with the flu, and I did get some cash for X-mas but now I have to put it towards the truck. That fucking *sucks*. I *cannot* get ahead. The paper dicked us on our article…it's just *not* there! The New Years Eve show is Friday. I wonder how we will sound. I hope the band aspect of my life doesn't fuck up next. That would ice the cake.

Max is on the phone with Erik. I hope he is planning to play New Years Eve. I'm really nervous about this show. I hope I kick ass and I don't let them down. I'm SO not used to performing live—especially not without much practice. It blows me away how little this band practices. There is always *some* excuse—some reason to not rehearse. Fine with me—until it's time to play live and I am totally uncomfortable with myself. They have such a huge following. God, I hope their crowd accepts me. I talked to Hope. She sent me a bitchin' candlestick for X-mas.

12.29.93

Went to Memphis yesterday. Hung with Savannah all day and she spent the night with me here. I really miss my little sister. I didn't think I would. I am proud of her for leaving her dickhead husband. They are getting a divorce. Unfuckingbelievable. I got my truck back! It was $571.43 to get it fixed. Mother fucker. We are SO booked. The 1st, 4th, 8th, 21st, 28th and we are goin' in the studio the 15th and 16th of January. Hell Yeah! My head is spinning…things are happening so fast. We will be *really* ready for the Crossroads showcase in April. Crossroads is a three-day weekend/tax write off for A&R reps of record labels, but sometimes they go to see some bands. We practiced last night during the freeze warning. Practice is painful for everyone because of the stinging cold. If we could practice indoors we would get *so* much more done. At least what I do is physical and I move around a little bit…so after about thirty minutes into the set, it's not so bad...but I can't imagine being a guitar player when it's that fucking cold. The strings must feel like icy razors slicing into numb fingertips. Last night Erik was wearin' this *crazy ass* fluorescent orange snowsuit and he jumped up and down a lot tryin to warm up, oh yeah...he's doin the show! We are gonna practice tonight and hopefully I can get down there on my own tomorrow. I am gonna *freak* if we don't practice enough before the show. This is all *so* new. I want to feel confident with the material and right now, I don't. I need to get in touch with the dope man. Or hell, maybe I should chill out a little bit. I've been feelin' kinda nauseated lately. The return of this band rides on my shoulders alone, and I can feel it in every breath I take. I haven't had the nightmare since we have been practicing, which is good, but I'm still scared to death.

1.3.94

The hot lights were flashing from behind my head, and I braced myself during the first song, waiting to be impaled by flying alcoholic beverages...but that never happened. As a matter of fact, New Years Eve was an incredible success! I fucked up a lot here and there, but overall we fucking *smoked*. The band told me over and over that they had super dedicated fans and the place would be packed, and I remembered their following from years ago, but I secretly doubted the gig was gonna have a good turn out. I could not have been more wrong. The place was **packed**—you could barely move. I swear there were over five hundred people in that shitty little club. We were *way* over the fire marshals limit of 300. Sweaty bodies were crammed next to each other...drunk girls and rednecks and punk teenagers...I met *so* many fucking people. Apparently, they have a huge following in the small towns around here, which is where they got Adam and Wayne, their kick ass roadies who are *so* fucking cool to me. All night I was treated like *royalty*. I'm serious. It was fucking wild. Max and I hung out at the house till the first band was on stage. He came in my room and sat down on my bed and grinned at me. He knew I was freakin' out. I was *extremely* stressed. It wasn't the average gig. It was my opportunity to establish myself—*and* the Redneck Vampire's rise from the dead. I was carrying the return of this band on my own shoulders and I knew I could NOT make mistakes. I also *knew* I had not had enough practice and it freaked me out. If I had had enough rehearsals I would have felt better—and max tried to tell me otherwise, but reassurance in words meant nothing at that point. I knew I was playin on luck alone. Twenty-two fucking songs. He told me I was gonna do great and not to worry. It was hard to not worry. We didn't get to practice worth a shit! But the show was unreal. All the bands I've ever been in *never* achieved such a following…Hell, my last band was so damn anal about being perfect that we would scarcely do any shows at all. The night I quit my last band we'd been together six months and we were just getting ready to do our first show when I quit. I quit the day after I joined the Vampires. I broke it to them over a huge fatty sitting in a circle in the band room. They couldn't believe I was quitting. **I** couldn't believe I was quitting! I guess I wasn't the only person who didn't think I had the guts to do what I did.

The whole night was just SO cool. People slammed and dove off the stage and smoked dope right in the fuckin' club. These people were like shaking my hands and hugging me after the show. I was to scared to get high during the set. I didn't want to take any chances fucking up. We played for 2 hours I think, and this is not lightweight drum shit. It wore my ass out. I tried to pretend I could handle it. I know it's not gonna get any easier. The show seemed to go by real fast…I didn't realize we'd played two solid hours until much later.

We got a commitment from Erik on Tuesday…or was it Wednesday? Anyway, he's back and it kicks ass! Were playin' tomorrow at Stage Stop in Memphis—which is nothing to write home about, but I'll fucking play *anywhere* to get tighter. Everyone is comin' to the show. I am SO sick…I'm home from work. My throat is sore and I feel weak all over. Our article came out today. It's cool! It's so amazing to see us in the newspaper. I'm cutting out the article and I'm gonna keep it and everything else press related. I made some silly ass flyers for New Years Eve with cut outs from the Enquirer all over it. I'm gonna keep everything we do and make a scrapbook. I wish Erik had been in the photo in the paper. I gotta get some rest for tomorrow. I work from eight in the morning till five at night, and then drive the hour to the show, sound check, play the show, the hour drive home, and work again. Hell. No wonder I am sick.

1.7.94

Stage Stop was fuckin' *great*! **EVERYONE** was there. Stage Stop is like this conglomerate of redneck rock glory. It's in a part of Memphis that is kind of going down; you can frequently hear the growls of cherry bomb mufflers on the highway, seedy pool halls hide next to coin op laundry's and check cashing places…yet Stage Stop has somehow stood the test of time. The doorway is a photography treasure trove of one-hit-wonder bands in crappy dime store frames; autographed copies of glossy 8 X 10's of bands you never wanted to hear of, stuffed in spandex and frozen permanently in time, courtesy of aqua net super hold.

It feels so good to be a part of this band. It's like I'm a part of a movement or something. Like I'm finally getting respect as a musician. Hell, maybe I finally respect myself. Justine and I rode together. She calms me down. The hour drive to Memphis offers me *way* too much time to think. It's a mild form of self-torture. I go over the set in my head and have horrible thoughts about the mistakes I will make and how much of an ass I will look like. I am excited as hell and scared to death at the same time. Justine just looks over at me and smiles, knowing I am nervous. She has seen me go from garage bands to Serpentine, which was the band I was in with Hope. We did mostly covers of Iron Maiden and Metallica…I guess everybody has to start somewhere. Justine has seen me come a long way. She always tells me she is proud of me. She drove my truck to the gig. I never let anybody drive it. I was too nervous to drive. Everybody laughs at my truck. It's a black, 1989 Nissan with funny stickers all over it. There are so many on it I can't see out the back window. What people make fun of though, aren't the stickers. At work, when I have to take the trash to the dumpster, I just throw it in the bed of the truck, and then forget…uh…I am too lazy…to drive to the dumpster. So, I am frequently seen with trash blowing out of the back of my truck, leaving a trail through the streets of Jackson, stinking up the neighborhoods with rotten permanent waves and half-eaten, week-old lunches.

I got—or attempted to get—my eyebrow pierced last night. I swear this dude did not know what he was doin'. He used a 14k gold hoop with no point on it at all. Dumb ass. Hell, I'm the dumb ass. Just cuz he pierced Ruger's girlfriend's nose didn't mean he could pierce an eyebrow. Serves me right, I guess. He put a hypodermic needle through my face for fifteen minutes—handing me a mirror so I could see the shit. NOT a good idea. I started feelin queasy—but I pretended I wasn't. Then he took the hypo out and tried to push the delicate hoop through the hole. It totally bent out of shape while blood was running down my face. Even if he got it through it would have looked like a mashed up gold paper clip through my eyebrow. Somewhere during this process I recall telling him I was gonna pass out, and I did and the dumb ass let me stay out cold for like twenty minutes. When I came to, I told him to call Geoff and have Geoff come get me. Geoff got there in less than five minutes with a real concerned look on his face.

When he realized I was okay, I could tell he wanted to laugh. I was too scared to laugh at myself. All that blood took the humor out of it for me. Geoff and I went to the house and no one was home. Snow was lightly falling outside…and we turned out the lights in my room…lit candles and I rolled a joint. He moved his body closer and closer to me…and I moved into him. It was so *comfortable*. I sat there…with Geoff's arms around me…feeling so safe…and we smoked that joint…and enjoyed the silence of the falling snow out the window. When the guys got home from playin' pool, he jumped up as soon as he heard the door and quickly moved to the couch…like we weren't *together* or anything. What the fuck is up with that?

We are playin' Saturday the 8th at Rascals in Memphis…hell…that's *tomorrow*! I called The Studio in Memphis today and spoke to a piercer named Jake. He's gonna hook me up before the show. I was embarrassed to tell him I had an inexperienced dude pierce me. He didn't make me feel dumb though.

It's still snowing its ass off outside. Snow is so peaceful. So calculating.

1.10.94

The Rascal's gig was **KILLER**. Rascals is a seedy club nestled in the attic boughs of a two-story building in the heart of midtown Memphis. It's a real dive, but has always been a rock club and a staple in the Memphis music scene. It has shitty mismatched carpet under the equally mismatched tables and chairs…remnants from garage sales and clubs that went out of business. Dusty strings of Christmas lights connect one beer sign to the other, and a crooked pool table steals your money in the corner. I guess about two hundred people could fit in there. I think we had close to that the other night. It's amazing how word travels, because we really didn't get to promote the show much at all. Bands don't go on at Rascals till like eleven, and the club stays open till like four in the morning, so it is very much the *after hours* bar. The rotting wood walls seemed to cry out in weakness when we took the stage…Ruger's bass growls like a demon deep in thought…we are just so damn **loud**. I wouldn't have it any other way. With every double kick or triplet on my bass drum, I could feel the sound resonate through the weak, sagging floor. I had a unique conviction in my playing that night. Maybe I am getting more used to it. I fucked up a couple tunes here and there…but the show overall *smoked*. The good news is I don't have to worry anymore, because we are gonna practice in the house.

Justine and I rode to the gig together again. We smoked out and listened to Rage Against the Machine and Sepultura's Chaos AD. It fucking *rocks*. *Nothing* pumps me up for a show like Sepultura. We go into the studio *this weekend* and I am SO fucking excited. I cannot believe I am going in the studio. A *real* studio—not some dudes house or some dudes garage. I wonder what it will be like…I wonder if the engineers will think I'm shit. Sometimes I wonder if I really am any good. People tell me I am…like after the New Years Eve show people said we rocked and people said I was slammin'…but do they *mean* it? I know I can keep a beat—that's obvious—or I wouldn't be in Vampires at all. I know they were desperate for a drummer…I guess I just…hell. I dunno. I wonder if I am supposed to use my own drums in the studio or not…If so, I am gonna have to get some cash somewhere to get new heads…new heads are like a $150 investment. Somebody told me once you were only as good as your sound, so I know it's worth it. I need them for live shit anyway. I guess that half-ounce will have to wait.

It was *so* cool hangin' out in Memphis with everyone. Getting high on the balcony out back at Rascals is *so* fun. The balcony sags worse than the floor and I won't be surprised if one day I read about it's collapse in the papers. I *stayed* stoned from the minute we got off stage! The main thing about Rascals that sucks is the fucking *staircase* to get up there. It's like **straight** up and my kick drum is heavier on that haul than ever. I had some help, though. I can't wait for the day when maybe I won't have to lug my own shit around—when *none* of us have to. We could just take it easy and save energy. Oh! I got my eyebrow pierced for real before the show by Jake at The Studio. He came to the show! He is *really* cool. I may try to hook him up with Dru and Chaos at their new tattoo shop in Jackson. People are calling and saying we "mopped the floor" at Rascal's. Cool!

1.16.94

We braved the icy interstate to come all the fucking way home from the studio, and we gotta get up and go right back in the morning. Why we just didn't crash at Kathy's in Memphis I do not know. I didn't care though. I secretly wanted Geoff to come over and spend the night with me. Since my room is the old living room to the house, I also have the front door to the house in my room…perfect for him to slip into. I called him just now. I hope he comes over. We got to the studio at ten o' clock this morning (on time-*unbelievable*) and we started recording about one in the afternoon. The engineer dude was really cool and laid back. This Memphis music mogul dude showed up and listened to the tracks we'd laid down. At first I thought he really dug us, but he asked too many questions about the bass guitar, so now I suspect he was just trying to steal Ruger's trademark sound for the band *he* manages. Ruger just smiled and shrugged his shoulders in answer to dude's questions. We're gonna mix the tape tomorrow. We won't get a copy till the $700 debt is paid off, but the engineer dude said he'd enter one in Crossroads for us, which is super cool of him. We've got a show at the Daisy scheduled for the 21st. I fucking **love** playin there. Even with the shitty bands I was in,…I have always dug that place. It has a lot to do with bein' fifteen and going to all ages shows, dreaming of a day when I could even PLAY drums, much less on a stage. Now, I *can* play and it's on **THAT** stage. Unreal. I've played there with bands before, but not with THIS band. **THE** band. The Daisy is an old ass theatre on Beale Street…the ceiling over the stage is like three stories high and there's a dance/pit area in front of the stage and then tables and shit up to the bar. It kinda slants in like a theatre. It holds like a *thousand* people. It has the greatest feel in the world…blue velvet curtains line the huge walls that lead up to a shitty old bar…behind it in the lobby is a little old man who sells popcorn out of an antique machine…and on either side of him are staircases that lead up to the balcony, where everybody and their brother get high. The Daisy has the *best* acoustics of any club in the world. It is truly a place *full* of dreams and potential. The stage is *huge* and sits like four feet high and like thirty feet wide…oh I am so excited just imagining the power of this band on that stage…we are really gonna try to get a lot done for that one! We also need to prepare a bio for Crossroads. Crossroads showcase may be the thing to get Redneck Vampires signed. We will definitely see. It's fucking great to have Erik back. He belongs in this band. I'm gonna finish this bowl and crash…

1.17.94

The mixed tape sounds unreal! It turned out that Ruger had a copy of it. Well of course his sneaky ass did! After we had been home a while, he called everyone into the living room. We turned out the lights, lit candles in the living room, and smoked out-listening to it full blast. It sounds *so* unreal. *So* fucking great…I still can't believe it's **me** playin with this band. I absolutely cannot believe I am here and I am doing this.

Geoff came over that night. He is *really* impressed with the tape. He is such a cute mother fucker…I don't know what it is about him…we slept together for the first time…it was really…sweet…in a weird sort of way. He was so vulnerable…it's *such* a different side of him.

Looks like we won't practice this week. Half our gear is still in Memphis due to the blizzard of ice outside. Hell, I'm kinda sick anyway. If I wasn't stoned, I'd really feel bad. The Daisy show is Friday. We need to kick *so* much ass. I've got to get started on the band bio for Crossroads and schedule pictures and shit.

1.23.94

The Daisy show Friday night **SUCKED.** I am so damn disappointed. We were SO out of practice. We just fucked off rehearsals and relied on how "great" we are. I'm gonna start practicing with or without them. I'm **throwing** myself into my kit. Fuck everybody. They may be able to sound kick ass without practice but I apparently do not have that ability. I was looking forward to playin the Daisy *so* much. I am *so* disappointed in myself. It was HELL bein' on stage. I questioned **every** move I made. I could not relax. I was *not* enjoying it. I watched them looking for clues. I couldn't hear shit out of my monitor. It was a nightmare. Ruger kept looking at me, rolling his eyes and shaking his head in disappointment. Once he turned around and screamed, "WHAT THE FUCK IS WRONG WITH YOU?" It was *awful*. I cannot express how horrible him doing that makes me feel. It erases any confidence I have left in myself and when I can't fucking hear on stage I need to be at peace so I can concentrate on what I CAN hear. I don't need to be fucking screamed at and humiliated by Ruger during the set. Like that is somehow going to make me play better!! I am relying on them for help and then he turns around and bitches at me like that! I relied on prayer to make the licks in the right places…it apparently wasn't working. The guys ignored me after the show. Well, Ruger did. I would stand next to him or something…and he would just walk away…not even acknowledging me. The vibe wasn't the same. It makes me wonder if they are having second thoughts about me.

I miss Memphis SO bad. I'm really *really* homesick now. I went back last night and hung out and got high with everybody. Geoff was hangin at the house and kinda ignoring me. What the fuck is up with that? I mentioned several times that I was thinking about goin to Memphis. He didn't try to talk me out of going, which I was hoping he would. I think Ruger is catching on to Geoff and I and I think he is jealous. Not of Geoff bein with *me*, or anything like that, but Geoff is like his "little buddy" or something and I take Geoff's attention now and Ruger doesn't like it. Or, at least that's the vibe I get. Hope is coming home in two weeks. That's gonna make me miss Memphis even more.

1.26.94

Mother fucker. Geoff came over and Ruger pulled him back in his room for like an hour…it made me nervous…and the next thing I know, fucking Geoff comes into *my* room and says he needs to talk to me. He proceeds to tell me that we can't see each other anymore…that it's "for the best" and that he is very sorry. I am SO fucking pissed. I told him, "What are you, bailing now since you fucked the girl drummer? Is that all you wanted to do? That's not how you acted in my bed, you son of a bitch…that's not what you whispered to me in your most vulnerable moments…does Ruger control YOUR life, too?" I let him have it…and he took **all** that shit. When I was done, he calmly got up, said nothing, and kissed my forehead…real lightly and real slowly. Then he left. I feel *so* fucking used. I feel *so* fucking controlled. I feel like such a dumb ass girl. I am embarrassed that I gave him the time of day—knowing he said that shit about fucking me before he ever knew me. I am a stupid girl.

1.31.94

We played on the 28th with Bone Squad. It was at the shitty little club here in Jackson. I guess we redeemed ourselves somehow. Geoff got in a fight, I got strangled by a bouncer for slam dancing, our power blew out twice, I annihilated the last song, but other than that, it was cool. The place was absolutely fucking *packed.* It freaks me out the way people watch me play. It's like they are taking me apart. I feel I am under constant scrutiny. I realize I have put myself in this position...but it still freaks me out. Some people even stand over to the side...away from the front of the stage to watch. I swear can almost hear their thoughts sometimes...saying I'm not really any good and the only reason I am here is because I am a girl.

Geoff and I are civil to each other. It really fucking hurts...I guess I just would like to know if it was all a fucking game of his...or if he ever felt anything for me at all. I truly want to know-not so I can torture myself, but like for information purposes. If it *was* a game...knowing it would help me spot it when it happens again.

Tomorrow we play in Memphis at Stage Stop. Hope is here! She came home from Los Angeles, got settled, and drove to Jackson, surprising me Wednesday at work. It was *great* to see her. It was cool that she drove all the way to Jackson without me knowing it just to surprise me. Jake, the piercer who did my eyebrow, *moved* here. He's workin at Dru and Chaos' tattoo shop. We've been hangin' out a lot. I like him. He crashed here with me a couple of times but nothin's happened. We just get high and talk. It's cool. He brought me a surprise...it was an Iguana! I named him "Prince Albert" after Jake's pierced penis. One of my dope men has a lot of reptiles so I'll get him to help me with Prince Albert. I've got to get on the ball and get our press kit and photos ready for Crossroads.

2.4.94

Sadie, Rugers girl, and her friend Rita moved in with us. We get high, read tarot, and play with the Ouija board. They are lots of fun. I haven't seen or heard from Jake in days. I have become more and more resentful of Ruger and the fact that he runs up phone bills calling all over the country setting up "gigs" that never seemed to manifest. He doesn't work and he scams his poor Mom for money all the time. She supports him. I think she feels bad because his dad died. I couldn't *believe* it when I heard him say to her "I didn't ask to be born!" I said that to my Mom when I was like thirteen. I have to *work* to be able to do this! I get SO jealous of his easy ride. He keeps saying that the "band fund" is going to pay the phone bills. What fucking band fund? The one that pays for them to get drunk after each show? I think if they are going to drink that money that I should be entitled to spend a share of it on MY drug of choice. I am getting so frustrated with this. We have to practically nail him to the floor when he comes in to try to get the rent money he gets from her out of him before he spends it on beer. I have never known anyone to drink so much. I get jealous of Sadie and Rita getting to live here for nothing. Sigh. I guess this is what it's all about. I guess this struggle is "paying my dues". I should be grateful instead of bitching. I still have money for pot and cigarettes. *And* we leave for our first real road trip soon. It's gonna cost us like $37 each for gas and everything and Ian's dad says the Suburban will make it. We are lucky to have wheels.

I'm having strange experiences at night. I wake at 3:41 and feel like something black is trying to smother me. It hovers over me, as I lay paralyzed in my bed.

2.5.94

Last night was a *nightmare*. We were supposed to play Nashville for the first time and the guys cancelled the show at the last minute. That is **so** fucking unprofessional. I was SO fucking pissed. The guys had played Nashville before and apparently cancelled too many gigs up there or some shit, and this was our last chance to get in there. Oh well! I was **so** fucking pissed at Ruger. I drove around to cool off and when I got home, Prince Albert was dead. I felt so fucking horrible. I felt like I killed him because I didn't know what he needed. I buried him in the backyard. We don't have much else goin on this month until Dallas. I can see it now. We won't even practice.

2.15.94

I found out why Jake just mysteriously "quit" coming to the house to see me. Rumor has it that he's stayin' with some divorced groupie chick that has a house. Guess he couldn't get a free ride with me. It hurt my feelings a little bit. Okay, it hurt a lot. I guess my Iguana was some sort of a "parting" gift.

Sadie and Justine got jobs waiting tables at this *ridiculous* restaurant for practically nothing. Things with Geoff are getting better. He is just always around and I am going to have to get used to it. Justine says he is an ass and doesn't deserve me being nice to him. She also thinks Ruger *made* him end it with me. He cornered me in the hallway the other night and tried to kiss me. My body was very tempted...but my brain said no way.

Not a whole lot else is goin on. I'm goin' to Memphis this weekend for Savannah's birthday. She is having a psychic come! It should be cool.

2.19.94

The psychic lady held my house key and she said in a past life I was a child and died of pneumonia in the house. She said that explained the suffocating blackness that surrounds me at night.

I'm getting excited about the Dallas trip. We leave *Thursday*. We are still playin with the Ouija board every night...I know some mother fucker is pushing the damn thing...but I guess that's what makes it fun...you never really know...anyway...it's still a nightly ritual around the house. Saturday night we contacted...uh...well we *think* we contacted...the spirits of the dead people buried in the lovely cemetery next to the house. We were creeped out all night about it and decided to calm the spirits down we would clean up the cemetery. So our lazy assess were outside raking leaves today in the graveyard. You can see it really well now.

3.4.94

We survived our first road gig. Dallas was a *blast*. All I did was get high the *whole* time. That was a long ass ride, so I just smoked bowl after bowl the whole way there. I got *so* fucking stoned—Ian said I was just rambling out the window about some black lady I didn't even know. I have only been that fucked up around them one other time and that was the first weekend I was officially in the band. I remember being at a club drinkin' some girlie drinks and then I remember doin' shots of Jagermeister. The next thing I remember I was on the floor of a convenience store laughing my ass off, while Ruger watched from the check out line just shaking his head with a grin on his face.

We got into Dallas at five o' clock in the morning and barely got any sleep before waking up in excitement. We crashed on the floor in chick's upstairs game room…damn what is her name? She's somebody in Bone Squad's girlfriend. Anyway, she is like apparently rich as hell and her house is *amazing*. She has a *bad-ass* dog—it's an Afghan hound so it has really long hair. She just sat around, got stoned and brushed its hair. We smoked out with Bone Squad with my peace pipe. It was cool. We played Friday night at some poserish club in like a tittie bar district. We were shooting pool waiting to play when Ruger took my hand and led me over to this dude at another table. I didn't know what was goin' on. Ruger tapped the dude on the shoulder and he turned around and I was shocked. It was Vinnie Paul from PANTERA. I could *not* fucking believe it. They live in Dallas and they used to play at the same club. He was just shooting pool with his friend. No shit. So, he signs this Pantera thing for me and it says "Eat Pussy…Vinnie Paul". Now what the fuck? Why do people assume I am a fucking dyke? What the fuck ever. Saturday night we went to a club with the Bone Squad's dudes and their Dallas friends and saw a band that Ruger and Max knew. That club had these cages everywhere with scantily clad drunk chicks dancing in them. The bar sold these huge ass bottles of beer…man what was that shit called…anyway it had some Indian dude on the bottle and they were cheap as hell so you can imagine what condition everybody was in. I kept finding Ian leaning against the wall with that three-year-old stare on his face…drooling over the chicks in the cage. I *really* freaked out when **Pantera** showed up for the world premiere of their video on Mtv. The whole club stopped whatever they were doing and the owner put Mtv on all the screens and everybody watched it. It was *awesome*. The band just drank and hung out like everybody else. They didn't act like rock stars at all. Later on, we all went out to Bone Squad's van to smoke out. They have a CB radio and there just happened to be a poor, innocent trucker in his rig out in the parking lot. Joseph and Erik got on the CB and talked like they were gay and they were looking for a date. They sounded *so* insane on that damn CB that poor trucker may have been afraid of who was watching him! I must say it was **so** fucking hilarious.

Our performance that weekend, on the other hand, was *murderous*. I fucked up one song so bad on stage that I thought I was out of the band. It was *truly* that bad. I am *so* glad that Vinnie Paul left before we played. That would have been *so* embarrassing. I don't know what is wrong with me. It's like the song has these amazingly difficult 36th notes on the ride cymbal-hell…I wrote the shit so I know I can do it—just hitting the cymbal that fast makes my muscle burn *so* bad…it's *excruciating*…and then I just grit my teeth and try to make it through the pain till the chorus is over. I played it fine in the studio. I listen to myself on the tape…I know it's *POSSIBLE* for me to do it. I have *proof*. The proof is in the tape. I just don't know what my fucking problem is. The guys are worried about it. Ruger didn't even talk to me after the show, or hardly at all the way back home. I've got to do *something*.

2

Fifty Bucks Plus a Sack

3.12.94

Last night we all went to this club here in Jackson…it's like one of the only clubs in the damn city…anyway, this band played and the guys made fun of them *all* night, especially the singer. They knew him, and the rest of the band, and when the band took a break, they introduced me to everyone. The singer is beautiful…his name is Riley…and he may be cheesy, but he is *so* polite and kind and beautiful…I did not get a bad vibe from him in any way at all. Usually singers are assholes, but he is cool as shit. We talked his whole break, and I hung around till after they were done, and we talked for another hour. I am so totally smitten! He walked me out to my car, and I was leaning against it facing him when he asked me something that I absolutely cannot remember, because as I answered his question, he interrupted me by putting his lips over my mouth, *kissing* me. In the middle of my sentence! It was the best kiss of my **life**. To have my speech interrupted with a passionate, heartfelt kiss…I tuned to butter right there in the empty parking lot. I don't know how to express in words what it was like. It made me like him even *more* that he had the guts to do it. In the silence that followed it, he asked what I was doing tonight. I told him nothing, and as I write, he should be here any minute! Max and Ruger think he is a pussy, and maybe he is, but he sure is nice. And *so* damn romantic. God…I am so nervous. I am going on a *date*! With a *nice guy*! That I *like*! God, I am *nervous*…I am wearing a black dress…Justine said it looked good…and my big ass cross around my throat…and black tights…and my shiny green combat boots. Do I look stupid? Oh, God I am so nervous…I'm gonna pack a little bowl…

3.13.94

Oh my Gods. I am a naughty girl. I cannot believe what I did. I cannot believe it. Riley got over here…and well…we went to liquor store…but that's as far as we got…we sat on the couch in my room and talked for hours…and started making out…and one thing led to another…and the good little girl within me…she left the room. She fought me for a while and finally gave up…I had **sex** with Riley…*on the first date*! I have *never* done that in my life. Never! Hell, he is only the fourth person I have ever been with…What is wrong with me? Why was I a bad girl? I really like him…and now he is gonna think I am a slut…that I do this sort of thing all the time…I feel kind of ashamed of myself. God, I hope nobody *heard* us. I wonder what everybody is thinking. I had a boy here in my room all night long! Oh, God!

3.18.94

Riley has called several times. I am so embarrassed for sleeping with him on the first date that I am afraid to face him. I feel like a slut. I am anxious about Crossroads. Max and I and some other people went to see the Pumpkins and someone came up to us and told Max and I congrats on the "cover". We were like, "What cover?" We made the cover of a magazine about bands appearing in Crossroads! It absolutely *rocks*! It is a needed boost. We tried practicing in the house, which worked for about fifteen minutes till the cops came. So now, we aren't doin shit as far as rehearsing. The band recorded their first demo here in Jackson, and Max said he is gonna call the dude who runs the studio and see if we can rent it cheap just to rehearse. Things with Ruger still suck. He's a great bass player but a nightmare for a roommate. And just who's bright idea was it to get a big house for all of us? Mine, of course. And my dumb ass put all the bills in my name. So, the $700 phone bills are mine to pay.

3.27.94

We went to Nashville last night to see some bands. It was cool to get out of town and do something cool and different. I hung out with Slaphead all night. He is one of Ruger and Max's best friends from school. Why do their friends have to be so fuckin *COOL*...why must I be smitten with this boy? Why must he be so fuckin *sexy*...Goddamn he is just the *shit*...

4.1.94

Ruger and I had ourselves a little chat. He told me that this band *just isn't going to practice*. That I need to *adapt* to that. I am *so* fucking *outraged*. This is such **bullshit.** Well, then he and his big fucking attitude need to *adapt* when I have a shitty fucking night due to *lack* of practice. What the fuck! This shit makes me feel like I am some fucking incompetent musician because I want to rehearse with my fucking band. It makes me *tighter*. It makes *all* of us fucking tighter. And hell, that's where we fucking *write* is during practice. Some of the members of this band have everything they fucking need handed to them. Money for bills, gas, pot, equipment...so why should this band not get a record deal handed to them, too? It may seem strange to certain members of this band that they may have to WORK to get somewhere in this industry. *Somebody* needs to *adapt* to the fucking truth.

4.6.94

Getting ready for Crossroads...we've got a new song to play and it's my favorite one yet! Oh yeah...we've been *practicing* at a studio here in town. Imagine that. *Work.* Who would have ever thought? And *imagine* that out of *practice* came a bad ass new song? The dude that runs the studio is really cool and he slipped in a tape while we were messing around so we have our new song recorded. It's got a bad ass, choppy, gritty fucking groove to it and when it gets tight it will cut like a fuckin' knife! And Max and Ruger do their signature wicked fuckin' harmony thing…*man* it just *smokes*…and I get to beat the *shit* out of my drums in this breakdown…man…It's fuckin' *righteous*!

Wayne told me about this guy named Cal who lives thirty minutes north of Jackson where he is from, this little place called Walnut Grove. Wayne thinks we'd get along real well because this guy is pagan, too. He says Cal is real serious about it. I want to meet him. I could use some real conversation. Maybe this dude could help with the night visitors I've having. It's freaking me out. We are still doin' the Ouija routine every night. We tried to contact Ruger's dad. It was weird. Sadie and I both cried. She's cool. We listen to the Indigo Girls and get stoned a lot. Justine is working as a waitress in the biggest bar in town. She works her ass off, but is making *killer* money. I miss her.

4.10.94

I met an interesting fellow at the gas station. He was obviously pagan…big lapis and turquoise rings…lots of charm…about thirty five…with a gleam in his eyes. I guess I have a magnetism for really strange ones! We smoked a joint behind the store and he said there was a couple who were opening a Lapidary in town and that I should check it out. I pretended I knew what a Lapidary was—I didn't want to seem stupid. He said the wife's name was Janine and she was a High Priestess in Wicca. I **had** to check this out. Other than my sister, I didn't know anybody else who practiced. I've read a lot about the order of Wiccan clergy, so I knew a High Priestess was the person 'in charge' of a working coven, but I'd never really met one. I figured anyone who outwardly calls herself a high priestess must be very powerful and know their shit…or at least, have a **monstrous** ego. I was intimidated and a little scared—yet my curiosity won. I went down there and they had a *huge* collection of stones and jewelry. She watched me and I watched her. I didn't know what to think. Something about her intimidated me, yet she seemed gentle. Maybe it was the way she cuddled her children that gave her the gentleness. I dunno. She and I finally quit staring at each other and talked. She said she was accepting students and asked me if I was interested. I told her I was. She told me about another witch in town, a lady named Anna who was opening a bookstore. I decided to check that out, too. But she did "warn" me, so to speak, about Anna, saying that they had worked together a little and she did not agree with the way Anna "worked". Sounds like the fucking Baptists and the Methodists. Whatever.

4.20.94

Janine and I are spending more time together. I hang out at the Lapidary shop a lot and then at their trailer. It's a nice escape from the rock star house where I live. There are *always* people at the house, beer in the fridge, and some crazy shit going on. It's the official party house—complete with its own parking lot.

Janine showed me meditation exercises and suggested a book I should read. She showed me her copy of the book and she had crossed a whole bunch of stuff out in like every paragraph and told me she penciled in her thoughts about what the author was saying. She is very intellectual. Her dad was an Episcopal priest. She knows her Wicca and seems to know what she is doing. Her husband is pagan, too. He is real aloof. He has long blond hair and he looks really pagan. Janine has long brown hair and she wears hippie skirts and goes barefoot a lot. She doesn't wear make up and she doesn't shave. She's a granola girl. She's really into actually taking on the personifications of deities. That kind of freaks me out—not the deity part, but the *human* part. Thinking that a God, one that has a personality, is inside you and you are acting as if you are them—that's just bizarre and sounds more like multiple personality disorder than religion. I guess I could say it was working for her. One minute I think all this pagan stuff is horseshit and the next minute I am feeling the moon surge through me...I know something exists that is greater than myself...I just don't know if it's in a trailer in Jackson.

4.27.94

Crossroads is steadily approaching. I am excited as hell and nervous at the same time. In complete and utter defiance of failure, I set up my kit in my room and I have been practicing *every night* by myself. Fuck them and their practice-when-it's-convenient for-them-assess. Plus, I am *terrified* of re-living Dallas at Crossroads. I was *so* scared of losing my spot in this band after that serious fuck up. If this band goes down at Crossroads, *I* am not going to have had *anything* to do with it. I dissected the song that has been giving me so much trouble. To figure out what I was doing wrong I've been playin right along to the tape. It blew me away when I realized how much faster we play that song live...*that* is the whole problem. The natural high of the stage makes all musicians play a little faster, and as it turns out, we are just playin it at a faster speed. No wonder I cant do the 36th notes! Ru starts that song off solo on his bass...so **he** sets the timing for the song. I had to prove it to him that we were playin it too fast by making him listen to the tape with me. Now, he is gonna look at me first, we will mutually set the timing with a verbal count off, and he will go into it from there. I hope we pull it off.

Elijah Young was in town. That man had my heart on a plate all through high skool. His job brought him out here for a couple days and he knew I was playin with the Vampire's and livin here so he looked me up. I met him at his hotel, and then he came out to the house and hung out. He has a girlfriend and he bragged about how honest of a guy he was; yet he asked me to keep my mouth shut when he called her. He said he'd be at Crossroads for sure. When he and I dated, his band was really popular...he used to come out to Hope's and jam with us. He taught us some Bad Brains and some Motorhead songs. That was back when I couldn't play with both my feet—and double kicks were all the rage. I was *constantly* intimidated by other drummers who *could* play double kicks. Wow. I had forgotten all about that. It's not a problem now. Seeing him tonight helped me to remember where I have come from as a drummer.

4.28.94

Crossroads weekend starts *tonight*! We play tomorrow night around nine. All the major clubs are housing Crossroads bands and a trolley takes people from one club to another. It's gonna be *so* much fun. I am *so* freakin' excited! I am driving to Memphis this afternoon and I'm gonna go down to the Radisson and check us in. I made some bad ass promo packs for the band...I worked my ass off on them. They look really professional. I also printed up some flyers to put on the tables in the clubs...just with band information, pictures, shit like that. I'm gonna pack up all that shit and hit the clubs early and flyer the tables. God, I am so nervous. I am so excited. I'm gonna stay at Mom's over the weekend to try to avoid all the partying…I'm gonna try to wait until after we play to get high. I feel like maybe I need a break. I am just *so* scared of fucking up I am willing to do *anything* to ensure I don't.

5.1.94

Redemption is so sweet. We *ROCKED* Crossroads. God, it was fun as hell. I feel *totally* redeemed as a member of this fuckin' band! The whole weekend was amazing. So much excitement in the air—and fear…fear of knowing that you have twenty minutes to play your best songs…and play them better than you ever have in your life…because you don't know who is watching…and you *can't* fuck up. I met the guys in town early for load in, and we fucked around on Beale Street for a while till the bands went on. Really it was like a big schmooze fest, musicians hangin' out talkin'…just ass-kissing other bands. Ruger is a schmoozing *pro*. Before it was out turn, at the last minute, I pulled my hair up into ponytails. It *really* seemed to help. I was cooler and I could **see**. I had no idea how much the sweaty curtain of hair got in my way…putting it up made it so much better. I cannot believe how much of a difference a fucking **hairdo** made. All my extra practice really paid off. The place was so packed full of people they were *turning them away*. It was like elbow to elbow in there—people from all over the country—bands from *everywhere*. A writer from RIP magazine was there and rumor was she *loved* us! My kit sounded *so* amazing. Each strike on my drums seemed to reach to the end of the earth itself. Words cannot do justice to the way it feels to perform live. No drug, no lover, **nothing** can replace the rush of that feeling. The intensity of the sound—and knowing that sound is produced by **you**—you and them. To think that five people can combine themselves and their intentions and talents and produce organized noise…and then to perform it in front of 1000 sweaty, screaming people. It's *unreal*. The twenty minutes we were on that stage is worth every tear, every fight, every moment freezing in the band room…every bit of it is worth it for moments like that. It's what keeps me going. It's magikcal.

I'd never made it to Crossroads with any band before. All the bands I was in before sent in tapes, but we never got accepted. It was a HUGE personal accomplishment. Janine and her husband showed up at Crossroads and she gave me a fairy earring. She told me it was alive and had been charged in a ritual they had performed just for me. Hmmm.

I got SO fucked up after Crossroads. But before that, I had a little "moment" by myself. I just sat a moment after the rush and hustle of getting all our shit off stage to get lost so I could be alone. I found a spot backstage between the amps where no one could see me. I sat there, just me and my sweat…and collected the moment. My first showcase gig. With a REAL band. *THE* band. Words could not express how happy I was and proud I was of myself. I thanked the powers that be for the talent I had been given and the gift of determination I had to carry it out. I had played my ass off and I knew it. I held the moment in a sacred space.

5.9.94

WE ARE GOING TO CHICAGO! Ruger called a band meeting at the house tonight and made the announcement. Bone Squad has been touring quite a bit, and they are headlining a kick ass club up there and they got us on with them! Holy Shit! I've *always* wanted to go there…we've got to figure out how we are getting all our shit up there plus all of us. I've always wanted to tour, it didn't really matter where I went. Dallas was cool but I didn't think we'd really start going a lot of other places so soon! I've just always wanted to be on the road…seeing the country…the world…and yet not just as a tourist. I guess this really isn't "the road" yet or anything, it's just some gigs here and there but it feels fucking great to me! Ruger has been trying to hook this up for a while. He is *so* determined to get this band on the road. That scares me a little cuz…well…where are we gonna get money to live on? If we are exclusively on the road, how are we gonna pay the rent at the house? I can't work and be on the road at the same time. Local gigs barely pay enough for gas money to get home and maybe dinner for the band and Adam and Wayne. It's obvious we are not in this for the money. Yet leaving for like a month…how in the hell am I gonna pay my bills? I can't call **MY** Mommy every time I need cash. Hell, my parents are so disgusted with my rock star shit they don't even want to hear about it—much less fund it. Gonna smoke this joint…

5.16.94

I went down to Anna's bookstore and met her during my lunch break. It's a cool little shop. She has lots of cool stuff in addition to books. I bought some patchouli oil from her. I think she knew why I was really there, but neither of us let in on it.

We are getting *really* excited about Chicago. Savannah and Justine are goin with us. Savannah is gonna drive her car, so some of us will ride with her, and the rest of the guys and our gear are goin in the Suburban. We are splitting the cost of gas like we did for the Dallas trip, and we'll get a big ass room for that night, and then the next night Jesse's band is playin' in Chicago, too, so me and Justine and Savannah are gonna stay for their show. We are SO psyched.

5.30.94

We survived road trip number two. We got home from Chicago yesterday after-noon. It was **so** fucking fun! The show *kicked ass*. The club was called the Avalon and it was right in the middle of everything! We met some cool people at the club and hung out with Bone Squad at the show. Max and Ruger met this chick named Cherie who does promotion for bands in town and she is gonna hook us up with some more shows. Savannah and Justine and I went in on a half-ounce for the road. Savannah hid it in her underwear for the drive and when we got there, it ***wasn't in her fucking panties***. I was **so** pissed. We had stopped for a pee run somewhere in bumfuck Illinois and apparently, she forgot about it even being there. I was practically in tears because I wanted to party after the show and we barely had enough cash to get a room for everybody—much less buy some more smoke. Justine had a big surprise for me when I got back from sound check, though. She *found* the bag of dope on the bathroom floor in the hotel room after Savannah took a shower. Hmmmm…I don't even want to think about where it really was when she thought it was missing…but I didn't give a fuck! I was so relieved! So we played a trick on Savannah and told her we sold her car to a dude on the street for $50 plus a sack…the look on her face was *priceless*…it was fuck-ing hilarious. The staircase to get up to that club was the steepest staircase I have ever seen in my life. It was like looking up into a vertical hole into the darkness. I don't know how we lugged our shit up there. We played in the "lil" room, while another band played in the big room. Word is you gotta play the little shitty room a dozen times before they will move you to the big room. I guess you have to earn your way in there or something. That's fair enough I guess. We had a pretty good turn out. They say Smashing Pumpkins got huge before they even made it to the big room. That's food for thought. I met Taime Downs from Faster Pussycat at the club. I bet he feels like an ass. What a stupid band. Hell. I guess I'm stupid, too. I bought their stupid CD. We went to the suburbs to some poser ass club…the Thirsty Whale…I think…to see Jesse's band play. They had no one—I repeat *no one* in the club when they played. They were *so* disappointed. We were the only people in the club at all. They rented a minivan to make the trip and it was so small that Jesse had nowhere to sit—so he **laid** on an amp all the way from Memphis. Damn. No fucking shit. He is the sweetest guy.

Max just told Justine some bad news. It appears that the Sheriff's office came by looking for her while we were gone and left a business card for her to call him. Holy fucking shit. What is that all about? I'm gonna take her down there in the morning.

6.2.94

I took Justine to the police station. It was a nerve-racking adventure for me and I wasn't even the one they were after! I can't believe what they wanted her for. *Late fucking **videos**.* No shit. Some fucking video place filed criminal charges against her for not turning in some fucking movies. What is this world coming to?

We are playin at a local festival at the end of the month. We have a little spot on the radio. Every time it comes on at work and I hear us on the airwaves, I get all excited. Bone Squad's stage tech recommended some dude to us named Cade for a stage manager. I'm picking him up at the bus station at the end of the month.

6.4.94

Wayne brought a group of people from Walnut Grove to the house to hang out and party. Ruger said they were our "fans". Saying that makes me feel like such an idiot. When they arrived, and my eyes were drawn to this guy in a Misfits shirt with shaggy brown hair and a great smile. He smelled like earth; like a combination of really good mud and the street after a summer rain. I was not surprised when Wayne introduced him as the pagan guy he had been telling me about. Wayne was right about Cal. He **is** serious about studying. It's interesting having met so many people in such a short time who are pagan. I immediately invited Cal to leave the mass of people and slip into my room. When he walked in, he read the signs I had made in runes. No one had **ever** been able to do that. He recognized my altar and nodded at it respectively. I was SO impressed. I packed a bowl in my peace pipe and we got stoned and talked about magick. He had the most calm...no...safe is a better word...he had *safe* energy, yet...I dunno it was like something powerful under the surface. Something lurked behind his ocean blue eyes...something I want to know...to experience. Hangin with him was so refreshing. I told him I'd come to see him out in the Grove. We had some shows booked at a bar they were putting together out there and we would need to come out and check the place out anyway.

6.15.03

Cal and I dosed together in the woods by the saloon. He lives in the little room upstairs. It's a witch's *paradise*. He has tree branches everywhere. Runes fashioned out of sticks line the eaves of the ceiling. A huge circle has been cast in the center of the room...thirteen feet in diameter...salt...chalk line...It's all done correctly. He knows what he's doing. I am *smitten* with him. Just being in his presence makes me feel...completed. His eyes are *so* blue...and when I stare into them, they become waves of the ocean...and twinkle like the sea when the sun shines upon it. I've been going out to see him *every* day. The band is practicing in the bar now, so afterwards, we hang out with everyone and then run off by ourselves into the dark woods and just talk. It's a whole new world in Walnut Grove. The air is cooler and sweeter and it's so full of life energy. I've never spent any real time anywhere that resembled "country". Trees spill for miles in all directions. Wildflowers and creatures…gentle hills and winding roads…No wonder he's pagan.

Cal and I end our evenings with the same routine. We don't even have to plan it anymore…we just look at each other and we both *know*. Then we head out to the middle of the street. Its smooth, black asphalt cradles us, and we stare into the night sky together. The street was never a place I had ever felt safe before. Cars are very rare in the Grove. We can feel their vibrations in the road much quicker than we can see their headlights. I think I missed stars all my life. We point to various constellations, as he fires up the biggest joints I've ever seen. Then I somehow drive my truck back to Jackson…seeing Cal under every tree and in every starlit field on the way home. I'm falling in love with him and I know it.

6.18.03

I'm working on a wand for Cal. It's a gift for him…for Summer Solstice, technically called Midsummer, which is in three days. We are gonna do a circle together…I have never worked with anyone before…but I'm not nervous at all. I'm gonna go out there tonight. I love the way he stares at me. This confidence emanates from him that I cannot put into words. I can't stop thinking about him. I have so much respect for him and his knowledge. I am really feeling connected to the earth…like I never have before. I have been having this vision…of…being buried in the earth. I don't know where it is coming from…but I keep longing to do it. I've been reading Donald Tyson's *The New Magus* and I wonder if that has something to do with it. It has helped me become more aware and taught me to *pay attention*. I love Tyson's ideas. I am just longing to feel the coolness of dirt all over my flesh…to be blanketed by the mineral rich earth…to be a part of it. Maybe I will talk to Cal about it.

Our festival show here in town is the 25th. Some poser ass band from Memphis is doin' the show too. It's gonna be hilarious. Lots of people from the salon are coming and customers keep saying they feel privileged to have me do their hair. Whatever! Lucky for them I don't get high before I cut hair! That does not work well. I learned that the hard way years ago. I got stoned as hell on lunch once at my first haircutting job. When I got back from lunch, I had to roll a spiral perm and it took me *three hours* to do the one-hour job. I couldn't quit staring at the rollers! It was hell and I vowed *never* to do that again. Everyone there got fucked up *all day*. Not me! I am gonna get the chicks I work with high one of these days though, after work. Things here at home are bad. We are all spooked on the house being haunted, that is, Justine and I are.

6.22.94

Last night, we practiced, and as I drummed…I visualized I was drumming up energy from the earth…and it twisted in spirals above my head…and out the building…and over the trees…and into the brilliant sea of stars above the Grove. I imagined being on the back of a bird, flying around and playin in its mist…and did all of this while I beat the *shit* of my kit…playin in some sort of automatic drummer mode. It was Summer Solstice, and Cal and I headed to the woods right after practice. We sat down in a spot where the path branched off into two. We called the quarters, and sat in our sacred space. I gave him his wand. I also had a ring for him…it matched the one he already wore. I don't recall how I came across the ring…but it was in my box. What I didn't know was that he had made a gift for me as well…it's beautiful…it consists of feathers…bound together with leather and a stick for a handle…used for distributing incense into the air. I told him about the vision…about being buried in the earth. He told me I should definitely do it. Part of me *needed* it somehow, he said, and I was being shown what I needed via the vision. He said he would help me…he would dig me a spot in the woods…we are doing it tomorrow, when the moon is completely full. I am nervous…but I trust Cal to take care of me while I am 'under'.

I've got to remember to pick up that dude Cade, the road manager dude from Little Rock, at the bus station on Saturday. Hell, he's jumpin' in with both feet—cuz we will probably go from the bus station to the show.

6.26.94

I am sitting on my bed…it's early in the morning…somebody is crashed out on the couch in my room…I wonder who it is…anyway…the festival gig was last night and it was a *riot!* Oh, man…so much has happened. The poser band from Memphis got practically *booed* off the stage and they were *real* jerks to us. It was *so* bad ass playin outside…in the daylight. When we got up there, the pit was so huge and the crowd rushed the stage with such force that they *almost pushed it over*. Some 'head of the festival' dude climbed up on stage and started screaming at me to stop playin. What the fuck? *Stop* playin? That's like one of the rules of rock and roll. You don't stop playing during a song. I frantically looked for a signal from the guys that this was okay but with their backs to me, they had no idea I needed them. I know I pissed that guy off cuz I just kept right on playin' with him screaming at me and waving his arms wildly. Eventually, he grabbed Max, which freaked Max out real bad, and made us quit. The crowd went fucking *crazy*, booing and shit. This dude had *no* idea what he was getting into. He seemed scared…listening to the ranting crowd…scared that if he pulled the plug on us, he'd get killed or something. So, he politely told the crowd to calm down, and they did, and the show *rocked*. I picked Cade up at the bus station yesterday around noon. He is really cool! Adam and Wayne showed him the ropes and he caught on pretty well. Kathy and everybody came up from Memphis and we partied at the house. It was great. I think that's her on my couch.

Thursday night, I went deep into the womb of the earth. I did it. I cleansed myself in a bath, got some candles, and drove to the Grove. Cal was waiting for me. He led me down the path and to the right, going deeper into the woods than I had been before. We called the quarters. My body was throbbing…pulsating like…it was weird. I took off my clothes and stepped into the huge, rectangular shaped hole that Cal had dug for me. It was about two feet deep. I laid down in the soft, moist earth and he slowly covered me with dirt…gently packing it on me with the shovel. I asked him to cover my face too. When I was completely covered, the pulsating feeling through my body continued…but this time, the earth that surrounded me became like a choir…it complimented each pulse with its own…I was *convinced* Cal could hear this drumming…this rhythm of the earth and I…it had to be disturbing…but I laid still. It continued to throb in unison with me. Cal said I laid there for about fifteen minutes. When I came up, it was like coming up out of a swimming pool after a dive. He was standing there, smiling at me…candles blazing…the smell of incense sweet on the air. He handed me my clothes and helped me dress. He did not plague me with questions. We dismissed the quarters and packed up. We went to this little place in Walnut Grove to get some food…I was starving after this experience. I asked him about the pulsating sound…and he said he heard *nothing*. He said even the air was still until I came out. Then he said *he* wanted to do it.

The evening ended with him walking me to my car. We just kind of stared at each other for a minute. I thanked him for helping me…and he just stared at me and then he cradled his hands against my face…gently pulling me into him…and he kissed me. It was magickal. I floated all the way home.

7.5.94

Last night was *incredible*. Cal and I went into the woods after practice and sat in the stillness. Then we did our usual trip to the street, but this time we started fooling around…he was kissing me so passionately…as we laid there on that asphalt blanket. We went back to the cabin, lit candles, and called the quarters…and there was where we made love for the first time. I felt so completely…treasured. The *weirdest* thing is that while he was inside of me…I saw something…it was a vision I guess…it flooded my mind and took over my body…I saw *him*…but with some headdress on his head…it had these huge animal horns on either side of it…God it was so weird. It was like Cal was this half man and half…beast. God it was just so fucking weird. I didn't tell him about it.

I am more and more resentful of Ruger and his carefree lifestyle. The bills are piling up at the house and I know it's just a matter of time before we are gonna get kicked out. Sadie and Rita got an apartment in the hood in downtown Jackson, and they said I could live with them for nothing if I needed to. Mitch, the owner of the bar, is keeping the bar open during rehearsals. The area of the bar we are in has only three walls—so our practices are open for viewing. That pisses the guys off really bad. I don't care really. Personally, I cannot *stand* listening to other people practice. I don't know *how* it doesn't bother Mitch and the people in the bar. I mean we have to like practice certain *pieces* of songs over and over, which I know, has **got** to get annoying. The guys are pissed about it cuz they think Mitch is using us to attract business. I'm sure he is! But who in their right mind would want to hang out and listen to the same chord over and over? Well, maybe drunk rednecks. Mitch has decided to remodel the upstairs of the bar which means Cal has to move out. They are taking an old wooden shed and throwing some beds in it for him and a couple of other locals to crash in. It stinks and it's filthy. No air conditioning and cold water in a makeshift, bug infested shower.

7.7.94

We are getting kicked out of our house, and I'm moving in with Sadie and Rita. Ru is gonna live with his Gramma, Cades stayin' in the Grove, and Justine's movin' back to Memphis. I miss her already. I miss our silliness...our dice games...bein high...singing songs about crackheads. Things are really changing.

7.10.94

HOLY FUCKING SHIT! OH MY GODS! WE ARE IN FUCKING **RIP** MAGAZINE! That chick from the magazine that was at Crossroads wrote about *US*! We are in this section of the magazine that is about Buzz bands...so...does that mean WE are a buzz band? OH MY GODS! It is a little tiny write up, but who the fuck cares! It says: *"I also met The Redneck Vampires whose crushing heaviosity on their demo was impressive, as was their female drummer. They're top of the heap in their hometown, and ready to conquer further shores."* Then she gave our address...HOLY SHIT HOLY SHIT HOLY SHIT...we keep reading it over and over and over...I cannot *believe* it. I cannot believe it! And I *really* can't believe she said that about **ME**. Of all the cool things about the band she could have said, she wrote about ME. ME? ME! I mean...*damn*. She said I was IMPRESSIVE. Impressive? Me? I am impressive? I am impressive. I am impressive! **I am impressive**! I am trying this on like a new outfit. Wow. What a fucking huge compliment. How fucking huge is that. This has definitely been what we needed to kick our asses.

7.15.94

I cannot *believe* the amount of "fan" mail that has been piling up in our mailbox. I have been getting like five letters a day from people, mostly teenagers, from all over the country that saw the write—up in the magazine. They want pictures, tapes, t-shirts…it's blowing me away. I *never* expected this. What sucks is that we are all moving. I guess I can forward the address. I can go get a P.O. box. We are practicing regularly out in the Grove at the bar and writing songs out the ass. The RIP article really kicked us into gear.

Cal and I are so amazing together. It is *so* fucking great. It really is. He is so cool about *everything*. I guess my biggest fear about having a serious boyfriend is the whole cheating thing—it really hurt when the asshole boyfriend cheated on me. I have come to understand that all men cheat. They just **do**. My friends tried to tell me that if Sam loved me he wouldn't have cheated on me. I disagree. I believe he *did* love me—he loved me to the best of his ability at the time. So, I decided then that I would never tell another man that we were *exclusive*. I would tell my next significant other that he could fuck whoever he wanted. Perhaps this is reverse psychology—give him room to screw around and he wont—or maybe I am a dumb ass…but Cal and I talked about it and agreed we could sleep with whoever we wanted—that sex was just sex. I said this to him KNOWING I was not ever going to fuck around on him, but I wanted to let him know if he got the opportunity to get some while I was on the road to go ahead if he wanted to. Of course, I hope he won't.

7.17.94

We are playin at CMJ music showcase at the end of the month in NEW YORK CITY. I cant fucking believe it. I am *SO* excited. I am using the RIP article on flyers for the show. One of the bands we met at Crossroads is hooking us up. Okay, so we aren't *officially* in the showcase, but the chick that is managing this band we met says she knows people that can squeeze us in. Ruger has scammed some local girl into coughing up $600 to finance the trip. She is gonna draw up some damn contract, hell, I don't blame her, for assurance that we will pay her back. Ruger hooked all this up without asking ANY of us. He did this with this girl completely behind our backs. I would not have agreed to it at all. I know we can't pay that girl back. Ruger knows that too. We are still getting a ton of fan mail at the house. Amazing.

7.19.94

I moved in with Sadie and Rita yesterday. My room here is cool…this house reminds me of a Midtown Memphis house. My room has a window in it that opens out to the roof over the porch. You can crawl right out onto the roof and sit, get stoned, and watch the world go by. The girls listen to the Indigo Girls and Tori Amos and drink tea a lot. I feel comfortable here, but I feel disconnected from the guys and I miss Justine. I mean it man, she and I were close and I miss her a lot. Cal helped me move in and he spent the night with me. The vibe is so different here.

I got the P.O. box for the band set up and I made little slips to take with us to gigs for our mailing list. Lots of other bands have them and it is a really good idea. They send out newsletters and let folks know when they are playin' and where. I've got all the addresses from the letters we've received logged in a notebook so I'll put them on the list too.

The 22nd is full moon and Cal is going to go 'under'. I think I am more afraid of taking care of him while he is under than I was going under myself. Just being alone in the pitch black woods…with him so vulnerable like that…I mean…what if somebody followed us back there? What the hell would they think we were doing?

7.23.94

Cal and I are *such* a good team. He went under last night and it was so amazing. It was just as powerful of an experience on the outside of the event as it was on the inside. We are really good together. I've been spending almost every night in the Grove. I feel kind of bad about not hangin' with Sadie and Rita more. Rita was kinda seeing this dude in the Grove so she was ridin' out here with me a lot but she's not seein him anymore. They have been hangin' out with some new people at the house a lot. Maybe I'll stay home tonight and smoke out with them.

7.25.94

I cannot fucking *believe* it. Sadie and Rita just came up here to work to tell me THEY got kicked out of the house. I mean like KICKED out—where I need to go get my shit like *right now*. There is no way I can leave work! This is absolutely the shittiest. What the fuck am I gonna do? Where am I gonna stay? I guess I'm gonna have to go stay with Cal. Hell. I'm there all the time anyway. The shack thing that Cal lives in is not something I would want to write home about but I guess it will do. I need to call him at the bar…I talked to Hope…she's paying for me to get a tattoo!

7.?.94

I lost *so* much of my shit moving in with Cal. When I went to the apartment to get my shit I was able to pack up most of it, but I decided to wait till in the morning to go get the rest of it and when we got there it was on the curb. No shit. I'm glad I went right after work to get the important stuff. The "cabin" as I now call it is not that bad, but Mitch, the owner of the bar, is no fun to be around. He's like 6"4 and totally cut and he's a control freak from hell. He bosses Cal around. Cal is like his little slave. Mitch smokes crack and drinks all day and he is totally unpredictable. I am scared of him. He freaks out on shit and rages. He's got like one tooth that sticks out of the roof of his mouth and it kind of points at you as his eyes dance with fire about whatever bullshit he has cooked up. There is always a conspiracy…always someone after him, after his pot plants deep in the woods, some drama with his ex wife and kids…He is a really big guy…all muscle…completely violent. Something just isn't right about him.

New York was kind of a nightmare. I am embarrassed to say that we didn't get to play after all. No fucking shit. It took forever to get there…we ran out of money…but we did go sight seeing (the free shit) and we went to the Statue of Liberty and I Erik and I got stoned on Liberty Island! That rocked. When we got to the club the night we played, I had a funny feeling that their schedule was gonna run so tight that we weren't gonna play after all and I was right. It's cool to see other clubs in other cities and see how the scene runs in other places. I saw this dude…he was wearing a long black coat, but he wasn't all gothed out or anything. He had piercing blue eyes and long, black curls. He caught me staring at him, and I was embarrassed and looked away. I pretended to be watching the band playin', but I couldn't help but look over at this guy and I swear he was staring at me. *Through* me. I noticed he was wearing the Hammer of Thor around his neck. I smiled at him, so we could quit playing the "I'm not looking at you, you're not looking at me" game. I reached in my backpack to get my smokes, and when I leaned back up into my chair, he was standing there, in between the chair and the railing. I can't remember his name, but he told it to me, and I told him mine and he asked me if I was from there. I laughed. I told him about the showcase and the band and he said I had a southern accent and it was sexy. I commented on his Hammer of Thor pendant and he seemed surprised that even knew what it was. It looks like a drum key, actually. He told me he made it himself. We began talking about runes and rune theorists. This great conversation was interrupted by Erik. He kicked me under the seat and asked me what I was doing. What? Can I not talk to other people? I gave him the **look**…the look that said he needed to shut up…that I was fine and I could take care of myself. Yeah, right. But anyway, I cannot express how mesmerized I was by this dude. All the sudden the dude said he had to go, but that he would be back. It was weird. About an hour later he came rushing back in and he put both of his hand on my shoulders and lifted me up out of my seat and he fucking KISSED me. He fucking *kissed* me! Just like in the movies…when the guy just forces one on the girl. "I have to go…come with me", he said. I was *melting*. I couldn't leave! We hadn't even **played** yet. There was no way the guys would let me leave. *Leave?* With a *stranger?* Off into the dark, exciting night of New York? Ahh…I didn't go. Except for the tail of his long coat swirling behind him, I never saw him again.

I'm driving from the Grove to work everyday and back. It's **so** tiring. That long ass drive. I sometimes flinch when I get all the way back home to the Grove after a long day at work and I see the band's cars at the bar. That means we are gonna practice. I get so tired. It's weird with Cade and some other dude whose name escapes me crashing in the cabin, too. I just want to kick back and get stoned after work. I can't play well when I'm stoned.

Cal and I have bought all kinds of herbs and have begun studying about them and their uses. We make sachets and jewelry out of rocks we find in the woods. We are keeping all our supplies in a big black box with a lock on it. Together, we have quite a library of occult books! We've started hangin' out with Anna at the bookstore. I don't really see or hear from Janine anymore. Anna has taught us all about working in a coven, and seems real eager to get us together to start one. Cal and I have both worked solitary until we met. We don't know what to think about it. I mean, what the fuck is the point? To get together and play 'witch'? I just don't know. I know how I feel when I do what feels right to me. Like when I make amulets...I can *feel* them...and when I use candles...not just light them...but USE them...I can feel them too...I just don't know about *sharing* this feeling with a group of people. And honestly, I don't know how comfortable I am with the concept of two Gods, a male and a female. I have always thought that God was *above* gender...and that it is self-centered for us to think that the creator(s) looks like WE do. I don't know how cool it would be of me to commit to a coven when I am not convinced of the Wiccan beliefs. I definitely believe that the God has both a masculine aspect and a feminine aspect, and I have identified them as the god and goddess present in Wicca. But Wicca is really feminine based, which is the opposite of Christianity, and I think the goal should be balance of both. Another thing I have a problem with is all this power shit and this self will shit. Cal and I are both starting to study the *Golden Dawn* text and some of Crowley's stuff, which seems to involve the human will. If I want a thing...a lover...whatever...and I use the power of nature to accomplish it, and I have seen this done, how do I know I am not interfering with the natural flow of things? What gives **me** the right to interfere? Because I am special? Better? Because what I want is more important? Aw, *hell* no. I just think this is wrong. It's manipulative. It robs innocent people of their right to choose. So, if that's the case, what the hell **is** witchcraft...other than a sneaky way to manipulate the elements to get what you want? If so, it's not for me. If I can use it to bring some good into the world, that's cool...but hell how do I know that the world doesn't need the bad sometimes, too? To keep the balance of things? Fuck, man, I don't know what the fuck I am talking about.

Anyway, Anna has started carrying all kinds of craft supplies and Cal is real intrigued with some of the tools she got in from a dude from the mountains. Wands and athames. We also started hanging out with this lady from the Grove named Demi. She is *totally* crazy. She has a husband and two kids and she is like the husband that stays out partying and never comes home. She is sprung but she is fun to be around. She's really into studying with us and we took her to meet Anna. They hit it off right away. Anna gave us a tape of a Wiccan signing group called "Mother Tounge". I took my smallest drum that I'm not using and I've been playin along to the tape and memorizing every word to the songs. It takes 30 minutes to drive from the Grove to Jackson so that gives us plenty of time to sing and get stoned. We are going to Chicago for two or three weeks pretty soon. It's our first real road trip. I am so tired. I'm gonna finish this bowl and crash.

7.29.94

Man. Last night, this dude that's always at the bar came back to the cabin and offered to get us high. He packed a bowl and we all just started chatting about shit. He passed it to Cal, who took a hit, and then Cal passed it to me. Right after I inhaled, I felt this *surge* in my chest, and Cal started waving his arms around telling me, "**NO, put it *down*.**" I started choking and my head started to spin a little bit. I felt a warmth all over me. Cal said, "Dude, we don't smoke that shit, man". I was like "What shit?" Cal said, "Crack". I was so *pissed*. That dude put a fucking *crack* rock in the pipe under the pot. He apparently sells the shit. That must be the way he gets people, he sneaks it up on them. Mother fucker. I have smoked crack.

3

Natural Childbirth and Bunny Bread

8.2.94

I went to Memphis last Sunday. I got my tattoo! It's SO huge! I have a couple of others, but nothing as cool as this one. It is *so* cool. It's a big ass tribal angel. It's all black work. It's on my outer left leg under my knee. It' about ten inches long and five inches across. It *rocks*. It hurt *so* fucking bad. I mean it hurt to the **bone**. My freakin BONE aches. I am washing it three times a day and using A&D ointment.

I stayed with Hope at her new house. Hope wanted me to come and see the house she and her fiancé bought. They dated three weeks before she moved to Los Angeles to be in that band. Liam moved out there six months later and they've been together ever since. Anyway, so I get to Hope's house and we are just checkin' it out an shit and she tells me she wanted me to come to Memphis to do more than get a tattoo and show me the house. She says she wants to talk to me. I am sitting on the hearth of the fireplace in the empty house just staring at her. Then she starts telling me that the partyin' thing is cool an all that, but she never thought I'd take it so far. I told her it was just pot…and a little acid…but she said she didn't care and that I was going a little too far. She said that when I was with the asshole Sam, she wanted me to live a little and smoke a little bud, but she said now it was ALL I do and she thought it was a problem. I was like "Dude, don't worry about me." I know I will never take this too far. I know what **real** drugs are and I am not doing *them*. No one in the band does *real* drugs. That would really bother me if they did. I really appreciated her concern and I told her that, but she doesn't have anything to worry about. It still bothered me. I thought about it all the way home.

8.10.94

Cal and I started working in a coven with Anna, Demi, and this guy named Vince that Anna knows. Vince is okay, but I kind of get a weird vibe from him. He is really into evocation—and I suspect for all the wrong reasons. Anna said she was the Crone of the coven, because she is the oldest female. She wants me to become the High Priestess. I've been thinking about it a lot. Cal says it is an honor and I would be great at it. Demi agreed. I just take that so seriously. I mean I would be responsible for the spiritual development of everyone involved. I would represent the goddess during ritual, I would be responsible for the protection of everyone involved at all times. I would be responsible for the energies we utilize...for putting them back...it's a serious responsibility. We did a circle together for the first time in the bookstore the other night after it closed, it was really cool. There's this guy named Mark that has been hanging around at Anna's. He is an old friend of hers. He gives me the creeps. I don't know what it is about him...he just has this weird look in his eyes and he kind of shakes...like he is not balanced mentally very well. One thing that is really weird is that just out of nowhere he asked me why I have peacock feathers on my staff. Now how the hell would he have known that? Anna says he is psychic...maybe so...but she could have told him...and she swears she did not. Anyway, Mark is quite the authority on Crowley and Hermetic magick and Cal and I can listen to him talk for hours about it. He gives me weird looks though. Maybe I am just being paranoid.

8.13.94

Mitch freaked me out *so* bad last night. He and Cal were talking about the shitty ass stinky cabin and Mitch lost his shit and ran out there and like started throwing all our shit out and he poured straight bleach on the floor and started jumping in the puddles of bleach and screaming "How do you like it now!" Cal is allergic to bleach. Mitch knows that. Mitch is so big and scary. I think he loves to boss Cal around and he loves to intimidate me. Cal dyed his hair black.

8.19.94

Man. Anna is in the hospital. She came down with pneumonia just out of nowhere. We are getting the coven together and we are going to raise up some power together for her healing. Oh, get *this* shit. We've been practicing like every night to get ready for the road, and last night during practice Wayne said some guy nobody knew was sitting outside in a car for like *two* hours. They are always paranoid around here about shit, so Wayne went out there and asked him who he was and what he was doin'. He said he was just hangin out, which made Wayne suspicious. Then, Wayne notices the guy has a loaded fucking *crossbow* on the front seat next to him. Then he asks Wayne if *I* am in the building. Wayne said I was, which was obvious by the music. Then Wayne decided this was not a cool scene at all, and he walked inside to go get Adam and Mitch so they could tell the guy to leave, and when they went back outside, he was gone. Cal and I asked him what the guy looked like, what his car looked like, and Cal and I just looked at each other. We knew by the description of the guy and the car it had to be Mark—the creepy Crowley guy. I am pretty freaked out about it. The guy is not mentally stable at all, and combine that with the study of Esoterics and you have a recipe for disaster.

8.21.94

The afternoon was overcast, and a slight chill was in the air; the kind that isn't uncomfortable, but just bites your bare ankles enough to remind you you're alive. We did our circle for Anna. Vince and Demi met Cal and I at the bar. We donned our ritual robes, gathered candles and incense, and headed for the woods. We went *really* deep into the forest, to a new place we all decided upon. We found a tiny brook bubbling along next to an open glen. It was perfect. Vince started a fire. Cal and I measured out the circle and set up the quarters. When all elements were in place, we called the quarters as a group. We asked the earth for healing energy for our friend, and took elements from the circle and a personal object from each of us, and put them into a glass bottle. Cal sealed the bottle with wax from the candle for air, asking the power of air to assist in the healing of Anna's airway. It was a wonderful experience, with the exception of Vince wanting to evoke a fucking *demon* out of the fire. When he suggested doing that, I had no choice about being the High Priestess of this coven. I became her at that moment. I knew in that instant *exactly* what that was all about. I told him no very, *very* firmly, and when I did so, I could see a look of relief come over Demi's face. I did not realize until that moment that he was making her nervous too, and I felt really comfortable taking charge of the situation. I guess in a way I felt like the confidence to tell him no came from somewhere…from. something larger and bigger than I am…perhaps from the Goddess herself if I may be so blunt. I felt like it was my responsibility to lead the group in the right direction, which is what a High Priestess truly does. After the ritual, I made a bouquet of leaves and wildflowers for Anna and we went to the hospital to see her right after.

No one has seen creepy Mark's car at the bar. I told Anna about it and she said he was harmless but I just don't agree. Cal is concerned about it as well. I'm still reading Donald Tyson's *The New Magus* and it fucking rocks. I feel so comfortable with his ideas…especially his concept of God as "the light". Cal feels the same way. I just cannot express how awesome it is to have him in my life. He is *so* fucking cool. We get along so well. The band is getting ready to go on the road for a long time and it is gonna be so weird being without him everyday—but at the same time, I have nothing to fear…like I would with another type of dude. I am not afraid that he will cheat on me…or that his heart will be swayed…or anything. I just know completely and totally that the man loves me fully. He is sitting next to me now…surrounded by a pile of books…reading. He is so beautiful. His jet black hair twists around his white skin…framing the blue eyes that twinkle like stars in my sky…I'm going to kiss this man that I love.

9.9.94

I fucking *hate* them. They make me sick. *Every one of them.* We've been here for five days. We have over five more to go…All of us are broke…I've got a damn kidney infection...I'm miserable...we are almost out of bologna...and Katrina, the chick that is letting us stay here and all the guys just totally fucking left me asleep. I bet they went to the Tower. Fucking assholes. Ruger knew I wanted to go real bad. That *son of a bitch*. I am gonna *crucify* him. I wish there was a couch here. My legs really hurt from sitting and sleeping on the floor. She told us she was moving out this week and there would be no furniture...none of us complained. We don't even know her.

9.9.94 later

The view was like seeing a million fires burning from one end of the earth to another. I gave Ruger *hell* when they got back. I couldn't believe it when later that night he took me, just me, to the Tower. It was so beautiful. Absolutely amazing. I really love him. This has been an interesting trip. Mom wired me ten bucks—so I got to eat something today. The constant hunger has been really hard on me. I have just tried to stay stoned, which helps with the hunger pains. Yesterday Cade and I went to the library on the L and it was absolutely fabulous. It was the biggest library I have ever seen in my life. I didn't want to go by myself cuz I figured I'd get lost and Cade was the only one of them who would go to a library. Anyway, before I left, Cal copied the next few chapters of a book by Israel Regardie on ceremonial magick—well, I couldn't wait to tell him I found a *gold mine* in the Chicago library—they have a locked room—you had to have security access to get in—with all these old spiritual books in it. They have the whole Regardie collection! And the whole *Crowley* collection! They have an old copy of *The Golden Dawn* Cal would *die* for. They have real old manuscripts and really old Hebrew bibles. I was in *heaven*. I had four dollars left from what Mom gave me and I spent a buck on copies...*God* I wished I'd had more cash. Erik has gone back home until our next show. He is gonna drive all the fucking way home and then come all the fucking way back. I know his dad is giving him hell about the band and I assume his wife is too.

9.14.94

I was so glad I had brought my green boots and a black dress with me. Katrina, the chick we're staying with, had to work at this Goth club in town called the Neo. She volunteered to take any of us with that wanted to go hang. I was hoping to get to go out. Wayne, Ian, and Cade went with us. We parked her car and then walked down the street to an alleyway. Katrina led us down to the end of the alley where there was a fence and on the left of it was this *huge* black dude in sunglasses—just like in the movies. He smiled at Katrina and I swear he had fucking *fangs*. He let us all in for free. We went in and the club was kinda small, but cozy. There was a mix of the Sisters of Mercy blaring, and there were people...er...uh...*vampires* dancing on the dance floor. I don't know if you could call it dancing, really. It was more of a swooning, sweeping thing that did not flow with the music at all. They all had white faces and really blacked out eyes. One of them had this old fashioned gown on with ruffled cuffs and a cape lined with red velvet. The cape came up behind her head like Dracula's. I kinda surveyed the club. There were hunched over figures at the bar. The bartender looked like the rest of the people in the place. This one creepy dude stared at me when I walked by him. He came up to me later and pushed his mouth in my ear and said "you pull energy out of the floor like spiders"...I smiled at him, but I was kinda scared of him. He had fangs, too. He then told me his name was "Vlad". Oh God. The guys made fun of him for the rest of the trip. Anyway, I went to the bathroom, hoping I could find someone to smoke a joint with me. There were these Goth chicks in there, sitting on the counter next to the sink. They stared at me like "Who the fuck are you and what are you doing in our house?" I felt like an intruder in the fucking *bathroom* of this place. I asked them if they wanted to get high and one of them said she did. I pulled out one of the Walnut Grove joints I had, and she was like, "Uh...that's the biggest joint I've ever seen." Anyway, sharing my drugs with her did not make her any nicer to me. After becoming completely stoned, they handed me a card that was apparently an announcement for some birthday party for some Goth DJ lady they called "Scary Lady". The card was black and silver and it was instructing you on what kinds of gifts to buy this chick. I was like...these people must *worship* this fucking lady! Little did I know she was the DJ at the club that night. *She* was the Goth lady in the black gown with the cape. I guess my invite was payment for getting them high. I know I wont go to this event, but I sure would love to see what crazy ass shit goes on at a party like that. I am *so* infatuated with this lifestyle. Katrina says that in Chicago, you aren't accepted as a true Goth unless you dress like that all the time, not just when you go out. Like to the grocery store and everything. *Wow*. So, after she got off work, we went to another club. This one was called "The Gotham", another Goth club. It had these kick ass crucifixes on the outside of the club and a room inside that was *completely* lined in red velvet—I mean like the walls, the floors, the furniture, *everything*. Katrina bought me a couple drinks at the main bar and we watched what was goin' on. The place was *amazing*. There were these two guys dancing together that caught my attention. They were both bald and tall and semi muscular. They were wearing black patent leather pants and big chunky boots and had tattoos and wore black grease paint under their eyes. They seemed so...*dangerous*. There was this chick there with a snake wrapped around her throat...she wore a red leather corset and had black pants on and she had white hair. She hung with the bald dudes. I was completely enmeshed in watching them. We didn't stay there long. The next thing I knew I was waking up in the back seat of Katrina's car to the sound and feel of metal crashing on metal, and I started yelling. Katrina was like, "What is **wrong** with you? I'm just parking the car!" "Parking the car? You just *rammed* that car in front of us and pushed it up like two feet!" I said. She was like, "Yeah, we do it all the time. If you don't, you wont get to park anywhere. Hell, what do you think bumpers are for, anyway?" I was *shocked.* If you did that in Memphis, you would get in big trouble. We were parking to go to some other club I don't remember the name of. It was the most *amazing* place I have ever seen. It was the *hugest* club I have ever been to. It had three main stages in it; four dance floors, a viewing bar with these windows like in an air traffic-controlling tower where you could see the entire bar down below you. It had these staircases coming out from all over the place leading to God knows where. People were *everywhere*. All *kinds* of people. The line to get in the place was down the block, but apparently, if you work at a club in Chicago, you get in free at any club in town. Before I knew what was happening, Katrina led us through a dance floor to a tall staircase lined in red fabric. A man stood at the bottom of it and Katrina whispered something in his ear. The next thing I knew he unlatched the chain and we were walking up the stairs. We arrived in a room with soft music playin. A small bar was in one corner of the room and couches and chairs lined the walls. On my left was a huge pane of solid glass...some thirty feet high and twenty feet wide, overlooking the entire club. "The VIP room," someone said. *Whoa*. I noticed a man engaged in conversation with someone. He looked completely familiar to me. I suddenly realized he was Bruce Dickinson from Iron Maiden, one of my old favorite heavy metal bands. I decided not to annoy him.

9.17.94

Either I'm crazy, or that Detroit club is in the dark ages, or that *town* is in the dark ages because all the flyers up in the club were for poser bands. I mean like, big *hair* bands and shit. Spandex. That crazy shit. We are on the way home. We just stopped at a grocery store in Detroit and spent all the money we had on one package of generic bologna and a loaf of bunny bread. We made sandwiches on the hood of the truck and everybody was bitchin'. I'm just glad I have enough pot to keep me stoned. Being stoned hides the hunger pangs beautifully! Just fourteen hours and were home!

9.18.94

We just got home. The shit has really hit the fan here. When we were in Chicago there was a *huge* bust at the bar. Mitch's ex wife got pissed off at him for something and she ratted on him to the cops. Stupid bitch. Cal said they came out and all they found was a little pot on Mitch. They searched the cabin and they like freaked out on all our stuff. They photographed ALL our herbs and books and supplies. They took pictures of our big ass pentacle on the wall. I'm sure we are the talk of this backwoods ass redneck town. They didn't find shit on Cal, but they did take his scales. They have to go to court about it next month. I don't know how Cal managed to hide all his dope in time. It is *so* good to see Cal. I missed him like crazy.

9.19.94

I started breathing really heavy and I felt this blackness all around me. I was more afraid of the blackness than the pain. I woke up this morning at about five o' clock with the *worst* fucking pain in my right side. I have had these pains before, when I was thirteen and then fifteen, and they thought it was appendicitis, *and* they thought it was kidney stones, but they were never sure. Well, they are sure now! I woke up in *so* much pain. I went outside. There was this low laying fog all over the place. It was like I walked outside and walked into mist. I felt like I was dead…I was dead and this was it…then the pain brought me back to reality. Cal got up and ran to get Mitch. I laid there on the floor of the cabin for what felt like forever. I could feel the blackness coming back and I knew I was about to pass out. I was so afraid that they would not take me to the hospital if I passed out that I forced myself to stay conscious. Mitch came to the cabin with painkillers. I told Cal to take me to the fucking hospital. He had never driven my truck before. He swerved down the windy roads, doin eighty miles an hour to the hospital. The nurses took one look at me and shriveled up their mouths in smirks…like I was some junkie, making up some bullshit to get high. They put me on a stretcher in the ER and started asking me questions. Then I started puking. I have *never* felt my body contort in the ways it did that night—I puked with such *force*…and nothing but spit came out of me the first three or four times…and then this bright green stuff started to come out of me. Through the puking, I answered their questions. Yes, I had gotten high that day but it was only pot, and no, I didn't do any intravenous drugs. I told them my history with kidney stones…they started poking around between my legs. I don't really remember much after that. The next thing I remember is the ER nurse standing over me telling me that they had found blood in my urine and particles of a kidney stone. Then the doctor popped his head over and said something I will never forget. He said, "Miss, you are experiencing the pain of natural childbirth." I could *not* believe it. *Natural fucking childbirth.* No shit. I remember thinking that if I had known for nine months that I was going to eventually be in that kind of pain, and it was for the purpose of giving birth to a human, it would be worth it. But, it was *not* a cool experience to have that sprung on me out of nowhere, and all I had to show for it was a tiny piece of calcium. The nurse then told me that she herself had passed *six* kidney stones. Something about knowing that made me feel better. The next thing I knew, Cal was standing over me, and they said I was okay, and the pain was gone. Cal looked at me real weird. I walked to the bathroom and tried to pee. I looked in the mirror. I could not believe what I saw. My eyes...they are like solid blood from one corner to the other. I burst *every* blood vessel in *both* eyes from puking so hard. It looks absolutely disgusting.

9.29.94

Mitch keeps Cal and I high, but man, do we pay for it. Mitch got a slap on the wrist in court for the pot. I sent Cal up to the stand with a pouch of Indian herbal tobacco and told him to tell the judge he used his scales to weigh out his own cigarettes. The judge agreed and held up his own scales and said he used his for mail. Cal obviously got off. Mitch smoked a joint on the courthouse steps. He is crazy for real. Demi took me to a clinic out here. I couldn't remember how long it had been since I had been to the gyno. That lady begged me to let her give me a depro shot. Savannah got real sick from hers so I told the lady no. I told her about the kidney stone. She said I needed to drink more water and lay off calcium.

We finally paid off our studio debt so the tape should be ready to print soon. Ruger and I were tossing around ideas about the name for it. Everybody has been hangin out and our shows at the bar are a lot of fun. We do one once or twice a month, unless you count our unofficial practices. It's getting real cool at night in the cabin. Demi said she had a neighbor friend who might rent out a room to us. We went and met her tonight. She is pretty cool and her two kids are adorable. I've never lived with little kids before. Her mom lives in a house next door and she has a biker boyfriend who scares the shit out of me. He looks at me really weird. It freaks me out. Demi said to stay way out of his way. I'm planning to do exactly that.

10.14.94

Word is we will be on the road for the rest of the year so I don't know *what* I am gonna do about my job. We are getting T-shirts made! I am *so* excited. We have tapes now too and it feels so good...it feels...*professional.* I have worked hard on the mailing list too, trying to keep it going. I've been working my *ass* off at the salon, and we practice several nights a week. I am tired most of the time. Sometimes I just want to chill when I get off work. Today is my birthday! I am 24. Hope is throwing me a party at the end of the month in Memphis. She says it's gonna be the *shit* but she wont say what she is gonna do exactly. She is even passing out *flyers* for the mother fucker. I can't wait.

10.24.94

I have never seen so much dope being smoked in one room by such a large group of people. Last night was one of the BEST nights of my life. Hope threw me the most un**fucking** *believable* birthday party. Slaphead lovingly donated his house for the event, which she *completely* redecorated with black trash bag stuff and cobwebs and mummies and she made caves and crazy rooms within rooms and used fluorescent paint in spirals and she created all these visuals. She rigged up amps to the stereo and put up strobe lights...it didn't even look like a house. It looked like a club, but *better*...candles everywhere...and fucking EVERYBODY was there. You could hardly *move*! She even got me a crescent moon cake. It was the most unforgettable birthday of my life. And Cal *missed* it cuz he dosed the night before and he was too tired to go with. Mother fucker. I was *so* fucking pissed at him. Hope and I dosed together. She wanted to dose one last time before she started getting her body in shape to have kids.

10.27.94

Ohhh I cannot fucking *believe* them. They call this big ass band meeting...and they come out to the Grove...and Erik basically says he's out of the band...he just can't do it with the kids and shit...so *Ruger* joins in with this shit about how his Mom has offered to pay for him to go to college...and he's talkin about *doin* it. I could *kill* them. All this shit I am putting up with...and they are gonna walk the fuck out like that. I thought things were going good. I can understand Erik's position, but Ruger is just being a baby. I told them I was committed as hell to the band. Max and Ian said they were, too. I hope Ruger thinks about what he is saying. He does *not* need to plant the seed of doubt in my head like this. He should listen to his own fucking lyrics.

4

Cooler-Water Hot Dogs and Hot RC Cola

11.24.94

Pretty soon I will need to light a lighter so I can see as I write. My flashlight is cruised. I am lucky to have a full stomach for the ride home. We played a few gigs in Chicago and we met this dude at one of the clubs who invited us to come to his folks' house for Thanksgiving dinner. It broke my heart when Ruger *insisted* we go on the road over Thanksgiving. I have *never* missed my family Thanksgiving before. It's not like it was a *showcase* gig. I cried about it secretly. It was really cool of this dude's family to offer to feed us. They even paid to replace our tire that blew out the night before. The blow out experience was REAL exciting. The guys fixed it in about fifteen minutes, though. I got out of the truck and stood there with them in the stinging air. They won't let me help; yet I know they expect me to freeze with them. Anyway, that dude's dad not only took the guys to a tire place to get a new tire but he *paid* for it AND put it on the truck in the cold, while WE ate yummy Thanksgiving dinner inside the man's house. I still can't get over it.

It's almost *scary* having so much luck. The dude's Mom even offered us a case of coke for the ride home. I declined. I couldn't *imagine* riding home on the tires they paid for, with the full stomachs they created…sipping soda they donated. I dread the drive home. Cal hooked me up before I left the Grove so I've got a joint left for the ride! I'm sitting in my spot…behind the passenger seat…with my window on my right and an ashtray built in to the door, my bag full of books and tapes at my feet…my pipe neatly packed under my seat…

11.24.94 later

The stench of burning rubber caught Ian's attention as we flew down the high-way and as I write we are stuck at a gas station. No one can recall the last names of the lovely people we just spent this holiday with, so calling them is impossible. I'm staying quiet. There is enough attitude in here already. I knew I had a scary feeling about all that luck. It looks like we can't call any of our Chicago connec-tions cause Ruger left his precious briefcase in Jackson. We don't even have that band Deviant's number with us. I should be the one bitching...I'm the only one in this band who has to be at work in Jackson, TN at nine o' clock in the morn-ing eight and a half hours away. Hell...I'm the only one with a job period. Well. A tow truck just pulled up. I wonder if he would grease our rear axle for a cooler-water hot dog. Or perhaps some stale bread and a hot RC Cola? We got $80 for the gig and it takes $60 in gas to get home. We are cruised again. Ruger keeps saying he knew we were moving to Chicago, but not this soon. Just that state-ment alone makes my stomach cringe. Move to Chicago? Why? Would it really help the band? Where would Ruger get money? I know I could find a job...but would I be supporting the whole band by myself? No one else works...except maybe Max...and I think he's dealin'. Would it be a huge mistake to move here? Or would it be the turning point for us? Am I being realistic? Or am I being chicken? Max and Ruger are *really* screaming at each other now. This makes me feel *so* uncomfortable. I am not gonna say a *word*. Max is mad at Ruger for screaming at Ian. Max is right, it's not Ian's fault. Hell, without Ian's dad we wouldn't even *be* in Chicago cause we wouldn't have wheels. Ruger just keeps bitching and whining and rubbing the situation in. It's not helping anything. Max just hopped back in the truck and said the tow truck driver laughed at our story and drove away cuz he knew we couldn't pay him. Where would we have gone anyway? A service station? And pay them with what? And crash where? In the truck, I guess. I feel so hopeless.

Ian just turned around and looked at me weird...and without saying a word he has cranked the truck and backed it up. Ruger is screaming at him and calling him a dumb ass. Ian is screaming right back telling him to shut the fuck up. Yay Ian! I love it when Ian stands up to Ruger. Ian is driving around in circles in the parking lot we are stranded in. I am holding my breath. Wow! On the third circle around the stench of rubber became almost unbearable and then there was a loud thud and Ian started to laugh. It was the emergency brake! The fucking *emergency* brake! The light to indicate it being on didn't work and the man who fed us and changed our tire that day had apparently left the brake on by accident. We had "cooked" it off the truck. I'm sure the guys are glad we didn't get in touch with anyone in Chi town now! They would have been *so* embarrassed.

I just caught Ruger pulling a macho stunt. He had just convinced me we were going in the right direction and that he knew exactly how to get home when I overheard him asking a store clerk for directions. Somehow, in the excitement of our "uncruisedness" we wound up in Indiana by mistake. Max just passed out a round of Xanax. At least I'll get some sleep! I'm never gonna make it to work tomorrow. If I get fired, I won't get my X-mas bonus.

It wasn't bad being four piece for the gigs this trip. We were a little concerned about it, but we pulled it off. We haven't decided if we are gonna work someone else in on rhythm or not. I miss the thickness of the two guitars. But we are pulling it off okay.

11.26.94

We gotta get a promo together for this kick ass booking agent. Bone Squad is using them and they've been booked solid for a year. I'm excited about it and scared shitless at the same time. I'd have to quit my job. I can't handle the thought of having to scrounge for cigarette money and for pot and food. I'd be stuck wherever I was. I'd have no gas money and no way to get to Memphis to get any money! I don't want to burden my parents with my unemployment and I know that's what would happen.

I've acquired a week of vacation since I've worked at the salon for a year. I can't *believe* I have had that job for a year. I can't believe I've been in this *band* for a year. I remember my "christening" party. Adam threw it for me. I didn't realize until later that the party wasn't even at his house—a group of people just all said "party at Sean's'" and they all just showed up at this Sean dudes house. Ruger and Sadie played this awful but cool trick on me. We were all fucked up and she decided we would play this game where we stood in a circle and someone would trace the outline of a symbol on the cheek of the person on their left. This would travel all the way around the circle and the object was to have the correct symbol drawn by the time everyone had a turn. I knew something was up. Fifteen minutes later, I realized I had black shit scrawled all over my face. I was the laughing stock of the party. At least it wasn't as bad as Max's christening. He got stranded outdoors after a shower naked. I 'm glad they didn't pull that one on me.

11.28.94

Just as I thought we had escaped our road trip unscathed, I realize I have yet again been "cruised". I left $500 worth gear at the Chicago club. I can't *believe* how fucking stupid I am. How can this be happening? *What am I gonna do?* We were all unloading the suburban getting ready for practice at the bar when I couldn't find my blue case that holds my double kick pedal. *Motherfucker.* It's gone for sure. I know the guys are *so* fucking pissed at me because we can't practice now. I *hate* this. I *hate* feeling like this. It was an *accident*! Ian's little brother Couch plays drums. He said he'd ask his brother if I could use his pedals. I had a bizarre dream that night on the way home…it could've been the Xanax…but anyway I dreamt a whole bunch of us were hanging out at a truck stop off a highway at night. I glanced over at my truck and a huge Tuba case came slamming down into the hood. It dented my truck all up. I opened the case and inside it was a severed elephants head. Hmmmm. Don't they say elephants never forget?

I had another surprise waiting for me when I got home. I don't live in the cabin anymore. Cal moved us in with Lana, Demi's neighbor that we met a while back. He and Mitch got into it about some shit, and it was time anyway. It was getting cold. We have a small bedroom in her house and it has a twin bed in it. He managed to cram *all* our shit in this little bitty room. We have to pay a little rent now, but Cal said she will probably just want us to pay her in buds, which is cool. It's refreshing being in a real house again, but I am going to miss the woods.

11.29.94

We've been talking to Jesse about jammin' with us. He is *so* fucking excited. He's learned *all* our shit—just like I did when I auditioned for this band. I think he would be an asset. His sound, his musical ability, and stage presence—it all fits.

He fits. And to make it even better, he is my friend. He is coming out to jam with us this week.

12.2.94

Sitting at work. I sent off a check to Music Emporium yesterday for $378.95. I *hated* doing that. A hundred bucks of it was to replace Max's mic stand I left at the Daisy. Jesse came out and jammed with us this week and it was fucking *awesome*! I mean it man...it just fucking fits. It really really does. He has the *best* attitude...he has the best *musicianship*...if that's even a word. He doesn't have any of that Ruger bullshit goin on. I have known Jesse for years and he has played in bands *and* worked at Fed Ex the whole time. I can't *imagine* bein in a band with a guy who has a job! I hope the rest of the band is a psyched about it as I am. I mean, to me it's glaringly fucking obvious that he fits...but Ruger still hasn't made up his mind.

12.3.94

I wish I could dictate my thoughts and they would just appear on this page. Writing is so lame. Biohazard is playin in Memphis tonight. My work is having a Christmas party tonight. Hmmm. Country line dancing or Biohazard's mosh pit...I wonder where I'll wind up.

Ruger and I finally discussed the problem we've both been trying to wish away. Ian has gone a little too far with his drug experimenting. Meth is as dangerous as crack to me. I'm not gonna tell anyone this but I'm practically dyin' to try it! I know I'd get fuckin hooked on the shit. Ruger views cocaine as being a natural drug, (I don't really) but he and I stand on the same ground when it comes to crack and crank and meth. Fuckin' shit. I'll die if my guitarist blows up. Max has been hanging out with this major supplier dude I call "The Man". This dude has a great ride and tons of cash and free dope for all us "celebrities". Max hangs out with him all the time and now Ian is hangin out with him all the time too. I told

Ruger months ago I was worried about Max. He calmed me and told me that Max was a disciplined vocalist and he wouldn't let things get out of hand. It's true that Max does get plenty of rest before shows and he refrains from pot before gigs because it screws up his voice. I was still concerned. Ruger is a major alkie. He denies it and true he has been refraining from drinking lately but that doesn't mean he is not an alcoholic. They don't think I know anything. Max has been *such* an asshole lately. He makes fun of me at practice all the time. I act like he is just playin around…I know he is…but hell…I swear there is something else in him now that I haven't seen before.

I can't help but blame Max for Ian's drug entourage. Ian is a big boy and no one is putting the shit up his nose for him but Max seems to egg it on. "The Man" is no help. Ruger said if it doesn't stop he's gonna confront "The Man" himself. Ruger talked to Max, who got defensive and made him feel like he was prying into business that was not of his concern. **I will be *so* furious if drugs wind up being the downfall of this band.**

12.4.94

I went to see Biohazard last night. The band members were fighting on stage. You had to really be paying attention to notice. One dude in the band looked like a skull with skin stretched over it. Not surprisingly, he was the one causing the trouble. They were bad ass, though. Jesse is officially our new guitarist! He is SO excited to be here. I hate that the drug problems are so apparent. He swears he's not going anywhere though. We needed Jesse as much as Jesse needed us.

We've been practicing *a lot*. Part of it was just to get to jam with Jesse. Tuesday we played the set over and over. We played like twenty-six songs. I was *dead* tired cuz I had worked all day and that was an extra long practice. The guys don't work so they don't have to worry about shit. Max quit his job and started working with a construction crew headed by a crystal/crack head. He worked them to death for a week and then blew everyone's pay up his nose and bailed out of town. Max hasn't worked since. It's been about a month or so. I don't know how he's paying his bills…hell I don't think I *want* to know.

12.5.94

I feel like shit. I think my urinary tract infection has spread to my kidneys. It scares the shit out of me. My lower back hurts really bad on both sides. To top it off I'm *sure* we have practice tonight. I'm obviously real excited about it. Man, my health is really suffering. I don't eat regularly and when I do its junk. I'm living out in the middle of fucking *nowhere*. I can't afford to eat today. Maybe I will make some tips. I really wish I was in a more stable environment. I remember what it was like before I moved to Jackson. I got up every morning, did thirty minutes of aerobics, ate breakfast, and went to work. Then I'd go to band practice and then hang out with my friends till twelve or so and go home and crash. I was happy, but I wanted a better musical project. Now, I have the better musical project but NONE of the serenity of my former life. I'm so tired all the time. I eat crap and smoke a lot of pot. Maybe that has something to do with it. I have to do something or I am gonna be huge and miserable. The drummer of this band should be energetic, attractive and thin. Not fat, ugly, miserable, and lethargic. I am so sick of looking at myself like this. Even I don't want to look at me.

12.6.94

Ruger just gave me our list of dates…December 10th, Memphis, Dec 14th Chicago, December 15th, Detroit, December 16th, Chicago, December 17th somewhere I cant remember, Dec 20th Indianapolis, December 31st home, January 26th, Champaign, January 27th Springfield, January 28th Chicago. Oh my God…I'm gonna have to quit my job.

12.7.94

Maybe today I'll fuckin quit. I've got this feelin' that everyone at work realizes I'm not takin any more shit. I cried all morning. I was so unorganized. I hate that. Cal saw the whole thing. I cry all the time. I don't know what's wrong with me. I could cry right now. For no reason at all. I'm tired and I want to go home. I'm meeting Mom at a truck stop today. She got me some antibiotics for my urinary tract infection. I love her.

The guys seem strange. Sometimes I feel like none of them give half a shit about me. Especially Ruger. I feel like they use me. It's easy to get me to do anything and they know that. I am overly co operable. I agree with all of Ruger's musical ideas. Sometimes I wish I could disagree with any part or something just to remind them I have an opinion. I don't argue cuz I don't have a reason to. Musically, things are *bad ass. That's why I am fucking here*! Ruger told me that the band fund has been paying the band phone bill at his Grandma's. I'll bet. This makes me feel *totally* taken advantage of. The band owes me $371 for the phone bill Ruger ran up on my calling card. He says it was my personal calls. That's BULLSHIT and he knows it. Sometimes I hate them. I hate all of them. They are mean to me and they run all over me. Hell, I'm to blame too cuz I let them. They have no respect for anyone including their band mates. Ruger is the worst.

12.9.94

My infection *definitely* spread to my kidneys. Lucky for me that I have such a sweet mom. Mom says the band is the root of all of my problems. Maybe she's right but she just doesn't get it. She says God's plan for my life doesn't include playin' in a band. I asked her if I could get a copy of God's plan for my life. That pissed her off. Shit, I have to believe that even if this isn't what "God" wants me to do, the experiences I am encountering are for a purpose and there is no doubt about that.

I found out how Max has been able to go without working. "The Man" is paying his bills. DAMN IT. Why can't I get a free ride? Why can't I get off so easy? I'm **so** fucking jealous.

I asked Mom if I could come home for a while. I know they would use that time to convince me to quit the band. Maybe that's not at all what I need. Maybe I could create a stable, peaceful environment without going home. But I need *money*. I'd like to quit smoking pot for a while and start exercising and eating healthy.

12.12.94

Jesse was *so* fucking excited. You could feel it all over him. Our show Sat night at Rascals in Memphis went good. It was Jesse's first gig with us. He was *real* nervous. I didn't expect things to feel different on stage compared to rehearsals but they **did**. Ian was on my right with Ruger instead of being by himself on the left, where Jesse now is. It was *weird*. I have a unique view of things being the drummer, I guess. I am so used to seeing them backwards from everybody else. I can make out faces in the crowd in between them, and I can tell how they feel about the show in the middle of the songs. Ruger spits a lot when he is thinking…or when he feels confident. Sometimes Max will turn around during a song and wink or smile at me when we are kicking ass. He is such a flirt. Rascal's was *packed*. We have acquired a new road manager from having Jesse. "Cornfed" is one of Jesse's best friends and he is a sort of "jack of all trades." Cade went back to Little Rock so we are gonna need Cornfed on the road. He is super nice to me.

I got totally stoned right after the show on the balcony, as always, and I was petrified when I found out we had to play an *entire additional set*. It was fuckin' two o' clock in the morning! The new owner dude was *crazy!* I thought the guys were fuckin' with me when they said, "Flo, get ready!" I was *so* fuckin' *stoned*. I can't play stoned worth shit. If I fuck up, they treat me like crap. It was *horrifying*. I pulled it off somehow. What a buzz kill. We made some cash off the gig. I overheard Ian telling Ruger he had $140. I heard Ru say he sold six or seven tapes. Ruger told me yesterday that he had $119. Hmmmm.

Cal actually went with me to the show! I had asked him to go Friday night and he said he might. I really wanted him to go. I am always talking about him but no one ever *sees* him. When I got home Saturday from work and asked him if he was going he said no. I lost it. I started bawling. I was just so exhausted and miserable. I dreaded the two-hour drive to the club; especially after working all day and driving the forty-minute drive home. I had no laundry clean and I had asked him to please do a load while I was at work and apparently, the washer was broken. I wont be seeing him for the next seventeen days because we are goin' on the road. I guess I thought he'd want to spend some time with me while he could. I was really glad he went with me.

We've been playin chess a lot. We just chill out together over a couple of bowls and play for hours. It's amazing how much that game seems to relate to real life. After playin a game I feel like I am still on the board…driving…cutting hair…playin' drums…staying in a safe zone. Moving my pieces carefully, I make decisions in life as I would on the board. I judge what my consequences are of each move on the board as I do in life. It's cool.

12.?.94

I feel like I am slipping away somewhere. Mom and Dad said "no way" about me coming home. It *really* fucking hurt my feelings. They absolutely *refuse* to offer me any help while I am in this band. No money, no place to live, *nothing*. My dad has never seen me play. Mom has been driven by guilt to show up a time or two over the years, and I'm sure Savannah talked her into it then. Ruger's mom is the *shit*. She is one of our biggest fans. She used to come to our shows in Jackson wearing the T-shirt! When we lived in the house, she would have us over every Sunday night. She would cook dinner and make us chocolate vodka milkshakes. I guess I just wish my parents would accept this is my choice instead of hiding from it and trying to *pray* it away. They are so different from me. They teach Sunday school at *Six Flags over Jesus* church. I guess I don't fit the mold they made. My dad has always been busy with his company, and mom started school when Savannah was born, and worked after that, and then went to grad skool, so my brother pretty much raised me. And *he* was living hell, because he was robbed of being a kid by having to be the parent. He beat the shit out of us on a regular basis; yet every Sunday there we were, in panty hose and shiny patent leather shoes, praising the lord in church. The happy fucking family.

All of the sudden my life doesn't seem to matter anymore. I mean my band, my job, my everything. It seems like I don't even care. I was SO moody last night. I wonder when this all started. I guess it started when we moved in with Lana. It turns out Lana just wanted some live in babysitters to take care of shit while she turns tricks. I thought maybe my dis-interest in the band was because I longed to spend more time with Cal, but even that isn't the same anymore. I don't feel like I belong anywhere. I just want to kind of hang out in my own shell. It's like my physical body is my own world and the limits of that world are my own physical body. I want to stay inside these boundaries and go nowhere. No one comes in and I don't go out. Fuck everybody.

We leave Tuesday at six to go on the road. I wish I could say I was excited about it and I feel guilty for not being excited. We are playin tonight in Memphis and I could care less. I'm really afraid that not working will leave me with too much idle time to slip further and further away into this dark place. At the same time, I am afraid that *continuing* to work will cause me to have a nervous breakdown. I can't work here anymore because of my band schedule and I can't get another job because of my band schedule.

I *won't* quit the band. That is not even an option. I could never live with myself. I'd really freak out then. I can handle this. I'll get some Valium to take with me on the trip in case I lose my shit or anything. That way I'll be sedated and I won't freak out.

I caught Ruger trying to talk Jesse into co-signing for him to get a new bass. Ruger gets everything he wants somehow or another. Poor Jesse. He would surely be cruised if he signs for Ruger. Ruger just has *no* damn respect for anyone. My dumb ass would have signed for him when I first got into the band, too. He must not have wanted a new bass back then.

God. I feel tears coming on. For no reason. What the FUCK is wrong with me? I'm getting pissed. I want to run away…far away…

12.?.94

Back on the road, headed somewhere up north. I have a feeling this trip is going to have some kind of major impact on my life. Maybe it's because I quit my job. Today was my last day! I still cannot fucking *believe* I did it. It was just getting to be too damn hard to do all of this. The band is more than a full time obligation…it's my **life**. The job is just forty-five hours that I found somewhere in between, but I don't even have that anymore. I feel so free but I'm scared shitless at the same time. I have not been unemployed since I was fifteen.

Just asked Ruger…we are playin' Chicago first. Chi-town feels homier each time we play here. It is such an amazing city. It's like it's another world reached only through the highest odds and hardest obstacles. This is our first trip with Jesse. I can tell he is *really* excited. We are covering four states in the next six days.

We have a U-haul trailer for the first time ever. It's weird looking behind my spot and seeing the rear window! Usually all our gear is jam-packed back there with barely enough room for a few duffels of clothes. Now it's somewhat…spacious? Ruger made the comment that the trailer makes him feel like we are a REAL band. I figured he felt that way.

I don't know if I wrote that they found my stuff at the club in Chicago. I can't *believe* it. I wish my new pedals were in. I got the mic stand and cymbal stuff. Ian's little brother, Couch, got his pedals back today. Good timing!

We are barely down the road and I still cant quit thinking about the fact that I quit my job. All the girls that worked there...they all wanted to do their own things, too, but the husbands came earlier than expected...then kids and not always in that order. Sometimes I wonder what I have done differently. Is it just fate?

12.11.94

Waitin' my turn for a shower. We're stayin with this dude named Wes who plays drums for a band called "Deviant". We met them the second time we played up here...during that two weeks we stayed with that girl, Katrina. The guys in his band didn't know what to think about us at first, but I suppose our southern charm won them over. It's become a ritual when we come up north to don these excessively *horrendous* southern accents. We talk in these accents *constantly*...to the club owners, to the bartenders, and especially to each other. This insanity does *not* stop. We rarely use our regular voices anymore at all. Hell, that's where my nickname, Flo, came from, from actin' like redneck assholes. There are people who think it's my *real* name! We call Ian Sody Mc Water...cuz when he gets thirsty he asks if we can stop and get a sody water, and Jesse is "the dog" but I guess he's been the "dog" for a long time...even before this band. Anyway, when we took the stage the first time we played with Deviant, you could tell they seemed really curious as to how we were gonna sound, bein' that we were super rednecks, but by the middle of the first song they were in the pit with fists flaring into the air...they apparently got the joke. I must say we hit *hard* and the music is powerful...slow, slaughtering grooves with Max and Ruger's thick, haunting vocals...and then Max just starts *screaming*...man I am rambling...anyway...Wes is really cool and has a nice apartment in the suburbs. It's a haul into town from here but awesome to have a free piece of carpet to crash on—plus it's a lot more comfortable stayin' with him than that chick we didn't even know.

I had a dream on the way here that the truck got wrecked. I think it was Ian and I alone when we hit. I saw the whole thing from like fifty feet above it. It's like I saw it coming and I flew away.

It appears it took like twelve hours to get here this time, instead of the usual eight. The alternator was apparently acting weird and Cornfed said we had to choose headlights or heat. The wind chill is *nine degrees* here. I don't know how I slept through the cold. Guess it was the Xanax!

Epic records is supposed to be coming to the show tonight. I talked to Cherie, the promoter chick, and she and I were working out how we were gonna get my drum shit to the club.

12.11.94 later

Its Wednesday nite "rock nite" at this club and apparently, this is a new thing so there probably won't be much of a draw. But we don't expect one, so it's okay. We are playin with some band from Indianapolis. Jesse's girlfriend is from here and her dad and brothers are supposed to come out.

Man! I found out from Cornfed exactly why it took so long to get up here. He said we had to stop *every thirty minutes* of the last four hours of our trip and *wait* another thirty minutes for the battery to re-charge. And I slept through it all. Cool! I missed the bitching! The truck would not start when we left for the club. More incessant bitching. We got a jump from a neighbor and barely made it here. The truck is now deceased. I'm sure we will make it home somehow.

I miss Cal. I thought about him on the way here. It will be weird not having to work Monday. Or Tuesday. Or any day! I'm halfway excited about it and halfway petrified. The band we are playin' with all work. Damn. I wish we could be an organized, realistic, practical band instead a bunch of spoiled brats. If they can work it out, we could too. I guess it's easier on them cuz they live three hours from here and can drive here and play on weeknights and drive home and still get three or four hours of sleep.

12.12.94

On the way to Detroit Rock City. It's hard to write cuz I'm wearing gloves. Ian cocked *such* an attitude earlier. I was *so* proud of him. Ruger and Max are always bitching about us smoking in the truck. They say I am *ALWAYS* smoking *SOMETHING*. I know it's true. I'll smoke a bowl...then I'll smoke a ciga-rette...then another bowl...then a cigarette to kick it in, and so on. They say I am like a chimney. When Max bitched at Ian for smoking just now Ian rolled his window all the way down (mind you there is NO heat in the truck and snow is *packed* on the highway here) and THEN he opened his fucking door! At seventy-five miles per hour! That shut Max up. It was great. I smiled secretly. We are lis-tening to the radio and that song by "Live"...lightning something...is on the radio. Ruger just turned it way up and everyone is silent. I wonder where it is tak-ing them. It's taking me...WHOA...I just glanced up and looked out my win-dow...and out in the huge, open, vast, snowy field...are two deer. One of them looked up...wow...how beautiful.

Our show last night in Chicago was DEAD. The opening band didn't even watch. I even gave them a joint! Inconsiderate asshole musicians. Well, I guess they did have to go to work. Our Chicago promoter, Cherie, was there and the Epic dude showed! He was impressed. The guys however said we had a bad night. Once again, I guess I have a different mix or they are being their extremely critical and perfectionist selves. Maybe both.

It gets colder as we draw closer to Detroit. More snow here. I look *ridiculous*! I've got my London Fog trench on and my Chuck's with fitted leg warmers over my entire shoes (Chuck's don't work in the winter) and gloves on and a big orange and blue scarf on and my headphones and my hat backwards. I think I'm wearing all of the clothes I brought!

We've got about five contacts in Detroit already. We should have a prosperous spring tour. Well, me and Cornfed are gonna smoke this joint...

12.12.94 at the club

Brrrrr...freezing in the backstage room. The club has heat, but not back here. I started my fucking *period* on the way here. I have no money to buy any pads or anything. This is gonna **suck**. I guess I could be the bleeding drummer. The bathroom back here has a scale in it and I weighed myself, which I know is not a good idea…but my dumb ass did it and I cannot **believe** how much weight I have gained. Oh my God. I've gained like thirty pounds since I joined this band. I can't *believe* it. Well, maybe I can. I mean I eat like shit. Not eating till midnight and then its fast food or gas station food. And then eating for a whole day when we have money. Fuck.

Wayne and I had an interesting conversation on the way here. We were talking about addicts and what defines an addict. I say an addict is someone who abuses unnatural substances. I know Wayne uses crystal. He doesn't seem to have a problem admitting he is an addict, but he doesn't feel that it is problematic. We discussed the word "abuse" in great detail. He was kinda starting to piss me off. He seems to think people that smoke pot are no better than people who do cocaine. Idiot. There is NO fucking comparison! Pot is a *completely* natural substance. It is not altered in some damn laboratory and does no harm to the human body, except maybe the lungs and hell, pollution does that. He just doesn't fucking get it. These dudes sure can press my buttons. A "pot' addict. Yeah right.

Detroit *has* to have some cool clubs *somewhere*. The opening act tonight is some really young local band. I hope people show up. The guys are shooting pool and seem to be enjoying themselves. We ran out of power again in the truck, but we weren't stuck as long as we could have been. Cornfed tightened the alternator belt. He's a *lifesaver*. The guys need to not be so fucking hard on him. They pick on him like *crazy*. It would not surprise me if one day he just doesn't pick the fuck up and leave. He showed me this kick ass sneaky ass trick. There is enough space between the stage and the wall for a drumstick to fall through, so under the drum risers and stages in clubs are *hoards* of lost drumsticks! I'm finding like three or four pairs a night…some slightly used…some brand spanking new. It's keeping my supply afloat! I found a brand new snare head under the stage in Chicago, so my snare will be snappin' tonight! We are headed back to Chicago after this show…I left my bag of clothes there since we are going right back. I will probably regret that. OOOOh! Ian's firing up a joint. **DAMN** it. I wish I could smoke it with him but I would cruise my whole reason for being here. Metallica is blaring through the club. Sometimes the music they play is so old.

5

The Devil Worshippers

12.14.94

Ridin' home to Dixie. I'm feelin' good. We had a good show in Detroit…but my timing was apparently *all* fucked up. Ruger is getting easier to figure out. I can always tell his opinion of each show by the way he acts immediately afterwards. If I am the last person he speaks to I had the worst show and he is disappointed in me. Then I start having these visions of being replaced and I fuck myself up. Hell. I was aware that my timing was off. I'm fucking human! I knew I would make up for it Friday night.

And I did. We *rolled* Friday in Chicago with Bone Squad. Deviant played too. They get better every time. It was cool seein' Memphis homies in another city. Bone Squad's van is **so** fucked up that they can't turn it off. *Literally.* If they turn it off…it's dead. So, they keep it filled up with gas constantly and they all have a key so they keep it locked and running while they do shows. It's *crazy*. Joseph, their singer, married some girl from here. He knew her for like a month. He is **so** crazy. They are all so cool and so fun to hang with. I learned all kinds of road tips. Lysol. Lice spray. Vitamins. Chewable Vitamin C. Washing pillowcases. Man. We are just babies at this.

At about three o clock in the morning, we were all packed up and we all headed out to this twenty four-hour burrito shop in downtown Chicago. "Burritos as Big as Your Head"…I think that was the name of the place…or maybe that's just what Deviant's drummer nicknamed it. Anyway, it was wild. The burritos really *were* the size of a human head…and they were good, fresh, and cheap. The place was *huge*. Gangsters huddled in a corner speaking Spanish. A group of elite gay men chain-smoking in the back. Drunk yuppie college kids. Quite a mixed clientele. An nobody fucked with anybody. I'd be lying if I said I wasn't a little scared of this big city. It's so overwhelming.

We didn't hit Greek town this trip. The guys managed to find a gyro shop but they said the food wasn't as good. I don't eat gyros. Something is weird about eating lambs.

It's hard to enjoy my buzz weaving in and out of Chicago traffic. It's two in the afternoon and people are everywhere. Richies in BMW's talking on cell phones. Poor people packed in the ghetto subways. Cabrini Green in its gray glory. People walking with their hands stuffed in their pockets...words freezing in mid air.

12.22.94

They didn't think we would make it. We got there at fucking ten after eleven! It was *wild* It was the *best* show of the road trip! We were scheduled to play in the Grove Sat night at eleven. We left Chicago Saturday afternoon around two and drove straight to the Grove. I was *so* exhausted. On Sunday, Cal and I went and got my truck and hung out at Anna's all afternoon. She gave me a job! Four hours every other day, twenty bucks a day. I worked Tuesday and Wednesday. Last night Cal, Ruger, Ian and I all went to Kathy and Justine's X-mas party in Memphis. It was rather cool! It was real laid back...friends...you know...not a fuck shit up party or anything. I got a bad ass candle from Kathy and a necklace from Mica and two from Justine. We are on the ride home from the party now. I've got some X mas shopping to do. Lana, the kids, Cal, etc. I doubt my measly check is gonna do shit. I heard so much silly gossip tonight, what Sam is doing...what the old band members are doing...more like WHO they are doing...The next few days are gonna be rough on me...Oh...can't forget Cal's Mom...I need to finish this bowl and write a list...

12.26.94

X-mas has come and gone. It was cool going home. My big brother, Joe, beat me in chess (for once without cheating). Hope gave me a cross that belonged to her Grandmother who died this year. Her Grandmother was a devout Catholic and I don't know if she'd approve of my pagan ass having her cross. I am so touched that Hope gave it to me. It's like it's a family heirloom or something. Cal and I watched The Wizard of Oz and crashed over there Friday night. It was cool. She liked her gifts.

I racked *up* at Moms. Dad gave me $100, Joe gave me $30, and Mom gave me a beautiful leather trench coat. I spent *all* my money today on all kinds of toiletries…I got toothpaste, new make up, q-tips, a new toothbrush, shampoo and conditioner, deodorant, pony tail holders, new nail polish, pads, hell you *know* you are stocking up when you buy pads and you are not even raggin'! No more socks to ruin! I cannot *believe* I am **this** excited about toiletries.

We went to Cal's parents Sunday. He got along with them and everything! Oh! Ruger's step dad is seriously considering a move to Miami soon. That means Ruger's mooching money would be *cut off* and he knows it and he is SCARED. Reality hits like a motherfucker! His Mom offered him free college and a free apartment if he would move there. He is considering it as I write. Fucker. I wonder if the band would stay together if he quit…Hmmmm. My new lil' job is pretty damn cool. It's fun working with Anna. Hangin' out, lookin' at books, makin cappuccinos…she says I make great froth!

I am enjoying being the hell out of the slave driver salon *so* much. I feel almost alive again. The—well, I would say the *depression* is over but I don't want to jinx anything. I braved Wal-Mart today. It was *so* crowded. Where do all these people come from anyway! I'm doing OK on my new beading loom and I made some pottery last night. It was cool! Cal loves the soldering iron I got him. He made me a beautiful dream catcher for X-mas. He also made me a handle for my athame. It looks like his copper wand. It kicks ass. Existence is cool right now. I better go before I fuck it up.

12.28.94

Cal is telling me to write this down. I lost my home in Memphis. I lost my kick butt job. I lost my chance for a college education. I lost some friends. I lost my sanity. I lost my new home in Jackson. I lost credit with the phone and utility companies. Then I lost my new apartment—which, during eviction, I lost my furniture (it was stolen from the curb at the apartment). Then, I lose the jam box in my truck (no tunes). Cal and I moved in together and lost some romance (no serious damage). I then lost a guitarist, and soon after $500 worth of equipment. I've lost books, clothes, tapes, videos, jewelry, etc. in all this moving around. I soon lost my sanity again when I lost my job to go on the road. Then I lost Thanksgiving with my family for the first time in my life. I then lost my health…(colds…sinus shit…and the urinary tract infection which spread to my kidneys) I then recently lose a kidney stone…I've lost touch with my sister and dear friends from home. I've lost my daily connection to the guys and now I've lost permission to go to the neighbors and use the phone and the shower and laundry and now the other neighbor lost *her* phone. I always said if I ever lost the one thing I had left…The one thing I haven't lost. My best pal. My most dependable friend. My **truck**. My ride. My ticket. It's dead and I killed it. The mechanic offered me a thousand dollars for what is left of it. He says it's got a cracked block. I think I'll dye my hair green. No, maybe purple/fuchsia.

1.13.95

We played a huge New Years Eve show. We played after Bone Squad got done. We had their back wash crowd. I stayed in Memphis for four days after the show. I hung with Savannah some. Mostly I stayed at Jesse's playin' Dungeons and Dragons with Mica and everybody. Mom almost saw my tattoos! I was showering in her bathroom in their clear glass shower when she walked in. I was almost busted! I had to hold my legs at really odd angles so she couldn't see. When I got back in Jackson, I went straight to the shop. Demi was there and she said Cal was a mess because he thought I took off with the ounce of dope he gave me to sell while I was in Memphis. *What the fuck*! You would think he knew me better than that. That blew me away. I actually smoked so much of it that the quarter bags were *real* skimpy...I mean *bad* skimpy. We usually get a fat ounce fronted; we keep a quarter and sell the other four. I split the keeper quarter with Cal before I left. I smoked it all, and then I dipped into it too much after that. The folks that bought those quarters **had** to do it out of sympathy for me. Mom bailed me out of the last of the cash that I owed Cal. I still can't believe he thought I would cruise him like that.

Anyway, Cal and I started making some cool ass mojo bags. Anna gave us a bunch of polished stones for cheap and we've identified their healing uses. I wrote out a little card to go in each bag to explain each set. Compiled, the bag is balanced numerically, as well as balanced with the appropriate amount of male and female energies. We sold two mojo bags for $20! We are gonna start a company. Three Pathways. We agreed on that name. It's religiously non-specializing. I need to write but I can't get my thoughts straight. We are playin' Memphis tonight...gotta go get ready...

1.22.95

I tried to dye my hair purple with Kool Aid the other day. It didn't work out to well. Black girls use Kool Aid all the time. I'm really ready to just do it. I need some Manic Panic. I'm just sittin' here smoking this bowl waitin' on Cal to get here. We are Memphis to do flyers. I saw a lot of cool stones at Mica's when I was in Memphis. He has this cool ass chime. The stones really love it. You can feel their energies resonate with the harmonies in the chime.

We've been playin' in Memphis *a lot*. We had a fabulous show Saturday night at some tittie bar turned club. But ooooh Friday the 13th earned its name. We were gonna play at the Attic (which used to be Rascals) Ian took off from the club a couple hours before the set with Cassie—nice girl but she's just a fuck to him...anyway they *fell asleep* in their motel room and *never made it to the club*...well...they did eventually but it was two thirty in the morning! OOOOooh, the guys were fucking *furious*. We had packed the house, at that! The PA wasn't working anyway.

1.27.95

It's *so* fucking cool to be on the road. I fucking *love* it. I love just watching the yellow dashes disappear underneath the truck…knowing that with each one that we swallow, we are truly…*living*. We are on the way to play in Champaign, IL. It's apparently about an hour or two out of Chicago. Bone Squad has an *amazing* following there…It's scary, though, too. I don't have *any* money! I am *so* not used to this! Cal gave me money for cigarettes, which kicks ass, and a little bag of dope, so I've got it rationed out for the next few days. I am truly a broke-ass starving musician. Well, I'm not starving right now…but shit, I guess I will be in two hours. Playin' a new town is *so* damn cool. We just got done doing mad libs. They are so fucking fun…they are little stories for kids with parts of speech missing. You ask folks for a noun or an adjective and then fill them in and the stories are fucking *hilarious*. The guys are ruthless when they get in racist-white-trash mode. They try to out do each other by saying the worst imaginable thing. If someone who did not know us heard this shit, **we** would be the ones at the gallows. They make so much fun of me for bringing all these games and notebooks and books and flashlights. But they **love** the actual games when we play them. I write the date on every game we play. I really wish I had a camera for these trips…something tells me I should be taking pictures of all this…hell, now they are singing David Alan Coe…

The prairie is so beautiful…the sky extends so far in all directions and it's so *flat* here. OH! Ian just farted. His are the absolute worst of all…especially since he never bathes. The guys are teasing him about his nasty ass shorts that he's been wearing everyday since last week. Yuck. Were getting close now…

1.27.95

Sitting at the bar in the "Five Points Saloon" waiting to play. It's cold as *shit* here. Some radio dude is talking to Ruger and Jesse. Max and Ian are playin' pool. It's nice to just chill for a minute. There is this group of dudes sitting behind me at a table and they all have on black and one of them is wearing an inverted pentacle around his neck. I think the pentacle dude is staring at me. Maybe it's my imagination…no…I *know* he is. I am sneakily watching him through the mirror behind the bar…Man! Real Satan people! Something tells me that real Satan people probably don't flaunt it with inverted pentacles…nor would they hang out at the Five Points Saloon. Ha! That's ironic…"Five Points"…like a pentacle. Here comes Ruger…looks like I gotta load in…I better throw my hair in ponytails real quick…

1.28.95

Last night was *AMAZING*…Our set was tight as *hell* and the place was *SO* packed that this dude got slammed into Max and the bouncer thought he was trying to grab him so he got thrown to the floor and people started pushing each other around…it was *insane*! We made all kinds of friends and guess who I hung with? The *Satan worshipers*, of course! It turns out Ethan, the 'pentacle' dude, is *super* fuckin' cool. I talked to him and one of his friends before we played. I can't remember what I said to them, but they were real funny and they are in a band. They play death metal…gee, surprise! Their eyes were glued to us, well…uh…me…during the set. It was creepy, kinda. Just the whole mystique of devil worship…and here I have met some people who just might take it seriously…and they are watching me…*me*…the good little witch…I knew from just talking to Ethan though that his heart is not black. He has a kindness in his eyes. I am so absolutely intrigued and fascinated with the whole Satan thing—especially with the fact that someone would want to flaunt that they were involved with such a thing. After the show, Ethan and his friend helped me pack up my shit and hung out with me and Cornfed in the Suburban and got us high. It was really cool! Everyone in Champaign has these little personal wooden boxes that fit in your pocket and they have a hollow shaft to pack dope in and a little metal pipe that you jam into the dope and then smoke out of the other end. Dugouts, I think…anyway Ethan packed me bowl after bowl and Cornfed twisted a couple fattys…it was cool…Meanwhile, the guys were makin' their rounds, too. They met this cool chick named Sabrina, who offered her place for us to crash at anytime we were here. The other band that played was called "Hammer" and man are *they* cool mother fuckers! After the show, they invited us to stay at their place, and practically the whole fuckin' club came over to their house. I could not believe my eyes when we got here. They live in a part of town that looks like Midtown Memphis. It's a real old house and it's absolutely *huge*. Three stories and a basement of nothing but one party after another. On the main floor of the house is the living room, which has a pool table in it and like beer signs and posters everywhere. Old, mismatched couches…spilt beer on the hardwood floor…nameless smiling faces crowded into corners…huge kick ass stereo system blaring away. The smell of dope knocked me out when I walked in so I followed my nose to the kitchen, which was equipped with two refrigerators—one for food—the other for beer. Yes, *beer.* They keep so much beer in the "Hammer-house" that they need two refrigerators. And even more amazing, their glass recycling refund pays their *electric bill.* Even Ruger's jaw hit the floor on that note. Everyone here is *so* enamored with us! They *loved* us! And they show it by getting *me* high! It rocks! I followed the singer dude (I think his name is Gary…I can't remember) to the basement, where they practice. The walls were all spray painted really cool and someone made a separate bedroom down there with plywood and 2 x 4's. Amazing. Anyway, a jam session emitted itself, and we all jammed some old Sabbath and Zeppelin an shit and got more fucked up. It was *great.* Their house was as packed as the club! I fell out in the basement floor and it was cold as shit down there. Max crashed down there with me on sleeping bags. We really didn't need to be sleeping in the cold air like that. I hope we don't get sick. I can't figure out how many people actually live here. There's the dude Eli, who is like a hippie "fix it" dude…he wired the living room stereo up to all the amps in the basement, rigged speakers into the halls and even in the friggin bathroom so in the entire house you hear whatever is on the stereo. And I think all the band members live here, so that's at least six…damn. Wait, and there's that chick, so that's seven…and that older dude with the big ass bedroom on the third floor…so eight…hell I can't remember. Anyway, we are headed out for Chicago today so I better get in the shower before everybody gets up…

1.30.95

There was some stupid girl bass-player chick hangin' out at the club last night tryin' to recruit me into her band. She got on my nerves SO bad. She must have been *real* obnoxious to get on my nerves, cuz I can find something to like about anybody. I guess it was her snootiness that bugged me. She kinda put down my band in a way so that must be what turned me off about her. Our show fuckin' *smoked!* We are at Wes from Deviant's apartment. Some big-ass football game is coming on today and the guys want to stay in town and hang out to watch it. That's okay by me. I told them if they wanted I would do a chick thing and grill out burgers for them, so I sent them to the store with a list. Ian and I are watching the Pantera video and chillin' out. Wes has his *own dope*! I am so proud of him! He came by the club last night and said he couldn't stay for the show but he told me where his sack was so I could twist one when we got home and he gave us his keys. I think he had to work or something. Anyway, I'm feelin kind of bad because it was a quarter ounce sack…and I can't remember how much of it I smoked or Ian smoked or WE smoked but I just packed a bowl and it looks like only a couple of joints worth is left. I feel kinda bad about this. Not working is making a tremendous effect on my supply and it sucks. Cal gives me what he can, but I'm out and this *sucks*. It might actually be kinda cool and different to drink some whisky. I don't have anywhere to go…nothing really to do…maybe that would be cool…there is a ton of it on the top of the frig…

1.30.95 later

We are not even out of Chicago yet so traffic is everywhere, even though it's really late, and Ruger is drunk as shit. I cannot fucking *believe* what just happened! He started freakin' cuz he had to pee *SO* bad and we are on the *interstate* **in town** and we could not get off *anywhere*. So, he had to get up on his knees and pee in a **bottle**…*AND* the rear window along side the back end of the truck is really low and there were these chicks in a sports car on Ruger's side of the truck so when he was peein' they looked up and *SAW him*! HA! OH, *man* we are *still* laughing at his ass! He and Jesse are both *so* absolutely shitfaced! We put them on the sleeping bags in the back of the truck and they are back there rollin' around. They are giggling about farting so much. It's pissing Max and Ian off. I'm just silently grinning about the whole thing. The round of Xanax is calmin' me down! Ah, shit, Jesse's gonna hurl…we're pullin' over…I am not surprised he is so sick. The guys returned from the store with only *two* of the items on my list and the rest was *beer*. Max and Ian drank a little, but the majority of it was consumed by Jesse and Ruger. That means Ru and Jesse drank *seventy-two fucking beers*. And to top it off, they bought this box of pre-cut burger meat instead of *fresh* ground beef for me to make burgers out of. So there is no telling what kind of fucking mystery meat they ate, and they ate **a lot** of it. My dumb ass didn't realize that in January in Chicago **NO ONE** grills out…seeing how there is fucking two feet of *snow* on the ground and the wind chill is like twenty below. Duh. So I had to *FRY* the nasty mystery meat…mind you, and Ian and I had helped ourselves to the lonely bottle of Jack Daniels on the refrigerator, so I was grooving when I started cookin', yet I soon felt kind of queasy smelling the bologna—like scent emitting from the pan. Ugh. You can thus imagine the smell of the farts in here—and the *heat* is on…UGH.

It's a trip how the meth heads are in the front seats, the stoners are in the middle, and the drunks are in the back. Jesse seems better now since he puked and they aren't making any noise any more so I guess they are asleep. I can't believe we left when we did. I felt for sure we would spend the night in Chicago but for some reason Max became hell bent on leaving at like eleven o clock tonight. I didn't really care if we stayed or not. He conned Ian into the idea, apparently gave him some meth to wake his ass up for the haul home, and started trying to convince me *I* wanted to go home. I told him I didn't really care. Ruger was pissed. He was all kicked back on the couch and shit. Whatever. I'm getting sleepy. I'm gonna curl up on Cornfed and crash.

2.15.95

I don't know where Marty came from, but he is a recording engineer and we've been recording since we've been off the road. He kind of floats around from studio to studio in town. He has great ideas and he is super cool to work with. He wants to sample these great techno-like beats behind the grinding chomp of guitar in our songs and it is the *coolest* fucking thing ever. It's very tastefully done. The awesome part is when I hear the techno in my headphones—I can play along to it! It's like a click track (metronome) with accompaniment! The only thing that bugs me about the recording thing is that Max's dealer friend "The Man" hangs around a lot. I don't trust him at all and he gives me the funny vibe.

We are promoting the *shit* out of the band around town. We are layin' low on playin' out till this big ass show we are doin next month at Rascals, which is now the Attic, which is under renovation. After that gig, we are goin' on the road again. There is a new underground radio show on Sunday nights that is doing a lot of promo for local music so we are hoping to get them a tape or CD as soon as we get done recording. We are also gonna start workin' on some shit for Cross-roads.

It is still sucking not having wheels…practicing at the bar is getting really fucking old…I haven't seen much of Anna since we've been on the road so much, and Cal and I are great as always. Demi has pushed it too far with her husband and he wants to get rid of her. She doesn't blame him.

2.27.95

Oh, **this** is fuckin' *crazy*. Cal was sick…I mean *violently* sick…puking his guts up for like two days…and then I wake up in the middle of the night like two nights ago with the same shit…I have not puked like that since I was in the hospital for the kidney stone…it was awful and it is just now goin' away. I was swimmy headed and dizzy all day and puking *constantly*. So Demi came by to check on me and she said she had a funny feeling that Cal and I were not sick with a virus…she says she thinks that Lana was more pissed at us than she let on. She thinks Lana *deliberately* undercooked the chicken that she so eagerly encouraged us to eat, which Cal ate one night and me the next night. I cannot *imagine* being so vindictive that you would do something like that to a person, but Demi said not to put shit past Lana. No fucking lie, man. That is fucking **crazy**. Lana disappeared for a few days after we were sick…and I mean she just *left*…and the kids were here and everything. We took care of them for two nights and then her Mom came over and got them. Her mom is here now. I feel bad for Cal. I mean, at least I get to get out of here and go to Memphis or on the road. He's *got* to be a lot more miserable than he lets on.

Oh, get *this* shit. Cornfed came out to the Grove with us for practice and he said he'd ride out to our house and look at my truck. There is something about Johnny the mechanic and his verdict about my truck that I do not trust, and Cornfed said I may be right and it may not be completely fucked. So he comes out last weekend, and looks at it a minute, and tells me that a plug has blown off an important part of my engine, giving the *appearance* that it is fucked, when it actually is not. He said a freeze plug will cost me about three dollars. *Three fucking dollars!* He said getting *to* the freeze plug was a bitch, an I'd pay about a hundred bucks in labor, but shit, that *rocks!* I am so glad I trusted my gut about the other mechanic. I am so glad for Cornfed!

3.16.95

On the road. We just stopped at Boomtown, the biggest fucking truck stop I have ever seen. I *love* going in there. I love all truck stops, but that one is like truck stop *Mecca*. I always beg the guys stop there for me. I think they like looking at the trashy shit, too. It's is *so* huge. Like the size of a department store…with these *fields* of aisles…full of really bad Native American figurines and factory processed dream catchers that say "I love Illinois". There are rows upon rows of bad jewelry, coffee cups, ashtrays and license plates. And *then* they have aisles upon aisles of *fireworks*! I could spend hours that we don't have to spare in there. Ah…thank you, Boomtown, for offering such tasteful goods and for being such a great deviation from the boredom and endless trail of thoughts from the road.

This will be a busy trip. We were planning to record *during* this trip, but we would have had to rush back home and then go right back out on the road, which is *crazy*. We're playin' tonight in Champaign, then we go to Chicago and play a few shows, stay in town for pub-crawl Friday, and then to Muskegon Saturday and Detroit Sunday. We are supposedly playin' with an all chick band Saturday night. That should be interesting.

We had a kick *ass* weekend last weekend. We did $940 before bills headlining the *Addict*, which is Rascals redecorated and with a different name. (It's actually really "the **Attic**" but I like my version better) We got plugged for Crossroads on 107.1, the new underground station in Memphis. We may be doing a live interview before our next show. We got accepted to Crossroads again. Our spot is Saturday, April 8th at nine forty pm.

I'm listening to Tori Amos on my headset and watching the world go by. It's so cool to get to see the earth change in a full year. There is a Christmas tree farm somewhere in Illinois and we pass it every trip up here. I've gotten to see them as babies, then adolescents, then in full glory. Then, we drive by and they are just gone. All of the sudden I remember the deer I saw that time in that field in Michigan. Ruger is talking about us going to Montana…I would just *die*. Joseph told me that when Bone Squad went through Montana there were these mountains on either side of the highway and fields of wildflowers were all that separated them. They were so inspired by the beauty of what they saw that they all pulled over and got out of the van and stripped off all their clothes and went running in the field. Wow. I hope that is a true story.

Trust Jesus is written everywhere. I haven't listened to this tape since I had my truck and I feel free. I think I am definitely ready to drive again! It was a fiasco getting my truck to Memphis. It took all day to get the U-haul. We ran out of money, we had to disconnect the drive shaft, we had to cruise practice and piss off the guys, the straps came off the tires, Ian fell asleep at the wheel, and I had to drive THE SUBURBAN! Holy fucking shit! They have never; *never* in three years **ever** let me drive. When we got there, we broke the fucking trailer getting my truck off of it and we had to wait three hours on a mechanic to get there to fix it. Sigh, I will be so damn glad to have wheels again. I cannot **stand** to be at the mercy of another driver.

Not much is goin' on now. Jesse is jammin' in the lair of loss, (the back of the truck) and Cornfed and Ruger are asleep.

3.17.95

Headed to Chi town. Stoned as a rat and lovin it. Jesse is watching me write. Wait—here goes Ruger with a news flash—were giving our Chicago promoter Cherie and her boyfriend t-shirts. Did I mention we got bad ass T-shirts done? We had a *great* show at five points. Tennessee was in the house! Hammer was *killer*. We are eating vitamin C and listening to the I-rock. They got a cool promotional thang goin'. We are playin at a club called Mabel's a week from today with Hack, this kick ass band in Champaign. It's their CD release party and it's gonna smoke! I smoked out with Ethan at the club and when we come back, he's taking us to this amazing park called Allerton. We are going to gothic night at Bedrocks tonight. Maybe I'll meet some 'vampires'. I smoked some bad ass skunk fuckin' weed with some folks who said they *deliberately* came to the Hammer house to get me high. Man. Was I honored! The pot was so good it was worth mentioning, anyway. I told the Hammer boys to advertise for me that I would do tarot readings and haircuts for cash when I was in town. Cool. I hope it works out. I brought some stones and some wire. I need to wrap some stones. God, it's a beautiful day. Motley Crue's Home Sweet Home is on the radio and no one changed the station. Now we're all singing it! Awww…cheesy memories! I'm just so high!

3.19.95

Headed to Muskegon. We couldn't go to Zorba's cuz of time, but we checked out the guitar center and the Alley before we left. Cool and expensive as always. It got really cold about an hour out of town. It was like seventy degrees in Champaign and it was thirty-seven degrees in Chi town. Gothic night proved to be more of *exhausted* night. I stayed at Cherie's apartment. I smoked bowl after bowl by myself and it was cool just to chill in the quiet. I ate some chocolate ice cream. I'm on the rag so fuck it. The guys are currently in the redneck phase of the trip—acting and talking like old redneck men. They say some **really** sick shit. As soon as somebody says something just absolutely fucking horrifying, something so hilariously terrible that they cant stop laughing, that person is subconsciously declared the 'winner' and the game stops for a while. Anyway, the boys came back from Goth night and said I absolutely **had** to go up there...they said it was right up my alley. So, I went for a minute, but they were tearing down when I got there. I truthfully didn't want to go out because I left my fucking *make up bag* in Champaign. I cannot believe I left it. Of all things. Max started the dyke jokes immediately. It seems like I woke up one day and apparently everyone is gay. Ruger just said I get more chicks in Champaign than they do. Damn. I guess that explains the group of chicks that follow me around wanted to get me high all the time. They think I'm a *dyke*! Gee, girl, girl on drums, girl must be a dyke! God, I feel so stupid. I had no idea those chicks were gay. I don't care if they are or not, I just feel dumb cuz I didn't know.

Ruger just called Ian a girl cuz he was whining about wanting to eat. I wonder if they realize I don't complain about shit. Hell. I wonder if I am the only one who thinks I don't complain.

People are everywhere and the river is green. Traffic is actually mobile, as I thought it would be jammed up. Indiana. Iowa. Wisconsin. Signs are everywhere. I think I'm gonna lay off the pot today till after the gig. I am reading a book on the Kaballah. I think the Kaballah is so fascinating. Something feels dangerous about it, though. I can't explain it. The Jewish mystics feel it is a pathway to God, however along the 231 gates are doorkeepers, who expect to see a "seal" before you can pass through. Maybe that's the danger. I find Hebrew to be the most beautiful language I have ever seen, **or** heard. Something is so *holy* about it. My book says it is the original language of God. I think I believe that.

3.19.95

Sitting in the backstage room in Detroit. I have adjusted to the coldness in here cuz there is no heat. It's nice to be out of the truck. I can actually write legibly. I am not, I repeat, **not** getting on that fucking scale.

Muskegon was a blast. The show was awful, but it was an interesting night. We had no monitors, no nothing. I am proud to see us starting to talk things out rationally and leaving the problems at the club instead of holding grudges for three days and not talking to each other and shit. The girl band was three piece and the guitarist sang lead. They were gritty punky choppy. Not as hard as us but cool and unique. I met this chick that is in a local Slayerish band. She sings for them and she was real cool. I had heard of her band in Illinois. She gave me her card. Maybe we will do a show with them or somethin'. When we got to the club, we met Leg, the sound guy. He had green dreadlocks…and only one real leg. He was real cool and he hung out with us cuz we got there early (believe that). Jesse started talking about wanting to shave the underneath part of his hair and Leg said he had some clippers so they went in the bathroom to cut his hair. When he came out, he told me that Leg picked up every strand of his hair and carefully put it in the trash. He told Jesse that there were some devil worshippers in town who hung at the club and would use his hair for evil purposes. Oh holy shit. Here we go again. What the fuck is up with the north and the devil, man? Or do we have devil worshippers in the south that I just don't see? Anyway, this incident led to a major discussion between Leg and I. He said that the Satan worshippers are very serious up there. Like, real, real serious. He said some of them would be coming up to the club that night. I was fascinated. They did show up, too, and there were like twelve of them together. They were clad in black, of course, and seemed to be all hangin' on this one dude who looked like King Diamond, from the death metal band Merciful Fate. Anyway, the King Diamond dude was pretty creepy and they hung out for the whole night drinking and cutting up. I tried to eavesdrop on their conversations, but I couldn't really make out much. They didn't feel like Satan people but I took Leg's word for it. Later that night, we went to Leg's house to crash, and the guys got a case and Leg had and acoustic so Jesse got his out and we all sang songs and smoked out. We piled up in his living room in sleeping bags. It was fun. Leg gave us all some painkillers...my back was killing me cuz I pulled something lifting my floor tom over my head (dumb idea) when we were unloading from the stage. After the case was gone and the guys crashed, Ian, Leg and I stayed up and I picked his brain about the Satan thing. He said that he used to be involved in it. I kind of figured he had been. He seemed to be censoring what he told me, and I guess I did seem to be a little over interested. But he said there were hundreds of Satan worshippers in the area. I just gasped. Man! He said that the crew of them that we saw that night didn't even leave the house on Sundays because it was a "holy" day and they refused to let the light of the holy day shine on them. Even Ian seemed interested by this point. Leg continued to tell me about the seven leagues of hell and how demons from each level of hell get steadily more dangerous and the goal of these groups were to harness their power. Leg said this was a really dumb thing to try to do. I agreed. I have read a lot about invocation of spirits and I know this is what Crowley was attempting to do. It's just so fucking dangerous. I can't believe there are people who take this so seriously. I asked Leg why he thought Cal was incapable of dreaming. He said dreams were the only time that negative entities can enter the body only when it is dreaming because it is absorbed in the unconscious dream state. So maybe Cal is protected or something. I asked him about the vision I had had during a bad trip. I saw a horrible face wearing a mask of...human flesh. It was awful and it scared the shit out of me. He said that one of the demons in one of the first leagues of hell wears a mask made of flesh. Great! I shall not forget Leg...

My hand hurts from writing all this shit. I'm gonna go get Cornfed and see if we can find some new sticks under the drum riser!

3.?.95

In Chi town at Wes'. Ruger and Jesse went sightseeing. I've been *pot* seeing! Thanks to Wes! I guess I conformed him when they played at home with us! We had great shows in Detroit. At the last one, only **one** person paid to get in! In other words, the turn out sucked, but **we** fuckin' **rolled**! The one person we needed to be there was there, though, the dude that runs the biggest club in town. Ruger talked to him and he said we may be opening for "Fight". That would kick **ass**! Detroit was cool. This time we went downtown and hung with the dudes in a band we met here. I talked to Cal this morning. I miss him so much. We are headed to Champaign either tomorrow or Thursday. I hope it's tomorrow but Ruger usually gets his way so it will probably be Thursday. He likes it in Chicago. I want to get back to Champaign cuz I want to go to Allerton with Ethan! I am completely broke and I have no smokes. I cannot fucking *stand* this. I haven't had my own cigarettes in *days*. I absolutely fucking *hate* that. Corn-fed is hooking me up, though. Let's see…I play drums for this band and I'm broke, but the roadie gets paid and he has cigarettes! That makes no sense! But he is hooking me up. That's **super** cool. Max is doggin' him out. He is getting so predictable. When he's high, he gets jumpy and hyper and he picks on me real bad. Now he's picking on Cornfed too. I hate it for Cornfed cuz I can tell the only reason he is here is cuz he is such good friends with Jesse. But, Ruger and Max know he is the most dependable and consistent roadie we've ever had. Cruising him would be outright stupid. I would miss him a lot on the road. He is really nice to me and he never dogs me out. I can always lay my head in his lap and crash and he kindly makes sure I am comfortable. He gets me high and gives me smokes. They guys are *never* that affectionate…well unless they are drunk. Well, I guess that's not all the way true. Ruger and I cuddle and giggle when we crash together. Sometimes it feels like we are an old married couple…and other times he's like my evil brother. Most of the time though, I am one of the guys. I like the fact that they treat me as equal, but sometimes it's *less than* and that's what I hate. I guess now they've got Cornfed to pick on. This pen sucks.

3.22.95

It's dark and cold and I've got my flashlight on. On the way to Champaign. Things are mellow. I had hoped to be in Champaign all day today, But Ruger and Max wanted to hang in Chi town all day so we stuck around until four and we hit five o'clock traffic like a **motherfuck**er. It was *so* incredibly jammed. Ruger and Max didn't even bitch cuz I guess they knew it was their fault we were stuck in it. The lightening is doing cool things in the distance. It certainly not heat lightning, cuz it's fucking **freezing** in here. I even have my mittens on! The prairie stands so desolate as the blue gray of night creeps in. I've been thinking about Cal a lot. It's not painful, really, I just long to kiss him across his cheek under each eye in my special spot. I can feel his skin on my lips. I can smell him. God, I love that man. We've been discussing Crossroads promotional ideas. We took band pics the day we left. We took some fish-eye lens shots too. I hope they turn out bitchin'. I'm gonna watch the lightnin'.

3.25.95

We just got back on the road again. Makin' our way back to Memphis. I had a *great* time in Champaign. We went to Allerton Park, I made some great friends, and we had a **killer** show. We kicked *major* ass! Allerton is **beautiful.** It was cold, but *exquisite*. Ethan and I hooked up and became good buddies and I heard his band, Audible Mercy. Ethan is savable. I just know it. I hope I have made at least one person "think". I hope that one person is Ethan. The Hammer's were magnificent hosts, even better than before. We *stayed* stoned. I'm serious! Ethan and his buds came over and we got a keg and we all jammed. I got to practice some. Me and Ethan went to a head shop. It was cool. The guys seemed to be bothered about me hangin' out with "I am Satan" (Ethan). I don't know if it's because they don't like him or if it's because of Cal. I have to admit I have a little crush on Ethan, but I would *not* go there. They didn't say much about me leaving with him for the afternoon. I thought I'd get a lecture. They call him "I am Satan" behind his back.

Speaking of "I am Satan", when I went over to his house he asked me if I wanted to see their "sanctuary". I was a little hesitant, but my dark curiosity won. He led me down his basement stairs, and it got darker and colder with every one. The basement, which had been painted black, had a pentacle on the floor painted in white. It was *huge*, like fifteen feet across. In between the top two points of the pentacle, against a wall, was a table covered with a black cloth, and on it were candles and a book. Above this was a black tapestry, featuring a Baphomet, the goat's head pentacle thing, in white. Along the walls were typical things you would find in a basement, brooms and toolboxes, which provided me a little bit of comfort. I wanted to ask him if they like really *do* stuff down there, so I said, "So, do you guys like..." and he cut me off by saying, "Yes, we do." Hmmmmm. We didn't stay down there long. It doesn't scare me that much. What does scare me is that he and his friends take the shit seriously, or at least **they** think they do.

So much has happened I don't know where to start to write. I'm *so* high. We have actually eaten at least once a day this trip! Crossroads is in *two weeks*. We all managed to escape getting sick. It seems like we bonded a lot. Max stayed at another dudes house this trip but the rest of us Hammer-housed it. Eli gave me and Ruger his waterbed. We snuggled every night and would just lay there and talk for hours about all kinds of shit. It was so cool. I love him even though most of the time he makes me sick. There is lots of gossip in the scene about us. I think its funny, although sometimes I think me and Ruger may wind up married for real. We went to a laundry mat today and did clothes. Our clothes were so funky they could've played the gig for us. Hell, they knew the set.

It's four thirty in the morning and we have to be in Little Rock for a sound check at six tonight. And we are somewhere in Illinois. We're *cruised*. I took half a Xanax to knock me out so I should be well rested. Jesse found out some shit about his girlfriend cheating on him and he is pissed as hell and counting every mile marker in his anger. He can't wait to get home. I'm so buzzed. I'm gonna get Jesse high so he'll feel better!

3.26.95

Goin Home. The weather is really nice. I wish I had another bowl. The Little Rock show was okay. I wished we'd had a better turn out, though. I can't believe this pen is working.

My truck is fixed! YAY! Mom said they put a new freeze plug in and serviced the transmission. I am **mobile**! It has been three fucking months and it feels like **forever**. We got in from Illinois at noon and I took a long hot bath before we left for Little Rock. I wasn't really tired but my Memphis friends who showed up at the club kept telling me I looked like shit. Motherfuckers. Hell, maybe I do look like shit. I'm a lot more tired than I thought but fuck it—I'd go play again tonight.

We stayed with Cade! Our roadie from way back! It was cool and it was great to see him! He told me if Cal and I go crystal mining we could stay with him if we want. I feel like maybe I should thank God for all my good fortune. My parents got my truck fixed for me—and without the "you need to quit this rock and roll shit" lecture. I can't handle that lecture anymore.

We're goin' back up north in April. We're playin in Wisconsin and in India-napolis. Cool! New cities! That song "Lightning Crashes" by Live is on the radio again. This is the ultimate think-about-being-on-the-road-while-you-actually-are-on-the road-song. I brainstormed like a motherfucker on the way to Little Rock. I smoked a bowl and stared out the open window at the trees. As the wind tousled my hair, I started realizing that it's my expectations of the world that fuck me up every time. If I would just open my eyes and shut up I would see the real-ity of life and my situation and I would appreciate it more because it is HERE. It's here, Flo. I keep looking for success with this band as being right around the next fucking corner. Well, on what scale am I comparing it? Isn't this what I said I always wanted? To travel the country with a kick ass band? Isn't that what I've been doing? I keep waiting and whining and changing what I define success to be. I am not allowing myself to fully enjoy the experiences I am having because I just keep my mind set on what's coming next. I am spending my time in a daydream of the future and its possibilities instead of looking around me, right now, and seeing the moment for what it is. I am the drummer of THIS band. I am riding in OUR truck. Surrounding me are the boys I love more than anything, and the music we make together is a love I sometimes take for granted. We are returning home from an amazing adventure that as a little girl I wanted more than any-thing. I met a young, aspiring drummer girl in Champaign and I recall telling her to keep at it…that I was having the time of my life. Well, perhaps I am…

6

Don't Bring a Fucking Bong

4.6.95

Crossroads weekend has finally arrived! The road *wore me out*—hey—I'll admit it. We were gone a total of thirty-three days. It's weird how being on the road gives me more energy. I can go all day on five hours of carpet sleep, but at home, if I did that I'd be exhausted.

We're playin Saturday nite at the Daisy. We've got a thirty-minute set so that's only six songs. Bone Squad and Hack play tonight. *Tonight* is gonna be *so* fucking cool. I'm so excited to get to see everybody. It's a big deal that members of fellow bands show up for each other's gigs. The more bodies you have in front of you, the better you look. I'm stayin at Mom's. I'm gonna try to avoid the party scene for at least three days before this gig. Cleanse myself, I guess. At least I will avoid all pot smoking on the day of the show. It'll be like a sacrifice. I give up something I love and I get health, endurance and agility as a result. I don't look at pot as being something super bad for you, but I admit, I do abuse the drug. Taking a break can only be good for me. Plus, it shows me I can stop if I want to.

I hope that store in Cooper Young opens soon so I can get my hair color. It's the grooviest little place. I'm coloring it purple! I can't wait! Oh! Mom saw the top of my tattoo last night—the angel on my leg. I told her she didn't want to see the rest of it. She didn't flip to hard. She said it really hurt her though. I hope she knows I didn't want to hurt her. I guess it blows the plans she had to create the model daughter she was hoping for the week in Hawaii we are spending in July. Oh, I guess I forgot to write about that. My brother got his Masters degree so they are taking him to Hawaii and they invited me to go along. They said I can't go unless I color my hair to a normal color, I take out my eyebrow ring, I wear clothes with color in them and I leave my green combat boots at home. I was hoping they invited me because they 'accepted' me…but now I'm starting to suspect they are taking me to brainwash me. She literally said to me that she and dad were hoping that by the time we got home that I would have decided to quit my "ridiculous" band and decide to go to college. I better watch what they feed me.

Things are not working out with Lana at all. Ever since the poisoning incident, we have both felt the need to get the fuck out of there. Mitch has closed the bar and he is living in a trailer and offered to let us live there with him. Cal thinks he has calmed down a lot, so he says we might as well. He's gonna move us while I'm gone.

I just called that shop and they have the stuff for my hair. I'm outta here.

4.13.95

Getting high in Mt. Ida Arkansas with Cal! My arms are *so* sunburned! We've been crystal mining all day! It was a blast! We're gonna have jewelry supplies out the ass! We got loads of copper pipe and tubing and wire and six hundred feet of leather cord. We're on our way!

Crossroads was so **unfuckingbelievable**. I went to the seminars all day on Friday and Jesse went with me. He shares my enthusiasm for music business education. At least someone else in my band does. Ruger wouldn't set foot in a seminar. It might make him look like he doesn't already know everything. If anyone is interested, we haven't heard about it yet. I haven't heard if Bone Squad heard anything yet, either. Those lucky Motherfuckers. They just happened to get a gig in Seattle that someone cancelled out on at the last minute and they met Dimebag Darrell at the club and recorded a song with him for some movie sound track.

The show itself was so **incredible**. Staying sober for three days helped me as a drummer so much more than I expected. I wore my purple hair in pigtails (as usual) and this cool shirt that says "Stop staring at these" across the tits. I played so easily and this huge grin would not leave my face. I know I looked like an idiot up there smiling. I really don't know where it came from. I was so comfortable up there. I was excited as hell, but not nervous…well, a little but not like paranoid like usual. Usually on stage, this is what goes through my head:

"Oh *no*. That cymbal is an inch to far back...I'm gonna miss it in this chorus...my palms are all sweaty...I'm gonna drop a stick. **Fuck**...there's the drummer from Hack looking at me...He is such an amazing drummer...I bet he thinks I'm out of time on this song...shit...Am I playin this too fast? Too slow? Oh Damn that hurt...I hate it when I slam my finger on my snare...Oh god it's *throbbing*...What's Ruger doin'? Is he spitting? Does he look happy? Oh god did I *break* my fucking finger? Oh...I *hate* this songs chorus cuz the cymbal work wears out my arm...oh...just a few more seconds...oh...will this be the night that the drummer falls off the throne in sheer muscular agony? Wait—chorus over...*I made it*! My arm is still connected to my body. Look, look down at your arms and legs. How does your body do that? I'm not even thinking about it. I'm on automatic drummer. I'm gonna look out in the crowd. Look at all of those people! Their sweaty and hopping up and down and loving this! I am the beat that they hop to! Am I playin to fast? To slow? Oh shit...I fucked that tom roll all up. I hope reverb covered that up...I need to let the sticks do the work. Here it comes. Lower your hands. That's it...Yeah...Good one! I can do this! This is ME playin! ME! Oh, this sweaty piece of hair is sticking in my eye...it only does that in heavy parts where I absolutely cannot stop to pull it out...God the sweat stings my eyes so fucking bad...God I am so thirsty. Please song...please end...I'll dehydrate right here...I can read the headlines "local wimpy drummer Flo fell to the floor tonight during a song at Club Loss" "She just couldn't handle it and dehydrated to a lump of flesh on stage" Song over...wipe sweat out of eye. Grab water...ahhhh...thank you Cornfed ahhhh...ready for next song—wait—do I cue off this one? What song is next? Where's my set list? OH shit. I kicked my water over on it. . Ink is bleeding titles of songs together. What does it say? Can I see Jesse's list? Oh...Okay...I'm good here we go..."

Man, that sounds so awful. I'm not a paranoid person, but pot smoking five hours before a show does not help to avoid this kind of self-torture. Avoiding pot for three days **did** help me to avoid this torture. I was content. I was convinced. The random thoughts I wrote about above just weren't there. I played with conviction and the cool thing is that I was able to enjoy every minute of it. It was such a fun show. No wonder I smiled so much. I felt free.

It's so cool to have had a chance to get away with Cal for a couple of days. We have had such a good time together reconnecting to nature and mining together. We got some kick ass crystals. I'm gonna crash. I keep feeling like I need to call the guys and check in. It's probably just because I am so used to being with them every day and I haven't talked to them in a few days. I just can't help but feel like I should call them. I'll call in the morning.

4.14.95

Boy, were the guys glad to hear from me. I am **so** fucking glad I called them. It seems as if Manny Burton from Reel Studios called and wanted us to come in and record. TODAY. Marty, the engineer who is doing our record, works with him some, he had a band cancel, and he wanted us to get their spot. At one o' clock this afternoon! So, Cal is driving right now and we are en route to Memphis as I write. Jesse cannot get over the fact that his **wanting** me to call him actually worked. They found out last night and had absolutely no way of contacting me. Hell, we just took off. We had no idea where we were going, either. They had called everyone we knew looking for us or for information on how to find us. Amazing. I can't believe it. Anyway, we will be arriving in town in the nick of time. Cal is kind of pissed that our vacation got cut short, but he understands. I'm so glad he does. I guess I'd better not get high this mornin'…

4.15.95

It's six thirty in the morning and I just got back from the studio. Just *now*. I am **so** fucking tired. We had a studio switch to this place on Beale, so we had to relocate and set up and tune and do all the preliminary shit and get everything mic'ed. I'm enjoying a tasty bowl at Kathy's and preparing to crash. We didn't start recording until like seven last night. The shit sounds **so** kick ass and it's not even mixed yet. Recording is really hard work, but I feel like such a "real band" that I get over the work part real quick. There is **such** intensity between the five of us when we are in the studio together. The moment before we are told to start playin' is *so* intense, because you are telling yourself not to fuck up, and it's like you can hear everyone else telling each other not to fuck up, either. It holds *everyone* back when you do. You can play your fucking best, and then it fucking sucks to have to re-do the track because somebody fucked up their part. Nobody wants to be the motherfucker that fucked it up for everybody else. It's so amazing to get to hear yourself when you're **not** PLAYIN'. At *super* high volume, too! I got way down in front of the control room and Marty cranked it up super fucking loud and I closed my eyes and pretended I was in the audience of a club and the music I was hearing was a band on stage. It's real hard to be objective to your damn self. Of course I like it, but like, if I wasn't in the band, would **I** be a fan of my own music? Recording is scary sometimes, because somebody always fucks up, and I hate it when it's me. We do really well, though, cuz we all take the shit very seriously and we all know this is not the time to fuck around. Each of us is playin our *ultimate* best. I used to have this intense fear of the studio because I was petrified of having to play with a click track. I'm still a little afraid of it, but not as much as I used to be. I've learned that all drummers are human beings, not machines. I still have **huge** expectations of myself.

Marty is so cool. He told me that he was recently featured in Mix magazine, but his article wasn't about his abilities as a recording engineer. It was about his experiences with the **ghosts** in the studio on Beale. I was *completely* transfixed. I had to hear **all** the ghost stories! He told me that several times he has been working late and alone, and he will feel like someone is watching him, and he turns around, and there is a woman leaning against the door frame wearing clothes from the early 1900's, with her arms crossed in front of her just looking at him. Whoa! The guys were all snickering at him and at me for being so into it, but I couldn't help it! Then he told me he saw a lady ghost in the reflection in the snack machine out in the stairwell. I went out there to check it out. I made Ian go with me. When we were in there Marty came bounding in and it scared the shit out of me! He told me all about how it happened. I am so into this! We are goin' back this weekend for mixing. It will be around full moon, too. I can't wait!

4.26.95

We kicked *ass* at this new club in town. We got $300 for the gig! Michelle Waters, my high skool best friend, was there. She said she was so proud of me! She invited me to come over and crash at her place, and I regret it was three thirty in the morning when I went by there. I decided not to wake her and I left. So many people showed up at the show! The drummer from Bone Squad was there, and he is hooking us up with shows out West, which kicks ass, and this dude Ruger knows is getting our demo out to Mercury this week. Amazing. I got **so** stoned after the gig. It sucks to have cotton mouth and not have fifty cents for a coke. Or to have a headache and be dyin' for a Tylenol…or to be broke and hungry…speaking of which, I found some peanut butter and crackers under the seat of my truck. Dinner is served! I went to a party at the Holiday Inn. I don't know who's room it was…we just got more stoned…

4.27.95

We finished mixing on Beale. We're probably moving to another studio. Marty is gonna try to get us hooked up again at Reel studios. I have a suspicion that "The Man" is footin' the bill for us to record, but I don't know for sure. They never really tell me shit. The studio engineer that works with Marty and I attempted to summon the ghosts in the haunted studio. Nothing happened, that is, until hours later. It was about two o clock in the morning when we were in the control room—just the guys and Marty and I. We were all facing forward and the door to the studio was wide open on our left. I could see out of my peripheral vision a figure moving—gliding—super slow down the hallway past the door. I remember it was about seven feet tall and it seemed to be hovering over the floor. I didn't get a good look at it, but from what I remember it had long blond hair and was wearing a flowing silvery gray cloak or gown. At the moment I turned my head to look, a chill air seeped into the control room. I felt my jaw drop and all the hair on my arms stood up. I swung my head around to see if anyone else saw what I did, and Marty said, "Did you *see **that**?*" I couldn't believe it. I had seen a *ghost*! And **he** saw it *too*! Marty told Max the skeptic to go check it out. He came back and said he didn't see shit. It really scared the living shit out of me. I thought I wanted to see one, and after I did, I was scared shitless.

4.?.95

We recorded at Reel! It's another studio in town, painted all kick ass and there are these plaster sculptures everywhere. I avoided getting close to them. I was *severely* under the influence. Ruger and I drank *straight fucking whiskey* together…It was fun! I fucking love Ruger. I guess I'm a lightweight when it comes to whiskey. Joseph from Bone Squad came in and laid some tracks down. I got to sing…well…more like *scream*…on two songs! I did this stupid thing where I pretended to have an orgasm in the background. Uh…I think I'm embarrassed about it now. Whisky gives me balls I would otherwise never have. I had such a hangover the next day. We recorded and mixed from two in the morning until daylight the next day. I was sick as shit. "The Man" has decided to form his own record label with Marty and we are the first band that is gonna be signed! My suspicions about his involvement are correct. Looks like a full-length album is in the works! Uh, is this real? **Fuck Yeah**! And probably tour support as well. Of course, I'll show my true excitement when I see it in writing.

4.?.95

Mad Season fucking rocks, man…there is something about Lane Staley's voice that is so haunting…it's beautiful…this album is so different, too. I feel *so* connected to him. His songs speak of feelings I find so familiar. I still love Jar of Flies best, though…well I dunno. I guess that collection of songs will always remind me of the days in the house in Jackson…we listened to it *so* much. It's funny how music takes you back…you can listen to an old CD and immediately be taken back to the time and place when you first burned it out…at least…it works that way for me…the studio is going good. Everybody is so excited about the record deal…I just hope they aren't running their fucking mouths all over the place…

5.5.95

Well, it's *still* happening! We played 616 this weekend and kicked **major** ass. 616 is this kick ass bar kind of between midtown and downtown Memphis. The stage is incredible…almost as cool as the Daisy, but without the personal nostalgia. We went back in the studio on Monday at noon and stayed until late Tuesday night. The guys were there until *Wednesday* morning! Cal came to the studio with me! I told him all about it and we decided it would be a great place to dose. I waited until they told me my shit was done till I dropped, and then of course when I was rollin' they asked me to add some shit so I attempted to put some tambourine shit in while I was trippin'. It absolutely did **not** work and Ruger was so pissed at me! Ruger wound up layin' the tracks.

It seems as though someone else is taking an interest in our band. Manny Burton who manages Reel has apparently asked Marty about forming a label and signing us. If he gets turned down he's gonna offer us his *own* deal. Max told Slaphead, Cornfed, and Jesse this information. Max better not be twisting a few simple comments this Manny dude made into "were getting an offer". I will be *so pissed* if that's the case. It's so easy to think you hear what you want to hear. Ruger is trippin' out cuz he heard Marty mention a figure with four zero's when talking about this label. Ruger was red all over with his jaw hangin' open! I hope this all isn't bullshit. We are all seeming to be taking this very seriously. I will hang Max by his ears if it's misinformation.

I have spent my tax refund runnin' for two weeks and I have nothing to show for it. Cal moved us out of Lana's and we've been living with Mitch and that needs to change. He is fucking *psycho*. He is currently covering his trailer's floor with pennies. *Seriously*. He is gluing them to the floor. I was gonna use my tax money to try to find us a trailer—hell *anything* to get the fuck out of there. This bitch in the Grove I talked to said the two she had for rent rented in thirty minutes. *Bullshit*. I'm guessing it's my purple hair and the witch rumors.

Cal and I had a beautiful weekend. We celebrated Beltane with thirty witches in Shelby Forrest. We only knew Savannah and her new boyfriend, but we met some new friends. On the last day, they did a drawing to see who would be crowned May Queen and King. I couldn't believe it when *I* got picked to be May Queen. It's like a really big deal to get to be her. They put a crown on my head of fresh honeysuckle and me and the dude who was May King led a procession around the field. Then we stood under the Maypole and ate of the fruit of Beltane.

I've got to figure out something about reading cards for people. I've got customers in Memphis out the ass. I just need to have a phone number. If people could reach me, they could schedule readings. I could be not so cruised. I just don't know what to do. I need a pager, I guess. I could scream I feel so stuck sometimes. It gets **so** old sleeping on someone else's bed or couch or carpet. Now Cal is living this life, too. We've been here in Memphis for eight days. I've washed my underwear in the sink twice and blown them dry with a hair dryer.

5.?.95

Well, *shit is still happening*! Believe *that*! It's **finally** happening! Reel Studio's manager, Manny Burton, and Marty formed a real label and *offered us a deal*. We'd have no debts, no serious strings attached, they take no publishing rights, we just sell fifteen hundred CD's and break even. **We can do that**! Wow! Man, this is so cool. And Marty told us another studio in town may be offering us a deal to beat *their* deal. Man. *A bidding war*. Over **US**. I learned all about this shit at Crossroads. I'm *so* glad I went to the seminars. I want to call everybody—but I'm not gonna. I'll wait till we sign it on the dotted line, like that stupid but true song says.

We've been here for almost a week. I'm ready to go home but I really have no idea where home is. We stayed up till four o clock in the morning smoking out and playin' Dungeons and Dragons. I know I'm a fucking dork, but it's fun as hell. I'm gonna take a long hot bath.

5.?.95

Headed to Chicago. Ruger and I were just discussing our record deal. I still can't get used to saying 'record deal' in reference to **our** band. Part of me is terrified to even run with this in my own head, much less tell anyone about it. I told Hope about it of course, but nobody else. God only knows who Ruger and the guys have blabbed it too. There are some things that were confusing me about the deal that I asked Ruger to set me straight on. I couldn't understand how we were gonna make any money from day one like they said if "The Man" has paid the three grand for us to record and we *owe* him that cash. Ru said that Manny doesn't *know* we had a financial backer and that if he *did* know it we wouldn't be getting a $ 2,500 a day studio for $400 a day. Oh. Gee. *Dishonesty*. *That* makes sense. Duh. So basically we aren't gonna make money right off the bat. First, we will pay "The Man" back. The idea of starting this label with things not all out on the table bugs me, but I guess in the music business you just kind of pull the strings you have to pull and work it out somehow or get totally fucking ripped off.

It's turning out to be a beautiful day. We don't have the luxury of having a trailer on this trip, so all our gear is behind my head. *Literally.* Jesse's cousin has joined in the foolishness (otherwise known as *th' road*) and they are following us in her car. Slaphead is crashed in the front seat. I love it when he comes with us. He is so fucking hilarious and he clips Ruger so bad and gets away with it.

Max decided to rent a car in Jackson to drive up here. He was still asleep this morning when we took off and he still had to drive into town to rent the car! That is fucking *insane*. The rumor from Ruger is that he's about to be cut off—for his own good, of course. Gee. How very thoughtful of them. How considerate and caring. Okay, so I'm being negative. I just hope he is okay for tonight. RoadRunner records is gonna be there.

There are so many shades of green I never realized before. They all make up green as a whole, yet they are each their own unique *version* of green. It's like a wave of color with varying ranges of darkness and light, warmth and cool…

We passed through Champaign about five minutes ago. We just passed a bus full of old people on an ultra-winning bus. I wonder where they are goin'. They looked so content in their air conditioning. But I bet they don't have a travel bong like I do! We've been discussing the future of the Suburban. You can see the fucking **street** through the floor in the back. I mean literally a *chunk* of the floor of the truck is missing. I swear that's how we all get headaches is from the fucking exhaust coming right back the fuck up in here. Ruger is sayin' we should trade this in and see if the label would sign for us to get a new road ride. I reminded him that this vehicle is not ours to trade in. It belongs to Ian's dad. Ian, on the other hand, is hoping to keep it and smash shit up with it. Make it a junkyard-derby vehicle. **Kick ass**! We could all get little helmets and shit! YEE—HAW! Speaking of Yee haw, the guys put rebel flags on the faces of the amps last night. They look *kick ass*. We talked about me covering my kit in crushed red velvet fabric. That would be *awesome*. We're passing around the Vitamin C. It's not so bad really. It's actually kind of smart of us to take a preventative measure. Hmmm. I wonder what else we could do…Hmmmm…I'm gonna make a list of road rules.

Flo's list of Road rulez

1. Wash your hands at truck stops. Even if you don't have to piss, wash your hands. Colds spread in enclosed places, and most frequently, from germs on your hands. Use hot water **and** soap.

2. Use Lysol in the van/truck. Spray windowsills, under seats, the carpet, and pillowcases. You can add a capful of liquid Lysol to laundry.

3. Wash your nasty, ass-smellin' pillowcase when you do laundry.

4. Bring a towel.

5. Bring a sturdy box for the loaf of bread, or it will be a tortilla.

6. Create a band shower bag out of a mesh laundry bag. Go in on shampoo, conditioner, razors, shaving cream, and soap.

7. Bring a jacket. You never know *when* it will be cold *where*.

8. Take pictures. Even if you cant afford to develop them. Take pictures and store film in a safe place.

9. If somebody takes your seat, kick their ass, and then take it back.

10. Write down the call numbers of the radio stations you like on the map by the cities name.

11. Keep an empty water bottle with a lid on board because some drunk somebody isn't gonna be able to wait to piss and it's rush hour.

12. Create a Riding-gear box. Keep band aids, Tylenol/ibuprofen, baby wipes, paper towels, Nyquil, chap-stick, sinus medicine, flashlight, batteries, visine, Rolaids, ink pens, drum key, pics, body lotion, Kleenex, fingernail clippers, antibiotic ointment, matches, tweezers, extra toothbrush. And I vote condoms, but ya'll won't use them…

13. Retired golf bags are great for drum hardware, extension cords, and cables.

14. Lice spray. No shit.

15. Spend a freakin' buck on a copy of the key to the truck/van. Give it to most responsible band member.

16. Keep business cards of people you meet on the road…clubs, bands, photographers…you never know.

17. Don't bring a fucking *bong*.

18. For short trips, if you have the space, invite a lifelong friend to go along. They share the adventure, can bail you out of big trouble, and you get to smell new farts for a change.

19. Don't expect Chuck Taylor's to keep your feet warm or dry in the winter.

5.25.95

In the truck, headed north with the boys. It seems like an eternity since I wrote last. So much has happened. In Chicago, we had our first slump show in a while. I got high twice that day, on the way, and I avoided pot on the days of the *last* two shows. Gee, what does that say? So, of course, I felt responsible for us having a shitty show. But it really couldn't be all my fault, right? There **are** five of us. We were *tired*. We haven't been on the road in a while since we started recording the album. Bone Squad played, too. They slammed as usual. Justine was there and she and I got to hang out! I drank Jagermeister—did I spell that right? We all went out and ate burritos. Pot was practically scarce this trip. Slaphead went with us and made a **total** drunken fool of himself. It was so entertaining watching him. We went to Zorba's and being potless I decided to spend the afternoon drinking whiskey! We took Slaphead to the Tower. Monday was drive home day, so the guys decided we should drink the whole way home! Joseph from Bone Squad rode back to Memphis with us and we all drank Jack Daniels in broad daylight and got sloshed and sang 38 Special songs at the top of our lungs. We were **so** fucking **lit**. It took us twelve hours instead of eight to get home, two of which were spent stranded in Kennit, Missouri. Thank **God** for 24 hour Wal-Mart with an ATM. Thank God for Slaphead having money in the bank.

I can recollect the past few weeks in order…I'm gonna try. We played Memphis at this new club and **stomped.** Cal is spending numerous long weekends in Memphis with me and we've been playin Dungeons & Dragons *every* nite with Mica and this guy named Dan. Ian played with us too! Ian kicks ass. It's cool chillin' and playin' that. It's a nice breather to get to be a cleric instead of a rock star. We've been crashin at Jesse's most of the time. Cal and Mica seem to really get along great. I knew they would. Mica and Cal and I spent an afternoon together recently in the woods at Shelby Forrest. It was so refreshing to get out into nature. Cal and I were so used to being able to walk outside our door and have the woods right at our feet. I can feel the city's influence on Cal, but it's not bad, it's just different. It was great to go out to the woods. We got high on a great big tree stump that had fallen into a ravine. We saw a lizard and we tried to get him high, but he declined. Anyway, when we were walking through the deep woods we saw what appeared to be a person wandering around. When we got closer, it was indeed a person, an Indian, to be exact, and he was erecting, no shit, a teepee. Deep in the fucking woods. We stopped dead in our tracks. I mean he looked so authentic. Like we were in a time warp or some shit. He looked up and looked as startled as we were to see him. We all just stared at each other in an eerie silence. He came over and spoke and said he was preparing the ground for a vision quest, an ancient Indian ceremony. He said he had been consecrating the ground there for days and to see us was very strange, which is why he seemed so startled when he saw us. We told him we were just hanging out in nature to get out of the city. He seemed pleased by this. He told us about the ceremony. A young adept spends three days in the woods, deprived of food and sleep, with no contact with anyone, in hopes that they will receive the vision, usually of their spirit animal. He invited us to come back for their opening ceremony. I was honored. I felt like that was probably a big deal. We didn't go. We fucked it off.

5.?.95

Relaxing in Champaign in Eli's room. It's cool to have a comfortable, private place to lay down and chill. I always manage to get to sleep in a bed, but not because I am a girl. It's because RUGER always manages to get to sleep in a bed, because he is clever that way, so I just charm him into letting me sleep wherever he is. I bet he tells people we are fucking, or at least he doesn't deny it if they ask. I don't really even care. I know I'm not fucking him, and I know I love Cal, and I really don't care what people think anyway. It is *cool* to cuddle up with Ruger. We just lay there, giggle, and talk about the band. He calls me baby. He is drunk as shit every night and pretty damn funny most of the time. He has never **ever** tried *anything* with me...and he has certainly had the opportunity to. *None* of them ever have. It makes me feel so safe with him.

The ride here was pretty uneventful. I read the whole way here. I must write that my friend Ethan from here is no longer a Satanist! I am SO excited. He did it all on his own. "Look! Look! I took it off!" he told me, when I saw him, talking about his pentacle. He hasn't had a chance yet to tell me exactly what happened, but his friend did. He said that Ethan had a strange experience in the shower. He looked down and thought his nose was bleeding because he saw blood dripping down on his chest. He rubbed his nose and it wasn't bleeding. He than realized the blood was coming from his necklace…the pentacle around his neck. I don't know if I believe all of this, but his friend said Ethan **really** freaked the fuck out. About a week later on two or three hits of acid, eyes appeared out of the darkness in the basement, and the Baphomet in their ritual area beckoned them and sur-rounded them in abyss. They couldn't even see each other for the darkness. Then, a white light crashed through the darkness, splitting through the Bap-homet. Then the darkness disappeared. Dude said after this shit Ethan said he was no longer a Satanist. He said Ethan has been struggling with major insomnia and he is really disappointed in himself for falling for all of that shit to begin with. It seems as if I have read that those are legitimate symptoms of psychic attack…Dion Fortune…to be exact. Anyway, I want Ethan to tell me about his experiences himself. I want to hear it from his own mouth that he's through with this. It still blows me away how serious they all were about it. Next, Ethan will feel like he is losing his mind. He will get confused easily, he will see shit, he will freak out on people, he won't be able to express himself clearly and he will quit making sense, and he will be a participant to all of this happening and be aware that he is losing it. It's the darkness working on him. If he's not careful, he'll wind up in an institution.

6.?.95

Backing out the trailer is always a huge event. The guys are poking fun at burn out Eli, the electronic guru who gives up his bedroom so Ruger and I can crash. The Hammer's aren't even home! They are on the road themselves! They had some trouble in the mountains, but they called and checked in and all is well. We are on the way to find something to eat. I am *so* completely stoned! Ethan came by to see me and we went to score some buds. We got to talk finally. He spoke intellectually of what happened. He told me he is worried about his friends. I told him not to offer any information to anyone, to be careful, and to cover his ass. I told him about the going crazy thing, too. I wanted him to be forewarned. I also warned him about keeping up with his hair if he gets a haircut, and his fingernail clippings and body secretions. Man, he gave me a weird look when I told him that. Oh well. It's the unfortunate truth. He told me that he has felt a darkness around him. He said it made him feel powerful. He said he could also feel coldness around him, and that he could walk in a room and it would **become** cold. He told me the whole story of what happened to him that made him give up the Satan thing. He said he started feeling a vortex of darkness emanating from the basement. He described it to me as pulling him to it…he said he could be anywhere in the house and he would be consumed with thoughts of the basement. He couldn't get it out if his mind. One night he crashed at some one else's house to get away from the shit, but he found himself obsessing about it even over at a friends' house. Maybe the two hits of acid didn't help, but he was still freaking out really bad. He decided the only way to deal with this was to just face it, so he went home. He went down into the basement with his roommates and they saw eyes looking at them from a dark corner. He said he felt and intense darkness creeping around him and before he knew it he couldn't see his friends or anything but blackness. He felt his heart beating incredibly fast…like almost about to bust through his chest and he started sweating profusely, despite the cold air in the room. He said he doesn't know how long he was surrounded in the darkness, but he said he felt like he was suffocating from it and he said at the moment he felt like he was going to die, a white beam of light crashed through the wall behind the Baphomet. Real light, like the basement window behind it broke in half and let the moonlight into the room. He fell to the floor gasping. When they pulled themselves together from this experience, he went upstairs to shower cuz he had sweat so much he soaked his clothes. That's when he noticed blood dripping from what he thought was his nose, but he realized it was coming from his necklace. I cannot fucking **imagine** how *terrifying* that must have been. He ripped the thing off his neck and decided he was done with it. He seems weak to me. I wonder about him. All I can do is surround him with light in my mind. At the same time, I wonder if all of this is bullshit…and we are just a bunch of kids who have watched too many movies, smoked too much dope, and have overactive imaginations. Sigh.

We are smoking some *kind* ass bud. Max scored us some of it. We are blowin' Ruger exhale hits cuz he got a fucking bronchial infection and we gotta record tomorrow. Ian is blowin' em on Ru and so is Max. Ian's rollin' the window up. We're gonna bake!

7

Panties in the Sink

6.2.95

Almost home. I forgot to write that dude from the drum shop showed up at the show and he gave me a t-shirt. Eli gave me a cool wool flannel and I'm wearing it now. I sold the Redneck Vampires shirt *off my sweaty back* for 20$ and I spent it on a sack, so I'm gonna get home with buds! That *never* happens! I made a sign to put next to our t-shirts to advertise for my crystal necklaces that I'm selling. It says, "Buy a $10 rock that's *good* for you". Ha.

I am getting so sick of my mind. I read a book on the way here that helped me to realize how I am focusedly unfocused. I lack direction with my own spirituality and I question it a lot. I guess that makes for a pretty rocky path. I am not getting any younger, either and sometimes I wonder if I will turn thirty riding around in the back of this truck, still daydreaming that we are really gonna 'make it'. Still playin' these clubs. Being fucking thirty years old and tattooed and having no way to take care of myself in the future if we don't make it. I think about that more than I want to admit. Oh, how the road makes you think.

The huge sky goes on and on. Blue gray clouds billow together creating a multitude of coolness. Icy whites, opaques, slate blues, endlessness. You could walk outside your house and see someone walk outside their house a mile away. AC DC is on the radio. Everyone is Yee Hawin! Everyone is *way* high and I bet Ruger's got a contact buzz. Highway to Hell. Ruger wanted us to cover this song. Ian is picking on me because he caught me washing my panties in the sink. Shit. I should be giving his ass a hard time. I don't think he bathed the whole trip. Cornfed is reading one of my books next to me. Light is peeking through the clouds. What an eventful three days. I have really been examining my body's reaction to certain stimuli regarding drums. Like caffeine and pot and alcohol. And how much sleep I get or don't get. Or what we ate that day or if we didn't eat at all. I talked to Ruger about it and he said he thinks I'm being way to fucking technical. He said that shit doesn't matter. Maybe. Maybe not. I just wish my mind would shut the fuck up sometimes. Just let it flow.

This is the last (supposedly) road trip in the Suburban. I'm gonna miss my seat! They guys say they won't miss shit about this truck. I am so set in my little area. I have my feet on my small drum case, and inside it, I have crystals, wire, and beads and snips, scissors, leather cord, pliers, all my jewelry shit. And I keep my travel bong in there. Then I have next to it my backpack, full of pens and my flashlight, and my Walkman and CD's and tapes and batteries. I keep books in there and mad libs, and a spare notebook for lists and games. I am prepared to face boredom. When I look up, I see the rusted red roof of this old truck. The leather and vinyl is ripped in most places on the seat and you can really see the road well through the whole in the back floorboard. The stories this vehicle could tell. On my right is my door, which has my own private ashtray in the door handle and my smokes lie safely in the crevice of the handle next to my lighter and that bowl I'm gonna finish in a second. The red metal of the door is chipped and rusted in spots and I have spent so long staring at it that I think I have its patterns memorized. It's gonna be weird getting a new ride.

Damn, I am so high. That joint kicked my ass. The lakes provide a mirror image of the farms and barns. The clouds all have a darker side on the bottom, like they are sitting on an imaginary shield or something. Maybe the Earth's gravity is pulling the moisture through them. The sky peeking through them is a deep mysterious blue, as if it is God himself.

Ruger just pointed out a cemetery standing all alone by itself. It's odd. Just a few trees line a perfect square and there are all sorts of high grave markers in bleached white, donned with plastic tulips and roses in shades of orange and red. In two or three seconds, the physical image is lost. Just keep movin'. And don't take your eyes off the road.

Off in the distance, through slightly open spots in the clouds shoot emanations of light. Individual beams; columns, if you will. Beautiful. Looks like a gate or a domain in itself. Do I think too much? I just had the urge to roll around in the soft grass. The wind just toys with it, making waves in the earth.

6.17.95

I feel bad for not writing in so long. Cal and I moved to Memphis unofficially last weekend. We are here so much working on the album that it made sense to move. Plus I wanted to get away from crazy ass Mitch and his penny floor. We are living with my brother's psycho-ass girlfriend. I didn't realize she was psycho until we moved in, though. Isn't that how it always works? She takes some kind of psycho drugs for agoraphobia. She has trouble leaving her house, which is dirty and disgusting. The worst thing about her house is the fact that she has no fucking air-conditioning and it's five million degrees outside and she has three fucking big ass dogs that have fleas so bad it is **disgusting**. I mean *really* fucking bad. I have to take a bath at night just to lower my body temperature (a *cold* bath) and Cal and I put a blanket under the door to keep the fucking fleas out. We put a pan of warm water in the floor and in seconds, the pan is full of fucking nasty ass fleas. They think the warm water is an animal and they jump over to the warm spot and drown. Fuckers. I was hoping to have a fucking phone too but she doesn't have a phone. No phone and no air. This chick is crazy. We have got to get the fuck out of here.

6.25.95

My period should start any day now. I hope to God that I am *not* fucking pregnant. We use protection but I still worry one will get away. I don't even want to think about that shit. I knew that pen was gonna piss me off so I got a new one. Again, I feel guilty for not writing. New rule number one. Journal keeping is a luxury and not a necessity. It will be done when I have extra time. That way I can't feel bad about not doing it. Of course, so much has occurred this month. I did an interview at 107.1 last Sunday night. I was plugging the show we are doing tonight. Dude told me if I ever wanted a career in radio, I could walk right into it. I love to talk. I can't believe Ruger let *me* do the interview—he **ALWAYS** does them. We don't know how our equipment is getting here. The Suburban is not doing to good.

6.30.95

Sitting at work. It's rare to be sitting! We are playin tonight at the Edge with Bone Squad and Mica's new band. Jesse said the radio spots are kick ass and the coolest part of one of our songs is slammin' over the airwaves. It's gonna be weird going to play after working all day. This band kicks so much ass. I fucking mean it, man. Other than the Bone Squad, we have the biggest draw in town, and hell, Bone Squad calls Dallas home now anyway. I guess I haven't written in here that **I got a job**. I went to a slave driver salon and they hired me on the spot. I can't handle the not eating, not having my own pot, and living in the flea circus. I need to do some more haircuts. If I'm here, I might as well be raking it in. I'm using Tony's drums tonight. That's saving me time and torture. I got a beeper. It's purple, of course. I am **not** getting high before shows. It kind of works with the whole job thing. Staying straight during the day while I am at work doesn't bother me but I really like getting high and chilling right after work, instead of running off to a gig. Sigh.

7.7.95

I hate thinking about money all the time. I'm turning into everybody else. Sittin at work again. We got more stylists so we are not as busy. I hope that doesn't affect my killer money. I've just *got* to get the fuck out of the flea circus house. They are making Cal and I physically sick.

I realize how inconvenient it is for me to look the way I look. My new boss asked me to remove my eyebrow ring. I didn't have a problem with that. She said she didn't care about the tattoos though. The girls at work said it would be stupid of me to sacrifice my trip to Maui because I wouldn't dye my hair brown. They said I can dye it back when I get home. They have a point.

Cal and I went to the Grove yesterday. We stopped in and saw Anna and we went to the tattoo shop and saw everybody up there. Everyone seemed happy to see us. We went to the Grove and saw everybody and then we went to see Cal's Mom. The pot plants got ganked, but I helped him to look on the bright side of it. I told him he could've wound up sittin in a jail cell *wishing* the shit had been stolen so he wouldn't be there. He smiled when I said that. I got a letter from Ethan. I'm gonna write him back.

Cal and I should be getting a place on Monday. The band is practicing tonight, tomorrow night, and we are playin' Sunday. We need to rehearse *so* bad. I will have a better show for it. I said something to the boys about how I know I have a better show when I don't get high during the day. **And they said they noticed it, too**! Now I feel fucking *obligated* to avoid it on the days of shows—now that I said something about it—Hell, I guess I **admitted** it. I *admitted* I'm not the best drummer I am capable of being when I smoke dope. I admitted it to them. So now when I get high, knowing I have to play a show, am I just saying, "Fuck you, I don't care about the show, I gotta get high…it's more important to me." Ya know? Now that I've admitted it, to get high anyway would basically be saying that it *is* more important to me! Sigh. I **do** play better when I don't get high all day. I am more focused. It just pisses me off that *they* don't have to lay off. It sucks to be me sometimes. Why am I the fucking one to be affected that way?

7.11.95

Oh, I am *so* pissed off! The guys have decided at the last minute that we are gonna fucking **record** tonight. I will be there *all fucking night* and I can't be high and that is gonna suck **so** fucking bad. I am gonna be there all fucking night and I have to **work** tomorrow. None of them fucking work. Sons of bitches. They don't give a shit about me. This absolutely sucks. I am *so* not happy about this shit. I don't understand why, when we are paying all this money to record, that we have to do it on someone *else's* schedule. It sucks. I am **so** furious. We have to re-record a whole bunch of shit we have already done, and four other songs. I could tear their asses apart. I just thought to call Marty and go the fuck off about this shit but I know it would only make the shit worse. I fucking worked all day Friday and then we had the studio Friday night and then I worked all day Saturday and then we practiced all night and then I worked Sunday and we had the show Sunday night and then Monday I rode around Memphis all day in my no air conditioning-ass truck in the 100 degree heat looking desperately for a place to live and now I am at work **again** and I have to go **re** record this fucking record.

I cannot fucking stand this hectic schedule and I am fed up with never being able to make plans or the ones that are made get fucked up. Just when it seems like I have time to get things done I find out someone else has other shit for me to do.

7.13.95

Why is it that I take so much shit for granted? Five years ago I would have given *anything* to be in a successful band and going into the studio like that—especially with someone else paying for it. I *did not record* Tuesday night. I told them *no*. I knew I would be there till three or four in the morning. I cannot **believe** I told them no. I *never* tell them no. I am always so afraid they will get pissed and tell me to hit the fucking road. We rescheduled for next month. I hate that we have to wait that long. It is all my fault that we have to wait.

I found out yesterday that we are playin a showcase gig up north somewhere on the 20th and we are doing two shows after that which are just ordinary shows. The showcase gig I can understand, but the two little shows after that are going to cost me my new job. I just fucking started here and now I'm gonna have to turn around and quit so I can play two little puny ass shows. If Cal would get off his ass and help by getting a job, I wouldn't be so scared of not working. But, God *forbid* he gets a job and joins the rest of society. I get so furious when he gets on his anti society kicks. The band is going to have to rent a van to make the trip because the Suburban is sick. That is gonna cost us big time. To pay *all* that money for shows we really don't even have to do is so stupid. I was planning to get an apartment TODAY and move out of the psycho flea circus. I hate being such a bitch to Cal about the working thing. Am I wrong to want him to work and do half? To meet me halfway? Is it wrong of me to want that?

It is so fucking hot. Yesterday it was 108 degrees in the shade. I betcha it's 90 degrees as I sit here and write this in this parking lot. Believe it or not, Cal is inside a store applying for a job. I hope they are interviewing him. I'm sweating all over. It's gonna *really* suck moving in this heat. I've got three or four places lined up today too look at…This morning I awoke at 8:30 to the sound of my own brain starting to stress out and worry about all these things…my job…having to quit it after just getting a place…my credit…Cal not working…trying to find a place to live. Maybe I shouldn't sign a lease because I am gonna have to quit my job so we can go play these two stupid gigs. If I miss for the shows on the

20th, the 21st, 22nd and 23rd, and then leave for a week and *then* go in the studio I am gonna miss eleven to thirteen days of work. If I am committed to a lease, I will be in *serious* trouble. I could quit and go somewhere else, but God that is *so* stressful. Cal has threatened to move in with Max. Max has no car and neither does his girlfriend so how Cal plans to make it and get anywhere with Max is beyond me, seeing how he would not have a way to get to work. How would he get the cash to move in anyway? People shouldn't write checks with their mouths that their asses can't cash. Cal and I fight constantly. I get frustrated and resentful so I am bitchy and irritable and I snap at him and say bitchy things to him. It's almost like I *provoke* the outbursts. Well, today he got really fucking mad and yelled at me. It scared me. He never yells so loud and forcefully at me like that.

7.17.95

Well, Cal got a job that day! As I sweated in the car, he got hired at an auto body shop. It's a hot and sweaty job. We found two apartments, one was cool and we wound up getting it! It's a second floor of a house made into an apartment kind of thing. It's a beautiful old house over by the University. I love the neighborhood. It's in the center of town. The house is not next to any other houses…and it's owned by a church across the street so a **Baptist church** is our landlord! It has this bay window in the living room that you see right when you open the door. A huge ass oak tree has grown right in front of the window and I swear the apartment looks like a tree house. It has ten-foot ceilings, hardwood floors, and an antique fireplace. It is so cool. It felt *great* to have a big ass paycheck and be able to pay the rent and deposit right away. After living on couches and bumming for so long, it is *so wild* to have a place of my own. I just sat in the middle of the floor in the empty apartment and soaked in the fact that it is **MY** space. No fucking fleas…no fucking pennies…no fucking kids…no crack whores…no other people laying around asleep in the floor…god I cant **believe** this. I haven't had a 'home' in over…a year?

I have been so busy with the band and finding a place and working that I haven't even thought about the fact that I leave for *Maui* in a *week*. I wish I had more time to get settled in. I'm wondering how in the hell I am gonna safely carry some smoke with me. I know it's not customs or anything, but they are real picky about people bringing animals or vegetation in and out of the island. I'm scared to do it and I'm scared not to do it. I keep seeing the look on my parent's faces when I get busted trying to get on the plane. They would be so fucking embarrassed and it would ruin the whole trip. I keep imagining myself being on the island, chillin and wishing I had a fat one and not being able to score anything and being miserable. That would suck so bad. I don't know what the fuck I am gonna do.

7.21.95

Somewhere on the road. Cal lost his fucking job *already*. I am so pissed. I leave for Maui on the 27th and I am worried about money. My new bosses are so cool. I explained my circumstances to them when they hired me and I guess I didn't think they would really be as understanding as they said they would. I'm really fortunate.

7.26.95

I leave for Maui *tomorrow*. I don't know what the fuck I am gonna do about the tattoos. Mom says Dad is going to have a heart attack when he sees them. I did color my hair back brown, though. They are coming to get me in the morning. I decided not to take any smoke with me. I can't bear the thought of getting busted in front of Mom and Dad. I guess I'll just drink the whole time. Yuck.

Cal got a job at art store near my work. It has been working out okay riding to and from work together. He seems to like it okay. I think he just fucking hates working period. He wants to lay around, smoke pot, and study magick all day. So do I! But who would pay the fucking bills? He told me there was a part time job at the library that he applied for. Motherfucker. Part time! That is not fucking fair! I asked him what he was gonna do with the rest of his time and he said he wanted to write a book. Well, I'd love to work part time and focus more on the *band*. Gee. What world does he live in?

One thing is for sure, having money is unusual. We have bought all the new Donald Tyson books, a new *Golden Dawn* text, and four other kick ass new books that I cant think of the names of. We've been buying a half-ounce every week, which *really* kicks ass. Having smoke of my own is the *shit*. But the more we buy, the more we smoke. It almost seems as if pot isn't cutting it anymore. It's almost like I need a bowl **and** a joint of my own just to get a nice buzz. It kind of bothers me. I mean, what's next? What's after this? Where do you go from the buds? To the needle? Being on the road, I am used to going without every now and then, but now that I have money I NEVER go without, which seems to have made me like more resistant to it. Oh, what the hell do I know? I analyze everything way to fucking much.

I have been intently reading my new book on the Kaballah. It is so damn complicated, but mysterious and beautiful at the same time. If I am not playing, recording, at practice, or at work, I am studying it. I have also been studying the signs for the various gates, called sigils, which have a beauty all their own. Cal and I have really moved away from basic Wicca and into a more ceremonial path. I love ritual, and ceremonial magick is all about that.

8

The Great War in Heaven

8.5.95

Maui was **unbelievable**. I have never seen nor felt any place like it. I scored some bud twenty feet behind my parents in a little village. It wasn't much, but I spread it out and smoked it in a pipe I made out of a toilet paper roll. We bought some rum and I managed to stay mildly drunk during the day and smoke out on the beach at nite by myself which fucking **rocked**. I spent a lot of time with my brother. He's a freakin' *counselor* now. He kept diagnosing me. He had some really awesome insight. He was right about everything he said. He said that people are like a car. Each tire on the car represents a part a person's health—mental, physical, emotional, and spiritual. If one tire is flat, it's hard to drive the whole car. It puts the whole car off balance. I rekon I have some flat tires. He also sincerely apologized for the shit that happened when we were little. I forgave him, mainly because I could see how much it was tearing him apart. Now that he is a counselor, he knows exactly what he was putting me through. He deals with the perpetrator and the victim in his job now every day. I guess everything truly comes full circle. My **parents** bought me a **drum**. I could *not* fucking believe it. It almost felt as if they were accepting me for what I truly was. Something tells me not to be so convinced.

When I got home and walked in the door of the apartment, it looked *beautiful*. Cal and Mica had stained the floors a dark cherry color and we had Mica's Mom's old furniture in the living room. Cal was asleep when I walked in the door. I saw a pile of dirty laundry in the bedroom, the same pile that was there when I left. I had asked to him to do the laundry so my uniforms would be clean when I got home. I was *immediately* furious. He was really acting weird and indifferent. It turns out that Cal read *THIS* journal while I was gone. In a weird way I have to admit that I left it out almost on purpose. If he read my journal, he would know how I honestly felt about everything, without me having to tell him to his face. Well, you get what you ask for. He was *furious*. Mostly about Ethan. We fought all day. I was really hoping to be a lot more nice to him, especially after the trip and all the therapy from my brother. What a homecoming. I have to go to work, and then go straight to the studio. There is no telling how late we will be there. It's like I'm walking right back into a big pile of shit.

8.6.95

At the studio. Max and Ruger are working on the vocal tracks. "The Man" is here and he has the kind bud. That is *so* fucking frustrating. I can't smoke the shit because I may have to play again. I am in hell. Since when is being in the coolest band in the city and being on the road and doing what I have always wanted to be doing the equivalent of being in HELL? I am already exhausted. It's already past one o clock in the morning and I still have tracks to play. And I have the nine am shift tomorrow. I cant call in cuz I just *got* the fucking job *and* I just missed a week. Fuck.

8.7.95

Sittin at work. I was at the studio until fucking *three o' clock* this morning. Luckily, we are not busy right now. I hope it picks up later though because if I sit on my ass all day I will be exhausted. Things with Cal are better. He was real nice to me when I got home late. He was up with a bowl packed. That was super nice.

8.10.95

Holy fucking shit. After Cal picked me up from work last night, we went to the grocery store. We were riding down Poplar and just as I was about to ask where the bowl was so I could pack it, I saw blue lights. I *freaked*. We got pulled over just inside the Germantown city limits, which was really fucking bad, because they live in an alternate reality in Germantown. The cop said it was because we had a taillight out, but I suspect it was the freaks inside the truck with stickers all over it. He asked us to get out of the car and I knew it was over. I knew Cal had dope in the truck somewhere, I just didn't know if it was the ounce we had just bought or just enough for a bowl. The cop began searching inside the cab of the truck and Cal told me quietly that he would take the rap for everything. *Every-thing*! Then the cop got out of the truck and pulled out his little walkie talkie thing and I heard him say to whoever was on the other end that he had found marijuana. FUCK. We got busted. We were finally busted. Me and Cal. The pot-heads from hell finally caught. Oh my god. I was going to *jail*. My new job. The band. *Everything*. He handcuffed me and Cal and we were put in the back seat of the cop car. Unfucking believable. When I heard those cuff snap on my wrists I saw my future flash before my eyes. We had been getting away with the shit for too long. Way too fucking long. As we sat in silence in the back seat of that cop car, the cop went through our things in the truck piece by piece. As I felt the cold steel of the handcuffs cut into my wrists behind my back, a funny sense of calm come over me. I just smiled and told Cal everything would be all right. I think he was as surprised as I was. Inside I was freaking, yet a funny calm came over me. Neither of us spoke in the cop car. It's like we both had enough smarts to realize that any conversation we had in that cop car may not have been completely pri-vate. I could see the cop going through our stuff. He had my purse and he was fishing through it. I knew there was a pipe in there. At that moment, I knew for SURE **I** was goin to jail. I watched him intently. He fished around in the bag, shaking it. Those moments were the worst. As the cop walked over to the car, I thought of all the things I wished I had done differently. He opened my car door and asked me to get out of the car. This was it, I thought. "I have the right to remain silent…anything I say can and will be…" My thoughts were interrupted as I heard him ask me where I worked. I told him and he asked me if it was in Germantown. I told him it was. He looked at me in shock…as if I was his own daughter and he said, "That's where *I* get *my* hair cut" I was SO fucking ashamed of myself. Shaking, I braced myself for the news that he had found a pipe in my purse. But he did not say that. He said he had found marijuana in the glove box and a pipe. He asked me if it was mine. Cal yelled from the car that it was HIS dope and pipe. I couldn't *believe* Cal was really saving my ass and taking the rap for this. The cop asked me if that was true. I said yes, that it was true. I lied my ass off to that cop. I felt bad for lying, but worse for getting busted. He told me that Cal was going to be arrested for possession and for paraphernalia. He told me I was free to go and he was taking Cal in and I could come pick him up in a few hours. He got in the cop car and left. I got in the truck and lit a cigarette. I could not fucking believe this had happened. I drove to the police station and I just walked around by the little lake. I could see the reflection of myself in the water, even though it was really freakin dark outside. I watched my image waiver in that water. I thought about Maui. I thought about the last night that I was there…and how I sat on what seemed to be the edge of the earth, listening to that song about changing the world. I thought about how I had cried, knowing that the cause I devoted my life to was not at all helping change shit…but about self-ishness…fame…and personal success. I stared at my wavering face in that water for what seemed like forever. My cigarette had burnt down to the filter and burnt my finger. I got up and went inside the jail and asked about Cal. He came out a few minutes later. He said he would have to go to court and he had to get a law-yer. We didn't say much on the drive home.

8.15.95

Max's girlfriend's best friend works for a lawyer, so we have made an appoint-ment for next week. We have practice tonight and I don't even want to go. I would much rather just stay home. I want a normal life sometimes. I just want to kick back, study, and smoke out with Cal. I am so fucking tired after work. I got a copy of the *Book of Enoch*, a book of the bible of sorts that was omitted. It explains the fall of Lucifer and the story of the Great War in heaven. *All* of this ties into the Kaballah. I have *so* much reading to do.

8.20.95

We have shows this weekend and we've actually been practicing. Cal has to go to court next week. The court is right by his work. I told him I would go with him, but he says he will go by himself. I don't know what excuse I would give my new boss anyway. I have been nervous that that cop is going to come in to the shop. I cringe when the door opens. I hope he switches salons. I am getting more and more frustrated with the band. Just the bullshit of trying to actually fucking practice. Max is late. Ruger is drunk. Ruger is drunk and bitches about Max being late. He takes it to the extreme and talks shit about quitting the band, which freaks me out and makes me worry. He bitches about how fucked up our band is, about how shitty our last show was. He talks shit about Max when Max isn't around. He talks shit about Ian. I'm sure, then, that he talks shit about me. It makes me nervous. I feel unstable. One minute he thinks we are the greatest fucking band in the world and the next he wants to quit. All the more reason for me to secretly consider my own plans to quit. I am so sick of their shit. I'm sick of them not working, or selling dope for a job, which puts the whole fucking band at risk. If Max gets caught, he goes to jail—and we have no singer. I'm sick of the mooching, the lying. I'm sick of their immature asses who cant even show up to practice having the authority over when *I* can get high. I just crave some normalcy in my life. Sometimes I think it would be cool just to see my own band perform. Literally, from the crowds view. It's like if I could do that then I would know if we were worth all the bullshit. It's like I cannot tell if we are really any good, because from my viewpoint behind the drums, we sound amazing. **I** would buy my own CD if I were not in my band. That's how I have always measured us. But sometimes I wonder if I think that because I get to beat the shit out of my drums, and when they are rigged up to the PA and I have triggers in my kick drum, aw man…it's just *so* awesome. Sometimes I just want to find out…just to make sure that my investment in all of this has been worth it. That I am not blinded by the ego's in my own band to believe we are great and find out once and for all if we really are or not. I am too jaded to really be able to tell, especially from the stage, where almost every drummer is given the power trip of a lifetime…

8.22.95

I've been trying to teach myself Hebrew. It's a bitch. I put my Hebrew flash cards I made up on the walls on either side of the window. They look cool. The Hebrew language is so beautiful…written and spoken. With Cal working things have been so much easier. We bought a hundred bucks worth of new books last night and he came home yesterday with an easel, paint, and canvas. Our little apartment has so much character. We really need a bookcase for all these books. Cal is doing a beautiful painting of Osiris. He is so talented. I never knew he could paint. It makes me want to try. I wish everyday was so easy. Maybe its just cause I am off work, high, and cuddled up with my new Kabbalah book, watching Cal paint. We haven't done a circle in a while and we have been talking about going mining or just going somewhere to get away for a weekend. It would be great to get out into nature together. Sometimes I miss our cabin. I do so well in the woods and around nature. When I get into the city, I get all funky and bitchy and miserable. Maybe it's the heat. I swear I think the asphalt makes a huge difference. I used to wonder how the Indians survived with no air conditioning in their teepees, but now I swear it gets hotter than it did then because we have stone, cement, and asphalt to suck in the heat. We cut down the trees and then wonder why it gets so hot.

I think I am so happy today because we don't have practice tonight. I swear. I just am glowing. I get to smoke all I want, read, chill, and relax. I think more and more every day about just wanting a simple life. I just want sometimes to leave all the craziness of the band and just chill. I think sometimes about going to college. I think about meeting new people and having new friends. Not that I don't love the guys…and not that I don't love the attention, because I'd be lying if I said I didn't. I just feel sometimes like my whole life is centered in a goal and that's why all of the people who are in my life are there. I wonder how many of them would be around just for me. For the real me…not just for Flo. I wonder how well it would go off if I quit the band and then showed up to the gigs to party with everybody. I just am tired, I guess. I am tired of everything being so crazy all the time. I'm tired of missing sleep and hectic schedules and crashing on couches and not being able to get high when I want to get high. Sigh. I am gonna share a bowl with Cal…I'm gonna quit writing now before reality ruins my good mood.

8.23.95

I cannot fucking believe this. I waited on them for three hours. *Three fucking hours*! This is he shit I cannot stand. They could've paged me earlier than they did. Fucking inconsiderate asshole musicians. *This is bullshit.* And then I'm a bitch when we do start practice and then I cop an attitude from hell when I get home. I give up so much for them. So fucking much. And they play with it like it's *nothing*. They don't give a shit. They don't care that I work forty-five hours a week. They don't care that I have waited all day to get high just for them. They don't care about shit. I could go to college. I could do so many other things. Instead, I sacrifice myself to four men who play with the sacrifice like it's nothing. They have no respect for me or for the band or for anyone. Fuckers. Cal went to court. He got probation.

8.27.95

We have to pay a probation officer every month. Cal got off pretty easy. We were lucky. We were *extremely* lucky. We're playin at the Shell soon...should be cool...outdoor gig...Got a haircut...gotta go

8.30.95

I am too fed up to write anymore. I just don't even want to admit what I have been thinking. It's *so* fucked up. I am just really, really considering leaving this band. I am just so sick of the bullshit. I don't want to go to practice anymore. I don't want to do the gigs anymore. We are playin the Daisy this weekend and I don't even care. I used to daydream about playin there. What the hell is wrong with me? I don't even care about it. I would rather wish them a good show from the crowd and get high with my friends. Just have a simple existence. This is so fucking difficult. I am just so tired of working, struggling, practicing, and worrying about everybody's drug problems. Why can't these people just smoke dope?

Why do they have to do that chemical shit, get all sprung, and go around geekin 'and snifflin' and talkin' all crazy? Someone told me Max had a fucking *seizure* the other night. I am really worried about him. About *them*. About the *band*. Am I on a sinking ship? Is all I have been working for in vain? Why do I resent them so much? I am tired of being angry and frustrated. I am just so tired. I am crying. I love them and hate them at the same time.

9.1.95

Man. Cal and I scored some mescaline last night after our gig at the shell. I had never done that shit before, until last night. It was awesome. It was a real different buzz…real laid back…kinda like trippin…kinda like shroomin. It was really cool. The gig was fun. It was really different playin outside at night in the open air…being able to see the moon from my drum kit. I played for her.

9.5.95

I talked to Hope about wanting to quit the band. She said she understood the stuff about wanting a simpler life. She definitely has a simpler life now. She is trying to get pregnant. I've only been pregnant once, that was with Sam and I miscarried at 7 weeks. I hate to say I am glad I miscarried, but I am glad I miscarried. Sam would have been awful to deal with for the rest of my life. I remember when I saw that positive pregnancy test. I cried and cried because I knew Id never be able to do all the things I wanted to do. I felt my life was over and it was going to forever be all about someone else. But I got over that really quickly. I was *devastated* when I lost that baby. I miscarried in the bathroom in the middle of the night. I remember waking up to a pain like someone had stuck a hot knife inside me and then stuck their whole fist in me and ripped a part of me out. There was blood everywhere. I put both of my hands over my crotch and ran to the bathroom. When I pulled my hands away, there was blood all over them and something strange. In my right hand, there was something light blue that was about the size of a large golf ball. I held it up to the light, dripping blood everywhere. Inside it was something that looked like my thumb…except it had an eye on either side of the top of it. It was my baby. I cried and cried on the toilet. The ass-hole Sam got up. I called my Mom and they came and took me to the hospital. It was so awful. Sigh. I know it's all for the best now. Nature has its way, I guess. I don't think I have ever told anybody that story. It's not good conversation.

It seems like lately I have really been thinking a lot about my life. The past…what I wanted to see happen, what did happen, and how it's different from what I expected. I guess I just never dreamed the band stuff would be this diffi-cult. I don't think my inner seventeen year old had any fucking idea what this life would be like. It looks so easy…even the parts that look hard, seem exciting. It's hard to get five people to see eye to eye on things, to agree on music style and to write songs together and play them well. But then to have those five people show up for practice and respect each other and respect the common goal? It's just a clusterfuck. I just don't know if I have it in me anymore. I'm just so afraid. What if I'm wrong? What if I really don't want a simpler life? What if I quit, then get replaced, and then wish I hadn't quit? Then I would have to live with regret, and that's the WORST. I just don't know what to do. I have also been thinking about quitting getting high. I just wonder sometimes if it has more to do with my mood swings and my attitude problems than I would like to admit. I have not gone one day sober in years…well…since Crossroads…but other than that, not one fuck-ing day. I don't even know what I would be like. If I would even be the same per-son. I know I play better when I am sober, even if I don't like to admit it. I don't even know if I could do it. I mean I know you can't be **addicted** to pot, but still it's such a huge part of my life. What would I do? I'm going to try to stop and see what happens. I can always start back if it sucks.

9.6.95

I am going to see what happens if I don't get high tonight.

9.8.95

I've had two busy as hell days at work. Our friend Trick paged us and we went by there and he had the kind bud, so what the hell! He thinks I kick ass because I can clear the chamber on his six-foot graphics bong in one hit without choking. He scares the shit out of me. He has guns and shit all over his apartment. He is from California and talks that gang shit all the time. He really scares me. The first time we went over there I was on my way to practice. We bought a half-ounce from him and we were about to leave when he said we should stay and get high with him. I told him I couldn't, that I had to go to practice. He said, no, you **SHOULD** get high and he pulled up his shirt just enough to flash his gun as he pointed to a chair. I caught on real quickly that he was **ordering** me to sit down and get high. One of those "You might be the cops and I don't know you and you are going to get high or you are not going to leave here in one piece" kind of things. After he came to our show at the Daisy, I became one of his favorite people. He still scares the shit out of me. I don't know about the not getting high thing. I think I am over analyzing.

9.15.95

Cal and I are going hiking at Fall Creek for the weekend. I could really use it. I am trying to convince him that it might be good for us to lay off the buds for a while, and use the weekend to try it out. He doesn't seem convinced. We are going to take some with us and just see what happens.

I just don't know who I am anymore. I feel so foggy. Like the world is not real. I guess I wish it wasn't. Maybe the trip will do me some good. I'm gonna think a lot about the band. Maybe it just isn't what I want to do anymore. Mom says the band is the root of all of my problems. I hate to admit she may be right.

9.19.95

We made it through the three-day trip sober. It was miserable. It really was. I managed to feel pretty connected at some moments, but for the most part, I was miserable. I feel so *uneasy* sober. I just don't like it. It sucks. But it sucks being high, too, mainly because it takes more and more just to get a decent buzz. It pisses me off. I'm sick of needing something just to feel okay. I don't even remember what life was like without it. I don't remember how I felt. It would be so fucking hard to try to abstain around the band. I just don't know how the hell I would ever be able to do it. I know I am a better musician when I don't get high. I guess I could just drink. I have never had a problem with that. But I don't even like it. I don't know what the fuck I am gonna do. I feel trapped. I am damned if I do and damned if I don't. I have practice tonight. I don't want to go. I want to stay home and just hide from everybody.

9.21.95

Before I crashed tonight, I was sitting in the big pink chair in the living room. I grounded myself. I opened myself up. All of the sudden I heard a voice in my head that was not my own. It said to me, "What the hell are you thinking…quitting the band? It is what you have wanted for your whole life…are you going to let a drug problem get in the way? Before you give up your dream, give up the drugs…

9.22.95

I can't quit thinking about that voice in my head. What the fuck would happen to me and Cal if I quit? Could I quit and have him still smoke it in the house? People that smoke pot do not have drug problems. What the fuck? Could it be true? It's all I have thought about since then. Marijuana is not addictive…yet **I** am fucking miserable with it and without it. I was *never* this miserable when I just smoked occasionally. When did I go from smoking occasionally to smoking all day every day? When did the lines get blurred? I smoke pot like a fucking crack head smokes crack. I always thought THEY were the drug addicts. I can't believe I just admitted that. How am I going to go back to the way I used to smoke it? I can barely go three days without it. I hate this shit. I fucking hate it. What the fuck is wrong with me? Why do I abuse it?

9.24.95

I have been crying all fucking day. I just hate my self and my life. Cal can't fix me. I can't fix me. I smoked out and **it did not fix me**. What the fuck is wrong with me? I dread dread dread practice tonight. I don't want to see anyone or do anything. I just want to sit here on my couch.

9.25.95

I am done with fighting. I cannot fucking believe I am going to do this, but I am going to go to one of those 12 step fucking meetings that sprung ass Demi used to go to. I went to the gas station and used the phone to call them. I got the recording that tells you about when these meetings are. There is one not too far from here at eight o clock. I just hope between now and tonight I don't lose my courage to go. I don't want to stop for good. I just want to get back to the way it was before it all got out of control. I just want to know what they are doing that is working for them and then I can do that some of the time. I know there is no way I could stop permanently—with my lifestyle it would be too hard to do that. But I do know that I have tried to stop, and I can't make it past three days. These meeting people have the magic secret to staying stopped. I hope they share it.

9

The White Rabbit

Oh, man…I went to that meeting…I found the place way early so I drove around for what seemed like an eternity but it was probably only fifteen minutes. I pulled up to the dark meeting place at like fifteen minutes to eight. No one was there but me. It was an eight o clock meeting and no one was there! I felt so totally cruised. I finally worked up the courage to get help with this shit and no one was fucking there. I was *so* cruised. I threw my truck into reverse, and started to back out of the parking lot to go home when a big hooptie pulled in next to me. There was a nice looking man in the car and he smiled at me. I felt like he could see right through me…that he knew who I was, that he knew I was coming, and that he knew to come at the nick of time, or I was outta there. Part of me cringed. I didn't realize until that moment that I **wanted** to leave. I **wanted** nobody to show up. That way I could still get high and any problems I had could be God's fault because I had tried to get help and I had been cruised.

The nice man peeked into my truck and said, "Goin' somewhere?" I shook my head "no". He smiled at me and turned away to go unlock the door. I reluctantly followed him in. I had missed my chance to escape so I might as well see what I had gotten myself into. The first room I was in was kinda cool. Big tapestries hung on the walls…there were posters with all kinds of spiritual slogans on them. There were old comfy couches and tables and chairs. In the corner was a big jam box, which he turned on. He asked me if I wanted some coffee. Coffee? I told him okay…and all of the sudden I was overwhelmed with tears…I ran to the bathroom so he wouldn't see me crying…part of me cried because I was so fucking scared…but most of me cried because of the kindness of this stranger. I forced myself to stop crying and tried to dry my eyes so he wouldn't see that I had been crying. When I came out of the bathroom, I heard more voices. There were four other people there. One was a big biker guy…one grateful deadhead lookin' guy who looked like he was about nineteen…one guy looked like he was probably gay—he was real clean cut and had nice clothes on, and a woman who looked like she'd had a real hard life. I slipped back into the main room and sat on the comfy couch next to the jam box. I was terrified. None of them seemed to really notice me. The nice man started the meeting. They prayed and then read a bunch of stuff. I could not believe what I was hearing. What they were reading described me completely. I cannot remember exactly what they read, but it was stuff about being miserable and being sick and tired of being tired and sick, and about feeling hopeless…and about how now there was hope. One thing they said really freaked me out. It was that **alcohol** was considered a "drug" and they don't do any alcohol or drugs at all. Holy fucking shit. **NOTHING?** These people do **NOTH-ING!!!** Then they asked if anybody was new. I raised my hand up. I told them my name. They told me they were glad that I was there. Whatever! They didn't even know me! Then they each talked for a little while…everyone was real quiet when someone was talking…I don't remember what anybody said really…except that it was a spiritual program and God was the solution. Well hell. I have the God thing down. I've been studying abut God since I was fifteen…I just wondered how the deadhead guy was staying "clean and sober" as they called it if he was goin to dead shows…I figured if he could still go to shows and stay 'clean and sober' that maybe I could stayin the band sober for a while. After everybody said stuff, they asked me if I wanted to talk. I said no. I left there terrified that I might be one of them. I could stop, but I could not *stay stopped*. They said to just try to not get high or drink for the **day.** To not think about it in terms of the long haul, but just for the day. I could do it for one day. I did not get high when I got home last night. I have not been high today. There is a meeting tomorrow night at the same place. I can't go today but I am going tomorrow. It helps to know I am not the only one trying to do this.

9.28.95

Cal is tripped out because I have not been high since Sunday. Hell, *I* am tripped out too. I went again last night. This time, the place was *packed.* The nice man was there again and there were some people that looked cool there…like this beautiful guy with long black hair and tattoos and piercings in his face. I couldn't believe that people like me were clean and sober. I heard more this time than I did at the other meeting. They said I needed to get something they called a sponsor…someone who would be like a personal helper. They also said you needed to avoid the people you got high and drank with. Oh yeah right. I was so scared when they said that. There is no way I can **avoid** *those* people. *Those* people are my life. My world. My BAND. It is fucking **FOR** them that I am here in the first place! If I don't try to get clean, I will lose *everything* I have worked for. There has **got** to be a way to do both. They told me there was a 'dance' going on Saturday night. Savannah gets married Saturday but maybe I will go to it afterwards.

10.1.95

Savannah got married last night. It was really cool. I went to the dance thing out in Germantown. I talked to the singer of the band that was there for a long time about music and not getting high and how the hell the two are possible. She said anything was possible. The beautiful tattooed guy with the long black hair was there. So was his beautiful **wife.** To make it worse, *she* is *really* cool. Her name is Natasha she has been clean almost a year. A fucking YEAR. I met another cool girl named Wren. They were apparently really good friends and they were funny. I just can't believe all these people are clean and sober. The beautiful guy came up and talked to me. He told me that there is a meeting on Monday nights at the same church that the dance was at. He asked me if I thought I might go to that meeting…and I told him yeah…he then asked me for a lift to the meeting. I thought it was weird, but I told him I would. I guess these people try to hang out with the new people.

10.2.95

I am *still* fucking clean. Yesterday before work, I went to the park and just sat there for a while. It is so weird to have not been high in almost a week. I have never gone this long before. I just keep thinking that it is just today, not next week, not the next gig, just today. It is working. Cal told me if I wanted to quit, he would quit too. Just like that. And he HAS quit. It seems to be SO fucking easy for him. I don't understand it. I am going to that meeting to night in Germantown with the beautiful Demetri. I am starting to feel a little better about life. I like all these new people. They seem to really like me, except most of them say I will never stay clean and sober if I go to clubs and stay in the band. They just do not understand how hard I have worked to make this happen. They do not realize that it is the only life I have ever known and how important this is to me. If I leave the band, I walk away from everything I have ever wanted. *Years* of hard fucking work. To give it everything I have got is exactly WHY I'm trying to get fucking clean and sober. I am not here to LEAVE it all behind. I am here to give it the one hundred percent of me it has deserved for a long time. I just can't do it on my own. I am so glad I am doing this. The band deserves it. I deserve it. I think this is what I have needed to do for a long time.

10.3.95

I went to the meeting with Demetri last night. I liked the meeting a lot. During the meeting, this chick with really long hair said when she was getting high she imagined she'd be an old lady growin' her own dope and stayin' high all day rockin' in a rockin' chair on her porch. I have thought *exactly* the same thing! After the meeting this weird man, who has a real thick northern accent, told me I needed a sponsor. We were all outside smoking and he pointed to the rockin' chair lady and said "Pick her...she *NEEDS* you". I thought to myself about that. She NEEDED me? What they hell did that mean? How could **she** need *me*? I needed a sponsor...but for a sponsor to need ME? I walked up to her and interrupted the conversation she was having with a girl I had seen at one of our gigs blasted out of her mind. I just said, "Um...are you Carey? She said "yes"...then I just blurted out "will you be my sponsor?" She looked completely startled. She said, "uh...*yeah*". The blasted gig girl smiled and excused herself. Carey asked my how long I had been clean and sober. I told her it had been one week that day. She gave me her business card and told me to call her the next day. When I looked at the business card, I could not believe it. She worked with my *brother*. They were BOTH family counselors. I said "Holy shit, Carey, you work with my brother!" She said, "Who is your brother?" I told her "Joe", and she knew him. It was *weird*. Demetri and I left and we had to pick up Cal from work on the way home. Cal looked at Demetri and all the color seemed to leave his face. I could tell he did not like me being with Demetri one bit. They seemed to hit it off, though. We drove to Demetri and Natasha's apartment. We went in for a minute. She was curled up on the couch with an astrology book, with her vivid red hair streaming down her shoulders. It did not seem to bother her at all that her husband had gone to a meeting with another woman. I guess that's how the program works or something. She and Cal talked about astrology, and Demetri and I looked at his set of Ninja swords. They are cool fucking folks. After the visit on the way home Cal seemed much better, much calmer. He liked them.

10.9.95

I have been talking to Carey everyday. She is SO fucking cool. She has been sober for FOUR YEARS. My god, I cannot even imagine a month, much less four fucking years. She is an old dead head, and the weird thing is she is seems to be older than me but she's not. She is younger than I am! She is like twenty-three! Her boyfriend Rickie has been clean and sober for like a million years. He is old enough to be her dad. He's cool. He's a biker. Carey sponsors Wren, too, Natasha's friend. Carey is so fucking cool about the band thing. She says I can stay clean and sober through any situation if I want to bad enough. I just have to understand that I am powerless over the 'disease', which is my obsession with using and the compulsion to do it over and over again. The powerless thing wasn't too hard to swallow. It's fucking obvious that I can't control it myself. If I could have, I would have been able to stop on my own. I have no power when it comes to dope. However, the powerless thing *is* especially hard for a...uh...witch. Admitting you have no power is absolutely the last thing any witch would want to do. I am just beaten. I give up. This is easier...giving up is easier than struggling and fighting. Cal has gone to a few meetings with me. He says he thinks the 12 steps are cool; he just doesn't like the powerless one. He said he is not powerless. With his ability to stop and have no problems with stopping, I have to agree with him. It does piss me off, though. I'm just jealous, I guess.

10.13.95

Natasha came over last week and we hung out. She is *so* cool. *Get this.* I went to practice last night and it was **great**. It has not been great to go to band practice in FOREVER. I played the *shit* out of my drums. I was so AWARE…that's the only word I can think of to describe how I felt. I just felt so alive…like I was playin them for the first time, yet not as bad as the first time sounded…I don't know how to describe it. I kept thinking the guys would notice something was different about me, but if they did, they didn't say anything. I have not told them. I know they are going to tease me and call me a quitter. I feel like the more time I have clean, the easier it will be to tell them. Then I can withstand any bullshit they throw my way. My secret hope is that they will all get clean too. We would be so amazingly unstoppable then. Mica still comes around, even though we aren't getting high. It's hard to be around him…I keep feeling like he is judging me for being a quitter. Maybe I am judging myself for being one. We are planning a trip to go crystal mining. We are playin the Daisy Friday nite and then after the show we are leaving with some folks and meeting Mica and his Mom at the campground. It's my birthday tomorrow. I will be twenty fucking five. It's all downhill from here. I am concerned about the buds this weekend. I know Mica and them are gonna get high the whole time. I'm just going to have to find some way to deal with it. Carey, Natasha, Wren, and a bunch of folks from the meetings are coming to the Daisy to see us play. That is so fucking cool. My first show clean and sober and they are all gonna be there for me. How fucking cool is that.

10.14.95

I have twenty days today. *Twenty fucking days*. I cannot believe it. I am so excited about it. I was **so** excited that I *told* Max. He and I rode to pick up an amp from Jesse's before practice...I guess I felt safe because we were alone. He just said "That's good, Flo...that's real good." I guess I am kind of disappointed that he didn't say a whole lot else about it. I am also disappointed that for the past twenty days they have not even noticed. They have not noticed from my playin', nor have they even noticed after practice that I am not getting high. It's like they don't pay much attention to me. Oh well. I guess that's really a good thing. It would be worse if they were all over me about it. We decided to do a cover song, which we never do. We are doin' "The White Rabbit" by Jefferson Airplane. We are rocking it the fuck **out.** It sounds **so** good with Max and Ruger doin' their harmony thing in the vocals. We made it into an *extremely* heavy mother fucker. Instead of the little snare rolls being done on the snare, I am doing them with my feet on the kick drum, and then pounding the **shit** out of my snare with rim shots. It fuckin' *smokes*. We are going on the road next weekend. Headed up to Champaign and to Chicago. I am pretty scared. This will be my first road trip clean. I have **so** many stoner friends in Illinois. All I do in Champaign is get high. How am I going to avoid everyone? Maybe they won't even notice—just like the band. I think what scares me the most is boredom...boredom on the road. Boredom leads to thinking and I am *terrified* to be alone with my own thoughts. I must have stayed stoned all the time just to shut up my own head. Carey says it is my 'disease' that speaks to me negatively and God that speaks to me softly, so soft that I can barely hear it. She said the loud voice will get quieter and the God voice will get louder. I just know I am going to be calling her from the road. Today is my birthday. And I have twenty days! That's pretty cool.

10.20.95

Awwww maaaaannnn...I have *so* much to write about...I wish I could write as fast as I talk. *So* much has happened. The show at the Daisy was like **redemption.** I have **never** *ever* played so well, so **confidently** on a stage in my whole fucking life. The Redneck Vampires has pushed me...molded me...into being the best drummer I could ever be…the music is so demanding…but that night at the Daisy I had something I have never had before. I had **complete** confidence in myself. I was *not* afraid. Of Ruger. Of dropping a stick. Of messing up. I was not afraid of **anything**. I had *none* of the voices in my head telling my anything negative. I was not intimidated by anyone. I was not afraid of any other drummers watching me. I was completely FREE. The most amazing thing about all of it was that I absolutely **loved** *every fucking minute of it*. It was the best show of my career. Being on stage was so much fucking fun. I felt so powerful. I was able to ENJOY it because I was so free. And, to top it off, Demetri, Natasha, Carey, Wren, and a bunch of other folks were all there down front in the pit. It was so fucking cool. And then Cal and I took off to meet Mica and his Mom in Mt. Ida. We got there at about five in the morning. Mica and his Mom got up and made breakfast. Then we all went mining. That night we sang songs by the campfire. Mica and them got high all day. It wasn't really even tempting. I was on top of the fucking world. I had played my ass off Friday night and I knew it.

The way home from mining was *not* as wonderful. We broke down inside Hot Springs. These dudes helped us out and offered to get everybody high. AND they had the kind bud. Sigh. It figured. But once again, I did not. We got about an hour down the road and broke down *again*. This time it was *really* bad. I called our road crew in Memphis and they came and got us! Luckily for me, they were awake and ready for the rescue mission. I got home at about three o' clock this morning and had to be at work at nine, where I am now. Sigh. I have twenty-five days today. That is fucking amazing. I just can't believe it. Cal had a good weekend too. He scored more than anyone did on crystals. We are boiling some on the porch right now. I had to go and tell all the neighbor kids not to touch to crock pot on the porch…if they did the acid would eat through their skin. It smells like rotten eggs an it's all green and bubbling, so I think they were convinced.

10.22.95

We are going on the road this weekend. I am kind of freaking out about it. I shared about it in a meeting, but I get the feeling that it annoys people in meetings when I talk about the band, because one of the 'rules' is to avoid the people and places that you used with. So, when I talk about my band problems I feel like they are rolling their eyes inside. Carey says that what they think about me is none of my business and sharing about fear is important, because just talking about it cuts it in half. She is so amazing. I talk to her everyday. And she is right about the cutting the fear in half thing. It's true. She told me that I will get through the road trip the same way I get through every other day clean, just an hour at a time. She says that the fear of it in my head is bigger and more awful than the real experience will be. There is just something so soothing about her voice. And the words she says don't hurt, either! I think I believe her. I am ready with my calling card, though, if I need to call her from the road. And I have a meeting schedule for the area but I don't know if I will be going to a meeting. I don't know if I will have a chance…or really I don't know if I will work up the nerve to ask the crew to drive me to a meeting. That's the real truth. They don't know I am going to meetings. I guess my pride has me on this one. Gotta do a haircut…

10.25.95

We have a new practice place. It is **so** fucking bad ass. It's right in the heart of midtown in the basement of a newly renovated building. The building is an office and it has a loft apartment in it. It has a Jacuzzi, a pool table, raw wood rafters and the deco is fabulous, down the light fixtures. The kitchen looks like one you would see on a cooking show. The guy that owns the building is one of Max's friends and he likes hangin out with the band, so he invited us to practice here. The practice room has a little room off to the side of it. Dude put two futons in it, and he bought big ass posters for the cement walls and metal tables and cool lamps. There is a big art deco rug in the floor and a TV, VCR and a stereo. It's a little hang out room. It's so fabulous. He is sprung as shit, though and a little unpredictable. I have a feeling we wont be here long. It's like we are his "flavor of the week". I think I heard Max say he has a wife and kids. Demetri paged me and I called him back. He wants to come to practice tonight. Why does he want to come to practice? I told him they get high and drink at practice and he said that was not a problem for him. I am picking him up after work.

10.26.95

Okay, what the fuck is up with Demetri. He started giving me that 'look' last night while I was playin. I pretended not to notice it, even when our eyes met a few times for a little to long. Hell, I have an awesome boyfriend. So, what the fuck am I doing staring into the eyes of a married man? Then when I dropped him off at his place, he asked me to come in. I asked him if Natasha was there and he said no, that she was at a meeting. I felt kinda weird going up to their apartment…but I figured he could not be dumb enough to think I would actually 'go there' with him when I am a friend of his wife. But, he kind of let the conversation die down to those spots where you just kind of trail off your words and stay locked in each others eyes…he sat next to me on the couch and he sat waaay too close for a married man. I have to admit that I am absolutely so completely flattered by this. It's flattering because his wife is SO fucking beautiful. I think I have a serious crush on Demetri. I need to talk to Carey about it. Hell, I need to call her anyway before we leave for the road.

10.27.95

On the road. I am really struggling sitting in my spot. I am so used to smoking dope here!! I feel so restless. I just seem like I need to relax and I can't. Nobody is burning any dope, though. I'm kinda used to not getting high on the way **to** a gig. I just always rest assured knowing the reward is coming after the show. This time, that isn't going to happen.

I talked to Carey before I left. She said Demetri is one of her good friends, but he has a reputation for being quite a 'player'. She said he started seeing Natasha when she had nine days clean, which is apparently frowned upon pretty bad. It's suggested that you wait a year before dating (because relationships are so emotionally overwhelming) if you aren't already in a relationship when you get sober. And people with time, like Demetri, (he has like four years) are not supposed to hit on newcomers. Sigh. She said he married Natasha after like two months. They've been married just about a year. Natasha has a little boy, Ivan. He's not Demetri's. He's really little, like a year old or something. Ivan stays with her Mom most of the time.

I have been reading some, and I twisted a few crystals with copper wire. I added some hematite beads; they look pretty cool. Sigh. We will be gone all weekend and get home in time to play Halloween at The Attic. That's gonna kick ass.

10.28.95

Unfuckingbelievable. I could not fucking believe it. The Champaign folks threw **me** a birthday party. I did not know they knew me well enough to even know it *was* my birthday. The clincher was the cake. Sabrina, the kick ass friend we stay with up there, made the cake. The cake had been dyed green and it had white icing on it, and smack in the middle of it was a huge pot leaf made out of green icing. In the middle of the cake was a big ass joint. She brought it to me with a lighter and they all sang happy birthday. I had no fucking idea what to do. I just thanked them and thanked them. Sabrina said "fire it up dude!" I felt SO fucking obligated to smoke that joint. That was so cool of them. But I know myself—and I knew if I had smoked it that I would be off and running all over again. I don't think I would come back to recovery when I got home. I think I would be too embarrassed…too ashamed. I had no choice but to tell her the truth—well, at least part of it. I told her how much I appreciated the cake and the party, but that I was layin low on the buds for a while…and that I hoped she would understand. She seemed shocked, but she smiled and said it was cool. Then she said not to freak when I opened my presents. Presents? Then she handed me a beautifully wrapped package. I braced myself. Inside the box was a videotape of us playin live in Champaign, and a smaller box. I opened the smaller box and inside of it was the most kick ass pipe I have ever seen. The bowl is bright purple and it has this bad ass green foil lookin stuff on it. It is all shiny…and the pipe part is titanium purple and green…it is absolutely the coolest pipe I have ever seen and proof that she knows me very fucking well. I could not have picked out a better pipe for myself ever in the world. It is fucking cool. It makes me want to christen it…but I'm not going to. The show last night was great. I have **so** much more energy. I managed to avoid my usual crowd of potheads. Every time one of them would approach me with the one hitter packed, I would escape by saying I had to go check on something in the van. Luckily, they all just forgot to find me. I got through last night unscathed. I had to lie my ass off, but I managed to avoid the potheads so I guess the lies were worth it. Now let's see if I can make it through tonight.

10.30.95

We are playin' some pre Halloween bash in some city that starts with an S. I can't remember the name of it. Sabrina and I are gonna ride together. I really like her. She is going to come down and stay with Cal and I one weekend when we play. I talked to Carey for a while on the phone. She told me she was very proud of me for staying clean. She freaked the fuck **out** on the cake and the pipe. I was glad she reacted that way! It was good to know that would be hard for another person to deal with as well. It was great to connect with her. I went into the back bedroom to talk on the phone. I didn't want the guys to hear me talk about the drug stuff...well, more about my feelings and how this has been difficult. The only one of them I have directly told about being clean is Max, that day in the truck. The rest of them have kinda caught on to it on this trip. It's kind of freakin' them out. They could not *believe* I did not smoke the cake joint. I don't want them to know this is a struggle. Hell...maybe it's my pride, too...I want to look like I can handle this...even though I am struggling. Somehow, I don't think I am completely fooling them. Maybe it's the drool that runs down my chin when they fire it up. I'm trying to not talk about it at all in front of them. I guess I am afraid I will fail and I don't want to look like a hypocrite. I don't want to have to put my foot into my mouth. Well, it's my turn for a shower.........

10.31.95

That mother fucker. I cannot believe he just did that to me...wait...*yes* I can. It is *exactly* something he would do. He's the one that has been the most tripped out about me not getting high. So of course it would be him. I was minding my own business on the way home...which has always been my *favorite* time to get high...and motherfucker hands me a sack...his OWN sack, which he NEVER had smoke of his own...and asked me to *twist him one*. Just to spite him, I told him I would. I was determined as hell to not let his dirty little trick tempt me. But it was SO difficult to not fire that fucker up myself. If I got high after abstaining for thirty-six days, I was sure to catch a kick ass buzz. And to make it worse, the pot was so good that you could smell it all through the van just while I was *rolling* it. The buds just stuck together with no effort...the shit was *loaded* with little crystals of THC...sticky buds. After I twisted it, I asked Ian, who was riding in the passenger seat in the van, to switch places with me. I got up front and rolled the window down. Max just stared at me like he could not believe that did not tempt me to smoke it. I literally stuck my head outside the window while they smoked that sticky joint. Fuckers.

10.31.95 later

Ever since I have been in recovery, I have this whole new concept of God. I am still my pagan self, but I am coming to terms with these new ideas. I have been working on the God thing for so long now...the ceremonial path is narrow and strict...yet the recovery path is also narrow and strict, except in ceremonial magick God is at the *end* of the road, and in recovery you get God before you even set *foot* on the road. The God thing about recovery blows me away. It just can't be this easy. It just can't. That concept is in conflict with everything I believe in. I just cannot imagine God just being there for the asking and the taking. Just admit you are defeated, and acknowledge that something exists that is higher than you. And then ask that higher thing to help you do what you cannot do. And then it does. How fucking simple is that? The strange thing is, it *does* work. Carey says the only thing my higher power has to be is loving, caring, forgiving, and greater than myself. I just cannot imagine that God is so simple. God cannot be that simple. Can it? I guess the only reason I am even willing to believe this is 1) that my ass is kicked and my own ideas of a complex God weren't working for me and 2) that this one IS in fact working. I guess I have spent so much time trying to understand God that I haven't asked the God I did not understand to **help me**. I felt like I had to *understand* God before I could *use* God. I felt like I had to be worthy of God's grace before I could ask for God's help. But the recovery stuff is showing me otherwise. I have found more relief in *trusting* a God I *do not* understand than I ever did trying to *find* a God I was *attempting* to understand.

11.18.95

I have not written in forever. I am **STILL** fucking clean. I cannot believe it. It's been almost sixty days. SIXTY. Playin on stage is amazing. It is so fucking FREE-ING. I absolutely love it. It is so much fucking fun. Looking down into the crowd and seeing the faces of people...some familiar...others not...but they don't know I am looking at them...it's just fun to watch them get into the music so much. The best part is when they sing along to the songs...knowing *all* the words...that just makes me play even harder and better. **I cannot *believe* I was going to quit this band**. I cannot *believe* I was going to walk away from all of this. Marijuana made me the most insecure, paranoid musician in the world. It relaxed the shit out of me when I smoked it...but it seemed like later, after the buzz was gone, was when I got paranoid. Apparently not smoking it the day of the show was not enough to keep the paranoia at bay. The bad thing was when all of that was happening I had no idea that it was the drugs. I knew pot made me lazy, but I did **not** know it was responsible for the internal, self-torturing voices in my head. I thought I needed MORE of it to calm me down!!!!!! I remember that year at Crossroads when I stayed with Mom to avoid getting high for three days before the actual show. I KNEW **then** it was my problem. It just wasn't BAD enough to make me quit altogether, I guess. I guess I wasn't in danger of losing everything. I was not convinced. It seems like I remember having a really good show that night.

We are doing so well and things are really happening. We have shows lined up out the ass and we are recording some more soon. I can't wait to record clean. It is going to be a much more enjoyable experience. There is a recovery convention here thanksgiving weekend. I think it will be cool.

11.21.95

I've been hanging out with Natasha and Wren a lot. Natasha and Demetri split up. She has a little apartment of her own now. She is really messed up about the split. He seems to be *fine*. That has got to make it even harder for her. I steer pretty clear of him now. I still have a crush on him, but I really like Natasha. I would not want to lose her as a friend for messing with her ex. Plus, I have Cal. He has been awesome thru this whole thing, except for the fact that he is still clean and doesn't seem to have as much trouble staying that way. I am *so* jealous of that. There is this coffee shop that some dude in recovery opened up. It's really cool and it is right in the heart of midtown. It has a huge porch with benches outside and inside it's got this bizarre garage sale décor and an old jukebox with the weirdest selection of music on the freakin planet. It is so fun to hang out up there. Just acting silly and meeting folks. It is such a different crowd from the band scene. It's rather refreshing.

11.25.95

Staying clean around the band isn't easy. I got so tempted at practice last night. I made up this excuse in my head of why it would be okay **now** to get high. That I just needed the 'little break' that I have had. And then I thought about how high I would get from just a small amount because I have gone without for so long. Sigh. What kept me from listening to the excuses is that I knew it would just get bad all over again. I know it would. I wasn't able to smoke "just" after practice and after shows. I was fucking miserable trying to do that. I hated everyone that could smoke pot. I hated everything. I was resentful. Bitter. I was a bitch to Cal all the time. I just know the same thing would happen again. Another reason I didn't smoke it is because of the band. I think my pride has been helping keep me clean. Sometimes when we practice, nobody gets high at all because since I am clean, nobody else has dope.

11.27.95

When I was getting ready this morning I put in that CD that I listened to in Maui. I was immediately taken back to the island…to the energy…to that place of healing. It's like that was the beginning of this new chapter in my life. In Maui, I was re awakened. It's like something higher than me put me there to plant a seed of change…and two months later, it blossomed. I changed. Two months after that experience on that island, I got clean.

11.29.95

I have so much more MONEY. I cannot BELIEVE how much more MONEY I have. It is a freakin trip. I had no idea how much money I was spending on the shit.

This weekend was *such* a freaking trip. The convention was unbelievable. There were *thousands* of people there. I just could not get over the fact that they were all clean. There were bikers. There were conservative businessmen. There were rave kids in big jeans and neon necklaces. There were hippies with dread-locks. There were housewives. There were skaters. There were old seventies rock dudes in Rush t-shirts. And the cool thing is that all of these people would have never associated together before. They all shared one common thing. They were all addicted to substances and now they were free. I was so overwhelmed. Seeing all of those people just convinces me even more that I can do this. If all of those people can do this a day at a time I can, too. This has been the longest sixty—one days of my life.

12.29.95

I haven't written in forever! We have been on the road, the album is being mixed, and I am STILL clean.

This dude from the meetings called Cal while I was on the road. He told Cal he needed twenty bucks to go to the dentist…he said it was an emergency. Cal gave it to him. THEN Carey and Rickie's house got robbed. Really bad. All her jewelry, the titles to their cars, everything. She seems to be able to accept it so easily. She sounds sad, but she is not out to kill, or throwing a temper tantrum, or cursing and screaming or anything. She is just calmly expressing her pain. Amazing. The $20 dude has disappeared from meetings, and Memphis as a whole. He was at Carey and Rickie's X-mas eve party…so he is starting to look pretty guilty of robbing them. It doesn't take shit for a crack head to get sprung enough to fuck over their friends.

12.31.95

We are headlining tonight at the old Antenna Club on Madison. I've been thinking of all kinds of cool shit we could add to the show…little dumb shit to give away…anyway; I am looking forward to it. It's gonna fucking SLAM. We have had radio spots for this for over a week and Ruger says EVERYBODY is going to be there. He said Bone Squad is off the road and they are all gonna be there…and Justine may be coming…and the whole crew from Walnut Grove and Jackson are headed up…it's gonna rock. It's my first New Years Eve clean. That's gonna be weird. Not throwing down after the show? Drinking water? Anyway…gotta go to sound check……

1.3.96

It is 1996. That is *so* amazing. We have all kinds of road gigs lined up and we will be gone for most of the next two months. New Years Eve kicked so much fuckin' ass it was unbelievable. I think we played twenty-two songs. I **never** got tired. We *all* had a ton of energy…it was a sweaty, tight, rockin' show. When the place is so packed, it really feeds the band. It's like this huge exchange of energy is going on between the band and the crowd. We feed them, and then they feed us back and it goes on all night. And I have a really unique view of the whole thing. My view is blocked by the Max's back for the most part, and Ruger walks back and forth a lot…and so does Jesse. Ian stays pretty much by himself. But over the rims of my two mount toms, I can pretty much watch what is goin on in the crowd. I can see my friends…I can see the faces of strangers signing our songs…that is so wild. It just re-convinces me how awesome we are. The crowd is just as sweaty as I am. I got REALLY sweaty last night, too. My seat had a wet squish to it as I bounced around. My pigtails had sweat dripping off the ends of them and the looked like a collection of sticks by the end of the night. My black eyeliner had run down my face under each eye kinda making me look like Alice Cooper. People slammed, crowd surfed, and dove off the stage. Joseph from Bone Squad came up and sang with Max. People smoked pot in the crowd, and Max smoked it right on stage in front of the whole place during our last song. I bought a jar of pig feet at Piggly Wiggly for the prize for our crazy contest, and this guy won for whipping out his dick in front of the crowd and showing us his piercing. We made close to a THOUSAND dollars. We never dreamed we would make that much money. *We each got a hundred bucks.* I could not believe it. Max says we owe the rest of the money for some studio shit. It's probably going to go up his nose, or be reinvested in the 'business'. I'm going to keep my suspicions to myself. Once again, Flo will just play dumb. The oddest thing was this guy in the crowd passed a note to me after the show. He was kind of creepy. I still have the note. It says that my band sucks; that we sound like everybody else. He said that if I wanted to play in a REAL band, one that was going somewhere, to call him and he put his name and number on it. It bothered me. It bothered me that he had the gall to say we sucked when the place was PACKED full of people, people that came to see US. Plus, we had an AMAZINGLY good, tight set. What *really* bothered me the most was that he had the balls to say that shit about my band, and then expect me to want to call HIM. What a dumb ass. When you recruit a person from their band you don't start by telling them their current project sucks. That is an insult to them personally. Why did he not just be more specific and say, "You and your ideas suck", "What you have been working on for four years sucks". I could go on and on. I'm not calling him. Who knows, I could be passing up a chance to move into something that really *would* be better, but not with a guy who has an ego that big and the gall to be so insulting. If he would write a note like that, so full of insults, that is a pretty good indication of how he would be to work with in a band. I have enough attitude in my own band to deal with as it is. But that guy ices the cake. I showed the note to Joseph. He just shrugged his shoulders and kept nursing his drink. I wonder what he was thinking that he was not saying.

After the show was over, I made sure my shit was packed up and I said bye to the guys, and left. I went home. *On new years fucking eve.* I just went home. It's the safest thing I could do for myself. When we are on the road, I don't have the luxury of getting to go to a safe place right after the gig…but when I am at home…it's so nice to get to do that. I remember what it was like to not even have a home. I love my damn apartment.

1.14.96

Cal got 'laid off' from his job. He hasn't really done shit since. It's getting old. I am SO freakin busy with meetings, new friends, band practice, gigs, the road…I get so jealous of him and his free time. He and Demetri hang out sometimes and he and Mica are still running around. Gotta go to practice.

10

Carbon Monoxide

1.28.96

We've been practicing in the cold basement. I am still fucking CLEAN. It's been four months. FOUR FREAKING MONTHS. I cannot believe it. I really cant. I just keep thinking this is not forever, it's just for this day…but I cant believe I have thought and said and done just that every day for this many days in a row. Unbelievable. Truly.

I am more and more put off my Cal's not working, and his ability to not have to do anything to stay clean. I am so jealous. I can see and feel a huge difference in him since he stopped. He is calmer. He focuses more on his studies. His skin is clear and glowing. His hair is shiny and thick. I wonder if he notices it. I am jealous that I do all this introspective work and look at my behavior and my ulterior motives all the time and he doesn't have to do any of that. I really have a hard fucking time being around the band and the scene and all that clean, but it doesn't seem to bother him at all. We also seem to be growing farther apart in our relationship. We don't have that common theme of smoking out and it has seemed to leave a hole between us. It's like he is still really focused on the road we were on together and mine has taken another turn. I don't work ritually anymore. I don't read tarot anymore. I don't read our books anymore. I am working with a God that I absolutely do not understand, instead of worshipping a mystery I am trying desperately to understand. Using the God I don't understand…asking for this God to shut up my head…it's working…when before I would have *never* gone to "the light" with such a seemingly petty request. But Cal goes on…his does his rituals every morning like clockwork…and I love him for it. He feels so damn powerful. He gets stronger on his path and I struggle on mine, even though when I use it, it works. I guess I am not in the habit of USING God. I think about God. I respect God. I thoroughly believe in God. I just forget to say "Hey, God, uh,…can you help me out? I have been feeling out of place lately around the guys and becoming obsessed with the stupid idea that they want to replace me. Even though I know I am playin better than *ever* before, I do freak out about that sometimes. Carey calls it "the old tapes". She says that when we hear horrible things in our heads about ourselves that it's like a cassette tape that plays over and over. It's the same "old" information. It just plays over and over again, and we listen to it and believe it and get all freaked out. She says that if I think the old tapes are bad to wait until I hear the "new tapes". I was like "What the hell are the new tapes?" She told me the new tapes are all about recovery and how badly you work the program. They say stuff like, "you don't share right in meetings, you aren't working the program right, people in the program don't like you", etc. Oh fucking great! I think I already have some of the new tapes playin…Carey also talks about the itty-bitty shitty committee…a group of people that sit around a table in your head and debate your decisions. They hardly ever have anything nice to say. I can TOTALLY relate to the itty-bitty shitty committee. They tell me I am going to be thirty riding in the back of a van on the road with the band, they tell me the band is the biggest waste of time in the world, they tell me I need to be in college, they tell me I am fat, ugly, and stupid, oh it just goes on and on. Luckily, I have the antidote for the committee. Carey tells me to thank them for sharing their thoughts, and to dismiss them. It works. I can almost visualize their faces…staring in shock at being silenced. It makes me feel very powerful and in control of my life. I just am not in the habit of doing it all the time yet. I just reread what I wrote. It sounds like I am a crazy person—talking about voices in my head!

2.4.96

Last night after practice, Cal and I talked about our relationship. I have been thinking more and more about wanting my space—not breaking up—but just having some time to be alone and see if this is what I want. We have really grown apart—he said he could sense it. He talked about going back to the Grove for a while. I think he wants to quit working and go back to the way things used to be for him. He called Mitch, who is coming to pick him up in a week or two. Sigh. Am I doing the right thing? Is this going to be the end of us? Is this really what I want? Is it the right thing to do? I am absolutely torn. The 'committee' is meeting in my head, saying I am a selfish bitch for wanting time alone. I feel so guilty. Am

I being selfish? Is that true? He doesn't seem to be really sad. Either he isn't really sad, and this will be good for him, too or he is sad but he just doesn't want to make this harder than it has to be. God this is so hard. I think my biggest fear in life has always been regretting something. That is absolutely the worst pill to swallow. Regretting a decision absolutely sucks. So, I have to be prepared to deal with the consequences of my decisions. I used to just get high and not really make decisions. Or if I made a decision I regretted I just got high again and that fixed everything. But it was a false fix. It wasn't real. Now I have to be prepared to deal with, and FEEL the results of my decisions...for REAL. I just don't know what to do. I want time away from the relationship...but I don't want to lose Cal. I have to accept that he may like the separation too. He may meet someone he would rather be with. He may discover he has made decisions based on me that weren't right for him, like not getting high. Sigh. I just don't know what the fuck to do. I want my cake and I want to eat it, too. I know I am supposed to "give this away" to God, but I am so afraid to. I have always handled everything myself. I just don't know how to "give it away". How the hell do you do that? I mean, I can see me stopping to think about it, and stopping the obsession with it, but what do I do when we sit down to talk and I have "given it away"? How do you deal with it then? I just don't know what to do. I love him. We are inseparable. We are such a good team. So, if all this is true, why does it feel so stagnant? Sigh.

2.18.96

This chick, Amy-we used to get high and play D&D with her and her boyfriend Dan-called me two days ago asking if I had seen him. I told her no, and she just showed up over here tonight unexpectedly, asking about him again. It was odd, like we were hiding him out here or something. Amy and Dan have a good relationship. It is not like him to bail like this. Cal is worried about it. He said he has a bad feeling about the whole thing. He is leaving in a few days.

2.20.96

Today is Savannah's birthday. Cal left today. It was kind of a good parting, if saying goodbye can ever be good. I am goin up there to see him soon. It's goin to be so weird tonight…sleeping here by myself. Sitting around by myself. I have never lived alone EVER. It's going to be good for me, but I am scared as shit. Savannah says I need it. She says it will be good for me.

2.21.96

Amy just called me. Dan is *dead*. Two men found his body in his car. He had driven into a field, put one end of a hose in the exhaust pipe of his car and the other end through the car window, and turned the car on. He died of carbon monoxide poisoning. My **God**. I just cannot fucking believe it. We all hung out so much and he was such an intelligent guy. The kind of person that is so smart you can *feel* it all over them. It is just awful. The worst part of all is that Amy had just found out she was pregnant, and Dan disappeared before she had the chance to tell him. I have to call Cal…

3.10.96

I cannot sleep in the house without the TV on. I need something to drown out the sounds I hear at night. If I hear noises I freak out trying to interpret them and then I get all spooked out cuz this house is so damn old. AND near Orange Mound.

I went to Dan's funeral. It was the saddest fucking thing **ever**. His *parents…Amy*…it was heart wrenching. I am glad I went to support her, but it was so fucking **sad**. Cal and I have been talking on the phone quite a bit. He was pretty torn up about Dan, but other than that he says he is doing good and he misses me. I miss him too, but at the same time, I know this was the right decision for me. I hate to admit it, but it's true.

3.14.96

Sepultura is coming with Ozzy to the Pyramid…on the night we play Cross-roads! How fucking cool is that! Fucking **Sep**, man. My *favorite* fucking band. They canceled when they opened for Pantera…which sucked…I am so fucking excited. We have scored this 'manager' out of nowhere. He represents several blues artists…a couple really famous ones. His name is Larry Graves and he's a real character. He is *always* on the road in his car…he calls us from his mobile phone all the time. This dude STAYS on the phone. *All* day. He knows a lot of people for *real*…it's not just talk. He has a cool apartment at 99 towers that's riverfront. Ruger says he just has that place for the address. Whatever. He has the *weirdest* voice. It's like he has been gargling razor blades AND smoking lucky strikes for 30 years. On the phone, you would think he is black. *And* from Jersey. *And* a smoker/razor blade gargler. *And* constipated. He has this crazy hair, too. It's brown and curly and kinda of in his eyes and all over the place. Ruger has kissed his ass pretty good and I think he's moving in with him. Ruger is learning a lot from him. It makes me feel kind of like an idiot music-business wise. Just hangin out listening to them talk makes me realize how little I know about the business side of this industry. I am definitely going to go to all the panels at Crossroads this year.

3.25.96

I have six months clean today. That is half of a year. HALF of a YEAR. That is so unfuckingbelievable. I am so amazed. My life has changed so much. I feel so much more in charge of my life. I am the best drummer I have even been in my life. I am more dedicated to my band than ever. I am able to accept responsibilities. I am dependable. I show up when I say I will. I am on time…well…okay *that's* pushing it. I guess I am just a better, more directed human being today. I am a better friend, a better employee, and a better drummer. I am *so* focused on the band. I am prepared to fight like hell for this. I have been through enough and I am ready to seriously do this thing. No one really thought I could do this. No one believed I could stay clean through all this. I didn't even believe it. Carey did, though. She told me she believed that anyone could stay clean through anything if they wanted to bad enough. The truth is that I miss the hell out of partyin'. I miss it really bad. I miss how close the guys and I all were when we would get shitty together. I miss curling up with Cornfed and smoking a bowl. I just don't miss the *consequences* of using. I **don't** miss how much I doubted myself. I **don't** miss how uncomfortable I was on stage. I **don't** miss questioning myself and being confused all the time. I **don't** miss the agony of a twelve-hour ride up north...counting the mile markers until I could get high. I guess once again, I want my cake and I want to eat it too. I want to get high and not suffer the consequences of it.

4.5.96

I am going to see Cal soon for his birthday. I got him a cool ass hourglass for his altar. He will love it. I am looking forward to the drive to the Grove. To reflect on everything...

4.8.96

It's a new notebook day. Hope told me if I didn't write all this shit that was happening to me down on paper that I was crazy because she said it was "good stuff". She said it was so good that it was making it into HER journal.

I don't even know where to begin. I've had this stupid crush on Larry ever since he came around. I always wanted to think it was mutual, but I figured he just wanted sex—which I still think...or I *think* I think that...Anyway, on the last road trip up north he booked us a hotel and met us there. We slept in the same bed and I wanted to cuddle up close to him...but I didn't. We have to remain professional...right? Anyway, ever since then we've gotten closer and we've been talking about the business a lot and I have become more motivated about this band as a result. I guess seeing someone with power and pull in the industry become this interested in us makes me look at the band differently. Anyway, when we were in Illinois he cruised me on taking me to a meeting...I actually overslept, but I let him take the blame for it, which was fun, and then he went to Chicago on business. When we got home from the road he called me from Chicago four times...each time it was just to say hi...and then he shows up at my door after practice on Thursday and stayed at my place till like four thirty in the morning. I did *not* sleep with him. I told him he was out of luck if that's what he wanted. He either thought he could change that, or he really didn't mind that I wasn't gonna fuck him. He told me all kinds of gossip that goes on in my band. He told me Ruger was going to give me an "ultimatum" of some sort, which involves replacing me with Hack's drummer. Mother fucker. He also told me that I better take a look at the publishing rights of our songs, because if I don't, I'm gonna get screwed over by my own band. He said Ruger owns all the music in the band, and if we get signed, he technically will own the rights to the music and any money it produces. He also said I cant say shit about it to the band, because Ruger will immediately think we are fucking.

4.9.96

I'm wondering what they are thinking after we kicked so much ass on Saturday. Do they still want to get rid of me? Do they still want to replace me? I certainly can't ask them about it—I'm not supposed to know. I got the band alone for 5 minutes before the show. I told them how much I loved the band and each one of them and how I wanted the "band against Flo" shit to stop and how I wanted the "Flo against the band" shit to stop. I asked them to support me as I go through a major change in my life...not abandon me. They said, "cool" and seemed glad to hear what I had to say. Ian even came up, hugged me, and told me he was SO glad I said what I did. I love him. The show *rocked*—we had about eight hundred people through the door and we wound up being the highest grossing local band in a year at the Daisy.

Anyway, Larry left at 4:30 am and I felt weird. I didn't touch him, but I know I have a stupid crush on him. I feel bad because my heart belongs to someone else. And to top it off, he is the best bullshitter in the music business—so how in the hell am I supposed to believe what he tells *me*? He is very manipulative and clever. He tried to convince me that he wouldn't get high anymore so I would hang out with him. Yeah right. So when I roll my eyes at his comment, he says "come sit over here, mama". Mama? What the fuck is up with that? He calls women "mama" in his scruffy deep voice. He has the weirdest voice I've ever heard. So, as stupid as it is, I *like* it when he calls me "mama" in his gargly voice. So I go sit with him and he puts me in his lap and starts to massage my back and then he kisses me on top of my head. I am loving all this attention. Absolutely loving it. Then he grabs the clean pair of socks I have brought into the living room and puts them on my feet and says "you aint never had anyone takin care of you, have you mama?" God, I just melted on the inside when he said that. Then he says that Ruger and the babies (his name for the band) don't need to know anything about "Us" because they wouldn't like it. Well, hello! Does he think I am that fucking stupid? And who said there was an US anyway? He really thinks I am going to fuck him! Of course, my heart thinks this is a perfect love story and my brain says to get him the fuck out of my house—that he is full of shit. Sigh. The ongoing struggle between the head and the heart. It is nice to have a man that drives to my house in his own car. I can't recall dating a guy that ever had a car, much less a job, and their own place, who calls me from big cities and brings me presents. So maybe I am just completely infatuated with his age, his attention, his gifts, buying me dinner, the fact that he is so much older than me. I feel like such a dumb ass for even letting him hang out over here and keeping it a "secret". He feeds me all this bullshit about moving me to Maui—it's like he is trying to come up with shit he thinks I would like and then spoon feeding it to me bite by bite.

Anyway, so Friday night we played this party. But it wasn't like just *any* party. This was a warehouse downtown that some very cool folks turned into an apartment. It is so fucking HUGE. Room upon room upon room. And the ceilings were like forty feet high and there was a bar and big ass windows...and that was just the *living* room. I was so impressed with this place. From the street, you would never know it was up there. I think the guy said like five people lived there...so when I show up at the gig there is a line to get it the place. That's always the hardest part. I *hate* walking past folks and like flashing my official 'rock star' credentials. So, I just wait in line with everybody else. Well this night of course, the bouncer doesn't believe that I am in the band. He calls Ruger over and Ruger just starts laughing.

So, the place is absolutely *slammed* beyond belief. I didn't even know a lot of the people there. I hung out at the bar watching people drink until the show. I secretly scanned the room looking for Larry, but I didn't see him. So, I found a bathroom and put my hair in pigtails and when I came out, I saw him. He winked at me. That was it. What the fuck is up with that? So we play, and I find myself watching him from the stage. He had some tittie dancer slobbering all over him and he was eating it up. I knew at that moment I could not by any means let this motherfucker come around me any more. He was a fucking sleaze. I broke a drumhead I was so mad. After the show, I pulled Jesse outside. I told him I had something personal to tell him. I didn't tell him anything about Larry coming over to my apartment, but I did tell him that I had a stupid little crush on Larry. He said he didn't want to hurt my feelings, but that Larry was trying to have as much sex as possible with as many women as possible. He said he knows what a womanizer Larry really is. He said he was so sorry and that it was men like him that ruin it for men altogether. Then he told me something that was shocking. He said that if Max and Ruger knew that he was fucking with my head, that they would fire him and kick his ass. "No", he said, "We'd probably kick his ass, and then fire him." That totally blew me away. I was shocked. I could not believe they would stand up for me like that. I had no idea that they had a band loyalty like that. Jesse said that to me so matter of factly, ya know? I guess I thought I could learn a lot from Larry…I liked having the inside scoop on the gossip and the business…we have not had so much interest in the band since he came around…I guess I felt like we needed to keep him happy so he would come around. I am SO glad I did not fuck him. So glad. So glad. SO glad. So, after the show I came home and slept for four hours, got up Saturday, went to work, and then went to the gig. Larry played the Mr. Manager role all night. It was making me sick. Cal was supposed to be there, but he didn't show up. The guys all wanted to go to this party after the gig. I really just wanted to get some food and chill, but I wound up at the party. Larry walked in; he walks right fucking past me, and *immediately* plays Mr. Manager to Ruger's rock star act. I was so absolutely disgusted. As soon as he turned his head, I was out the door. I went home, made Alfredo, and went to sleep.

So, at eleven thirty the next morning, there is a knock at my door. I sleepily answer the door, and it's Mr. Manager. He walks right in, and plops himself down on my couch. He immediately begins to complain to me about how I "cruised" him at the party last night. He was trying to lay a guilt trip on ME! I sat down on the couch and told him it was over. This whole thing, which wasn't even a thing, was over, that this was unprofessional. He looked at me and said, "Oh, it took you this long to figure that out?" Then he looks at me and says, "Look, I didn't come over here to get hit with bricks…I came over here to relax" and he goes into telling me how relaxed he is around me. "So, hush up and come sit over here with me, mama." I was so fucking pissed! Was he even listening to me? Then he looks me dead in the eyes and says, "Flo, your titties and your pee pee don't mean nothing to me. I can get that anywhere, as I have in the past. I'm an old man. And I get what I want and I don't let nobody stand in my way. And I don't want nobody all up in my personal affairs. This is between us and us alone." Hmmm…why did his eyes have to twinkle like that when he said that to me? So, dumb ass Flo sits in his lap. And then he locks me in his arms and won't let me get up. Then he puts some fucking sports channel on the TV. I really felt uncomfortable. Disgusting. I wanted to him to respect my choices and what I was telling him but like he said, he gets what he wants. I believe him when he said I relax him, but is that my fucking obligation now? To be available for him when he needs to relax? Motherfucker! So, I tell him again. He is not even looking at me…he is looking at sports on TV and says he loves me. Love? He loves me? Aw, man this has gone too far. So he finally leaves—I guess he figured out I wasn't gonna fuck him after all. So, I go see Hope and I told her everything. She is just as confused by him as I am; which makes me feel better to know that another chick would be confused by this. So, he called me three times last night, and I didn't answer the phone. And then I was in bed and the phone rang and the caller ID was in the living room so I just picked it up and It was him and he said "mama been out runnin the streets…" I was like, "yeah", even thought I'd been home all night…and he said, "Ruger isn't home, you should be over here with me" What the fuck? Did he just need to relax? Selfish fucker! How am I gonna get him to leave me alone?

4.10.96

I called Cal yesterday. I was pretty upset that he didn't come to the show. He said, "Don't call making me feel bad," I told him vaguely about the Larry situation. Then he had to go all of a sudden. That REALLY bothers me. That's not like him. Just hearing his gentle voice was good even if it was just for that moment…I really love him. I am starting to feel like I am getting sick. My throat hurts.

4.11.96

Made it to work. I am feeling really weak all over. I talked to Carey yesterday. I tried to tell her in an hour what all has happened with Larry and she basically said that I deserve all the wonderful things he is promising me, but that he is bad news. She said he is the WRONG MAN but that I will have someone that respects me in the future. She said that she would have slept with him by now and she could not do what I am doing at six months clean. Hmmm.

I talked to Ian and he admitted that the band has discussed replacing me—if I have trouble being on the road. Well, that makes sense. I am almost glad to hear them making arrangements—not because I want to be replaced—God knows I don't—but it's because it shows them taking professional responsibility to the band. Cal just left a real sweet message on my machine. He says he misses me and to trust my judgment where Larry is concerned because *he does*. WOW. That is so fucking awesome of him. I can tell how much Cal respects me by the way he treats me.

4.12.96

Sitting in the living room. I went to the meeting. I really enjoy being around people in the meetings. They really seem to like me…the *real* me. Being with music people is scary, cuz I never know what there motives really are. The goal of recovery is to help other suffering people and the goal of a rock star is to what…succeed and then flaunt it? Larry has been calling here *non-stop*. I guess it's really "love". Yeah right. I can't wait to go see Cal. I pulled out the couch bed and I have been sleeping here for the past few days. It's been pretty cool. When I pulled the bed out of the couch I found several drum heads under there with pot all over them…and I found Cal's old roach collection…it was all sticky and stinky. I just laughed when I saw it all. I was not tempted by it at all. Wren came by and I told her about it. She asked me where it was and I told her it was still under there. She freaked the fuck out and said I should flush it. I said "okay" and I flushed it. She seemed freaked out that I did not flush it immediately after I found it. It was no big deal to me. I see the shit everyday. Oh! Carey got an engagement ring! She is so excited. Savannah and her husband are home from Colorado. They had a great time.

4.15.96

Friday night all hell broke loose in this house. The neighbors that live in the studio apartment next to me had some dealer beating the shit out of the door downstairs. They would not answer the door. I went down to the gas station where the cops hang out and tried to recruit one of them to come help but he never showed up. The guy wound up breaking the glass out of the door downstairs. The other day I found a card from my grandma that had been opened. I found it outside on the ground by the back of the house. I knew then that the neighbors had opened it hoping to find money in the card. I was so pissed that I taped the ruined card and envelope to their door. When I got home from work, it had been taped to MY door. I was so pissed. I knocked on their door and told them I did not appreciate them opening my mail. The head crack head was like "are you accusing me of stealing" and I said "yeah, I am". They were pissed and slammed the door. Fuckers. I called Ruger and he came over and stayed the night with me. I didn't want to stay by myself. I slept so good. I even turned off the TV for the first time since Cal left. I called the landlord and told him everything. He said he would take care of it. The boys say I need to move out. I talked to my old friend Crazy Tracy on the phone last night. She did a tarot reading for me. It basically said Larry was a snake (big surprise) and that he is starting a communication breakdown in the band. Hmmmm. I think that's true. But the information that he has is both helpful and harmful. He came over here last night and tried all his tricks AGAIN and they didn't work AGAIN. He told me when he walked through the door that I was going to sleep with him. I laughed at him. Then I completely ignored him. He took off his socks and shoes and then he took off his shirt. That made me real uncomfortable. I pretended to be asleep on the couch, hoping he would get the picture. He eventually put on his shit and left. Sleep with him my ass! Ruger and I went out to dinner Saturday night and he told me he's gonna start working for Max. Great. Two dope dealers in the band. He tried to tell me that it's just gonna be for a while, but I know once he starts making all that money he's not going to be able to stop. Just like Max. Sometimes I think that

Ruger is jealous of Max being "th man". He has tried to avoid joining in on Max's crew but I guess he can't avoid it any longer. He's been making these 'runs' to Jackson an shit. Anyway, Crazy Tracy suggested I tell the boys everything and get it all out in the open. I think I'll keep tiptoeing around until after Crossroads.

4.16.96

Talked to Carey about my shit-tuation and she suggested I get the fuck out of this apartment. She said no matter what my landlord does, she said they will know I narced on them, and they will be back for revenge. Damn. That's true! I am scared. I prayed about it and I thought maybe I could go home…I mean like…with my parents. I don't get high anymore…It would not be inconveniencing my habit. I am on hold with the landlord. I'm wondering if he has done anything about the situation. I'm guessing he has done nothing.

4.19.96

Sittin at work. Me and Hope went to lunch. I went to see Cal yesterday. It was *great*. No one showed up for practice Tuesday and I found out from Jesse that Ruger was in Jackson drinking with Dru. *Oh*. So, it's ok for *Ruger* to miss practice to hang out with a friend, but *Flo* **can't**. I went the fuck off on him. He got real defensive with me. He said our situations were not the same. What the fuck ever. I feel like I need to discuss the situation with everybody in the band individually—just to see if they understand how I feel. I feel like they are all just waiting on me to make a bad move so they can say I have "priority problems". Why doesn't anyone think *he* has priority problems?

My landlord kicked the neighbors out. I have not heard one peep out of them. They have until the end of the month to get out. Mom and Dad said I could come home, but I couldn't bring my rock collection, my driftwood collection, my books. Mom says my apartment is a museum and I should charge admission.

She says it's all a bunch of junk and I can't bring any of it. She also said I cant smoke in her house. Looks like I'm staying here.

11

Tom Foolery and the Loser

4.19.96

Man...the drummer for this band...Jack...he is so fine and I think he digs *ME*.
ME. I'm the fat, weird, drummer girl. What the hell is up with that? I have never
dated another drummer. It might be cool. He thinks I kick ass. Me and Ruger
went by their band room and I jammed with his band and he said I showed him
up. Yeah, right. Sometimes I think people just say that shit. Oh hell, I guess I
wouldn't be in *this* band if I sucked. They are perfectionists in a twisted kind of a
way. I know I can keep a pocket, but that's about it. I'm more John Bonham that
Neil Peart. I like it that way. Anyway, when he smiles at me I melt. What the
fuck? What about Cal? Oh shit, man...what am I gonna do...

4.23.96

I have an appointment to get my hair colored. It will be good to see the old salon
crew again. Maybe I'll go blond. Maybe it will fry it. Larry has finally taken me
seriously and left me alone. He has not bothered me in a week. Thank God. I
miss Cal. I think of him all the time.

I started a painting. I did the background so far and it looks good. I'm excited
about it. It's nice to sit here alone and chill and paint, even though I have no idea
what I am doing. Somehow, I am able to apply paint to canvas without demanding perfection from myself. That is **so** not like me.

The band is SO excited about Crossroads. We wrote a new song for it and it is
our best song yet. It's really awesome. We did an interview for a newspaper and

the Memphis Musician put us in their magazine. Ruger suggested we all do a new "look". We are rehearsing every night. I am SO busy. I have had a million things to do every day. Jack has called me twice. I feel kinda weird having a crush on him…

4.26.96

Well, in twenty-four hours we will have played Crossroads. This moment…this very moment as I sit here in anticipation…will never be repeated. I can never experience this moment again for what it is. This moment is precious.

I am listening to Portishead and it makes me think about Natasha…it's like I can feel her pain somehow. She is really suffering through her break up. Demetri doesn't seem phased at all.

I did another coat of black on my canvas. I think it's black enough now. I'm going to paint those columns I saw in my dream. I'm glad I had this night to chill and just hang out by myself. Sabrina's here and I haven't had much time alone. I have discovered I really like being alone. I am so much more comfortable with myself. It's a great feeling. I know God is responsible for this…left to my own thinking I was a wreck.

I am so excited about tomorrow! Sabrina and I are goin to the Ozzy/Sepultura show at the Pyramid. We wont get to catch much Ozzy. I've seen him three times anyway…but I'm *psyched* about seeing Sepultura live. They are my *favorite* fucking band. Were gonna pass out flyers for our Crossroads show while we are there. We are playin like right at midnight—we could not have asked for a better spot…RIGHT after Ozzy is over…

Larry called me at work today and kinda bitched because I haven't returned any of his calls. Just when I thought he had got the message! I feel better about the whole issue now because Jesse knows everything. He told me tonight that Larry has a girlfriend named Marie. Jesse *also* said that Ruger would beat the living shit out of Larry if he had a clue that he had tried to take advantage of me like he had. Jesse made me feel *so* much better about the whole thing. He said he could kinds of see how I may have been infatuated with him. When I think about the time that Larry was over here he did everything he could to get me in bed. That *Motherfucker*. He wants me to come up to Chicago in June. He said he'd fly me up there. He's such an asshole. I aint goin. I can't believe I almost fell for his shit.

Sabrina came up to my work and she went to practice with me and then to the Daisy to see the bands playin' tonight. She rode with the boys and she's out with them now. I guess not everybody would prefer sitting at home painting when you could be at the Daisy. Am I just a nerd? Or am I just over it? I'm getting sleepy. I need to crash but I don't know if I should...I feel like I should be up when she gets in. I am hitting the crossroads music business panels in the morning. I hope they are cool.

4.29.96

Sitting at the park. So much has fucking happened. Crossroads was absolutely amazing. *Amazing.* The best night of my life. The best show we have *ever* done. The best crowd, the best sound—it was a perfect gig if there is such a thing. After our five song set I was ready to play more. It just warmed me up! I had these crazy ass big ribbons in my ponytails...it was wild. The place was packed—you could barely walk through there.

Word is that we are talking to three record labels. Roadrunner, Mercury, and Immortal. That *sounds* great, but I'll believe it when I see it. I'm not quitting my day job.

Sabrina and I went down to the Pinch, the bar scene down by the Pyramid, early on the night of the show to pass out flyers to the concertgoers. I saw this guy getting off a motorcycle. He was wearing jeans and a white t-shirt. I sucked in my breath when he took off his helmet. It was Graham Friedman from High School...the preppy guy that sat next to me in English. The one *cool* preppy guy that got high with me and my freak friends. He looked a lot less preppy getting off that motorcycle. He recognized me too. We talked and it was *so* great to see him. I told him about the show and he showed up! I could see him in the back of the pit from the stage. He was *all over me* afterward. I think I liked it. Anyway, Sabrina and I went to the Ozzy show. Sepultura kicked *much* ass. They did *Rata-mahatta* with big ass tribal drums. That was the best part. We passed out flyers for our crossroads spot before the show in the halls of the Pyramid. We probably hit three hundred people with them.

After Sepultura, we *flew* to the Daisy. It was already packed, and the Ozzy crowd hadn't even gotten there yet. You could've cut the excitement and anxiety in the air of the Daisy with a knife. The place was **full** of bands—bands waiting there turn to play, bands that already played, bands that were playin the next night and were there to hang out, bands that were checking out the competition. At a showcase gig, you are basically giving your entire career everything you've got in five songs, and they better be your best songs, and your live performance better be great, and A&R reps better come see you, and you better not fuck anything up. The place was *seething* in anticipation. Ruger was so pumped...and Jesse was *so* excited. Everybody was in the *best* mood. Ruger walked around with me dangling off him before the show. He just kept kissing my cheeks, calling me "baby" and telling me he loved me. Max was all happy and hugging me. God, I love them. I love them so much. I love this band SO much. I know that kind of bonding helped us when we were on stage...being so excited and happy. The boys looked great—felt great...and the rumors circulating about "who" was in the crowd kept us excitedly dangling on the edge. We took the stage and took over the place. My drums seemed louder than *ever*. It is *such* a power trip to be up there. One strike on my kick drum is like a thunderclap. It just fueled my fire and made me play even harder...even better. All I could see over the rims of my toms were bodies...jumping in the rhythm of our songs. I could make out a few faces in the front, but behind that, it's just shadows and fists in the air. I just beat *the living shit* out of my drums. Every couple of minutes some brave soul would climb on the stage and dive off into the masses...being passed around by faceless arms. Ruger was spitting high into the air...he does that when he feels good and confident. He would turn around and look at me and just nod his head to the beat and grin with his lips curled up...in 'stage language' that means "fuck yeah...we sound **so** good". Playin in the Daisy, the place I used to sneak into when I was fifteen to see bands, is *awesome*. I imagined my seventeen-year-old self being in the crowd when I'm up there...she is so proud. I played that night for everyone that ever said I couldn't do it...I played for everyone that said I couldn't do it and stay sober...I played that night for the kids that picked on me when I was a little girl...I played that night for the preppies in high school that made fun of my freak ass...I beat the shit out of those drums that night...I was avenged. I was redeemed. And the coolest thing about it was that I was aware of the whole thing.

4.30.96

I called Cal yesterday and told him I wanted to see other people. I could not go out with Jack unless I called Cal. I would have felt awful, not that I didn't feel awful anyway. He said he was coming to get his shit. Why did that just impale me with a hot knife when he said that? I want to date Jack, but I also want to be with Cal. But Cal and I are headed in such different directions. I guess I just don't understand my feelings. It sucked to tell him. I knew it hurt him and it sucked. I cried all afternoon. We are going on the road Thursday.

5.2.96

Sitting at work. Jack came over last night. We played chess and listened to Portis-head. The deal with Jack is I guess I am obsessed with him…no…I'm probably obsessed with the *way he makes me feel*. Anyway, it's the whole dating a drummer thing. It's like he dates the tittie dancer types…ya know…like exactly what I am *NOT*. Like he's used to these scantily clad beautiful girls falling all over him…and then there's *me*…in pigtails, cut off overalls and a t-shirt beating the drums in my airwalks. I guess this arrangement is really weird, yet at the same time I have always secretly wanted a guy like him to like me…I just never knew that until it happened. He's just **such** the rock star type…and I'm so **NOT** the typical rock star girlfriend type. I don't even wear *panty hose*. I don't even *own* any. I don't have short skirts…or dresses…I have a kick ass collection of t-shirts from bars…and drum shops…and bands…and shirts that say funny shit…like my "I aint afraid of no slut" t-shirt (it's my favorite). I have two pairs of cut off black overalls…I have glittery socks…I have my favorite riot grrrl t-shirts, and I have uniforms to wear to work…and that's it. I guess I'm just afraid that I'm going to get all crazy about him and then he's gonna bail for some 100 lb chick in a g-string. And when that happens, I will have a huge complex. Sigh. I am thrilled to be dating a rock star and terrified at the same time.

5.3.96

Graham called last night. What is the fucking deal? Did the floodgates open or something? Did I take the anti—ugly pill? The only thing different with me is that I'm twenty lbs lighter and Cal is not here, and I don't think a siren was set off when he left…but it sure seems that way. It's weird, ya know…being a fat girl sucks most of the time, but it's a GREAT bullshit detector. If your fat, and people hang out with you, you know they are for real. Well, unless you're a rock star…Anyway, there is something about Graham I do not trust at all. It's like he has a girlfriend tucked away somewhere…Anyway, I am totally wanting to sleep with Jack but I'm not doin' it in me and Cal's bed. I really like Jack…I like him a lot…but the whole spiritual element is *so* not there…and I am deceiving myself if I think I can live without that. Yet there are things about him that are *SO* charming…like the way he drinks his beer from the bottle…I can't describe it really…it's just sexy.

5.4.96

In Champaign outside the Hammerhouse. It's full moon. I am almost ready to crash. We had an *awesome* show…Jack gave me a ride downtown to meet the guys and see me off. I could sense how uncomfortable he ways being around them. I guess if I was dating the only *guy* in an all *girl* band, I would be uncomfortable around all those girls…like they were totally checking me out. I'm listening to Portishead in my headphones…it's nice sitting outside by myself. I can feel the thunder of bass underneath me from the party inside the house…I saw some interesting people tonight. The Hammerhouse drew quite a mix. There was this striking guy and girl at the club that came to the house. He was beautiful. *She* was beautiful. She had on these white go go boots and a white short dress and long blond hair. She was so seductively glamorous. He was clad in black and had longish blond hair and eyes so blue that it moved a part of me when I made eye contact with him. I was standing in the kitchen with the Hammer guys and Ruger and Jessee. The Hammer's got a *coffee pot* out for me and brewed me a pot! I held my cup to my lips and felt like I was being stared at from the living room. I turned my head and that guy in black was looking dead at me. He smiled…and when he did, his hair fell from the side across the left side of his face. I pretty much melted then. I remembered them from the club...they watched us play intently. About ten minutes later, the go go girl got up...took the guys hand...and they walked into the kitchen. I pretended I wasn't watching. They both stared at me as they walked through the kitchen and out the door. Hmmmmmm...

We had an absolute *ball* on the way here. Ruger spent $20 on country music tapes, which we sang to *all* the way up here, and they got drunk as shit, which the music kind of called for. They have become pros at pissing in bottles. It became sort of a competition. My 'disease' decided I should 'live a little' and just get high with them. I didn't. I got Adam to drive me to a meeting today here in Illinois. It was so weird to go to a meeting away from home. Dude from the tattoo place finished the drawing for our album cover. It kicks *so much ass*. Ruger wont let it out of his possession.

5.6.96

At some club, planet something, in Springfield Illinois. The van broke down last nite and it took *forever* to fix it. Sabrina and I rode here in her jeep. She is so cool. We sang Alanis at the top of our lungs and talked the whole time. I put on fake tattoos and Ruger loaded the jukebox in the club with Motley Crue. I've been thinking about Jack, of course. I am glad we are on the road. I needed to detach from him.

5.6.96

Riding home...what a *wonderfully fun* road trip...At this moment...I feel so amazingly free...I feel like the great ball of fire that is settling itself into the smooth, flat prairie. That a phase of myself has finally found its place. A burning part of me has been soothed. It is so wonderful to be alive and to be free from the grip of the chains that bound me...I am looking over the last year of my life...I have really changed. I cannot *believe* I am not getting high with them. I cannot believe that *it's not a struggle* to not smoke dope every day. I just glanced in the side mirror. The person in it isn't so bad. I remember a year ago today I was crowned May Queen. For the past year, I have worn that crown. I have really grown in such a positive, healing, and healthy direction. I would never have believed it a year ago…if someone had told me how I would be different now. Thank you, God…for releasing me from myself.

5.7.96

So here I sit…waiting on Jack. I am sitting by the fucking window *waiting* on him to pull up outside. I ought to not be doing this…I should have the attitude where I don't care. *I am looking out the window waiting on a dude*! Oh. I should have realized that dating was not worth the torture. Jack, am I going to have to come after you?

5.9.96

Well, Jack was sound asleep on his couch the other nite. I *did* go over there. He was so apologetic. He came over and we had a good nite. I colored his hair purple. It is REALLY purple. We went out last nite, too. We went to the North End and had dinner outside by candlelight. We actually talked about what was up with 'us'. He said somethin about me bein his 'woman'. He told me I was his woman if I wanted to be. I suggested we not put a nametag on it. He agreed and I feel a lot more comfortable with things. He told me I was the coolest chick he had even met—even cooler than he thought I would be.

5.13.96

At work. Jack took me to the movies this weekend and then Sunday we went to visit some of his friends out in Mississippi. We shot guns and went fishing. It was *SO* cool. I can't believe how it feels to fire a gun. Guns scare the shit out of me. My brother gave me a gun to keep in the house. It's not going to do me any good if I can't fire it. We went by Hope's and then we went to his folks' house. They have the *coolest* house and they are *really* cool people. Jack is totally his self around them. We almost did *it* on Saturday. I'm a chicken. In the heat of the moment I told him my heart said yes but my brain said no. He said "well, then…don't." Just like that. I guess ever since Geoff I am scared I will get used. I wasn't scared of Cal. I could feel how much respect he had for me. But I'm just not completely convinced yet with Jack. I think he intimidates the shit out of me. Friday I met this chick at the meeting from Germany. She is a *trip*. She is this blues singer biker artist chick. She is *way* cool. She is really new—she is just coming off kicking heroin.

5.15.96

At work. Monday I gave Greta, German chick, a ride to the meeting. She asked me to sponsor her. Holy fucking shit. I don't even have a year clean yet. I guess it's really good timing because Jack is really pulling my attention away from the program and she will help me get focused. I feel so much responsibility—not for her, but because *of* her. I feel like my own program is even more important now. I don't know if that makes any sense. It's really weird because Monday I got on my knees and asked God to relieve me of my obsession with Jack. That night, I became a sponsor for the first time.

I can't believe I did not write about this in my last entry, but I talked to crazy ass Demi Friday night. She told me that before I called Cal and told him I wanted to see other people, he was already fooling around with other chicks. Demi has absolutely no reason to lie to me. She isn't into starting rumors or any shit like that. I feel like such a dumb ass. He made me feel so terrible when I called him that day and told him I wanted to see other people. Son of a bitch. He was already sticking his dick in other girls. I am so disappointed in him. It scares me and makes me afraid. It makes me feel really insecure. It makes me want to throw in the towel completely, on the whole dating thing.

We met with the record label last night. It's all under negotiation. It looks really promising but I'm not getting my hopes up.

Jacks been stayin with me a little. He doesn't lay a *hand* on me.

5.?.96

I'm off work and up really early. I'm watching this news crew on TV fly over the Grand Canyon. They are playin' a new song by Enya. It is so beautiful. I have always wanted to go there. Maybe it's a sign that now is the time to do it.

I'm tired. What a weekend. Saturday nite Ruger and Sallie came over and Jack cooked lasagna. It was so nice to just hang out at the house with them. I told Sallie that Mica's tittie dancer girlfriend made me nervous and I thought she was flirting with Jack. Sallie told me that she is slick and to watch out for her. Oh *hell*. I do *not* like the way this feels. I don't *need* this guy! Why am I so afraid of another girl taking him away? If he would rather be with another girl than so be it. I know that intellectually—but walking in that knowledge is another whole thing. Last night Jack came in late. He woke me up when he got in and told me I was gonna be mad, but that he had been at the tittie bar with Ruger. I told him I wasn't mad. My guys go there all the time. I told him if he would rather have a tittie dancer for a girlfriend to go for it. I feel real close to Jack but I would rather have him bail now than later.

5.19.96

Watching Jack paint my bedroom. It's way cool of him to do this for me. I bought a new bed and I wanted to re do the whole room. I haven't heard from Greta in a few days. My wrist hurts to write.

I moved all of Cal's stuff into the other room. When I was doing it, I found a letter he had written to a girl named Stacy. It solved the mystery of the bracelet on his wrist that he never took off. She gave it to him. The letter spoke nothing of me. He told her in the letter that he was goin to skool and living in Memphis and that there was such a thing as perfect love. My first thought was that it was a phony letter—planted there to hurt me that way my journals about Ethan had hurt him. My second thought was that I was crazy and that it indeed was real. Cal has never been one to play games. It hurts…the letter I found. It also had the pentacle earring that I have the match to in the letter. He said it was a charm for her. She must have sent him a letter, too, because the way it was written seemed to be answering a letter from her. It bothers me that he could never tell me the truth about her. I guess one thing is for sure. She never got the letter.

5.26.96

Relaxing with my morning coffee and smoking a camel wide. I switched brands. I haven't done that in ten years. Jack is laying beside me. We played a party at the band house Friday nite. It was still goin' at four thirty in the morning. I actually stayed and hung out. I even made it to work the next morning! After work, Jack came over and we made plans to cook dinner. He went to the store, which took him *forever,* and then he cooked and cleaned it all up. Dinner was perfect…we lit candles and listened to the Cure. I am falling for him so hard. I slept so good. I haven't slept this much since I met him. I bet that's mutual.

We are gonna finish painting my room today. He came to see me at work yesterday and he took me to lunch. It was *so* cool. He kept saying he was gonna do that—I guess I really didn't think he would. I dreamed the crystal around my neck broke. Hmmmmm.

That letter thing fucked me up really bad. I'm dealing with my grief over Cal a little at a time. If it was his intention to plant that so I would find it and be hurt by it, then he was successful. I guess packing up his stuff hasn't made it any easier either. I can feel him all over this place. The eye of Horus that he carved stares at me from the corner of the room.

I missed meetings all last week. I am up Jack's ass really bad. I am not praying like I used to and I don't feel as close to God. I realize now how easy it is to abandon God for something that feels good. God is not a quick fix—or at least it doesn't make my toes curl like a dude does.

5.28.96

Sitting up front to avoid the reefer smell throughout the van. We are on our way to Little Rock. I went to a meeting today. I needed it *so* fucking bad. I've been doing so shitty. I am obsessed with this boy leaving me for a tittie dancer. I am obsessed that the boys are going to replace me. I am obsessed that my future with this band is not going to happen the way I have always imagined. This is the worst I have felt since I have been clean. I can't shut my fucking head up. I am stressing about some shit all the time. I always have something on my mind and as soon as I quit thinking about it, something fucking else comes up. Shit...we are about to lose the trailer...that would suck.

Hope came over before we left today. She is *really* showing. The baby has been kicking her.

5.30.96

My foot itches...Jack is not here and he was supposed to be here thirty minutes ago. He told me he was on his way. I feel like such a fucking dumb ass. He went to Little Rock with us. I laid in his lap on the way home, which was weird showing him affection while the guys were around, and I was of course staring straight up at his nose and there was white powder all over it. I reached up and tapped it and just smiled at him and said "I bet your feeling good" and he was like "I don't know what you are talking about." God. How fucking stupid does he think I am? What was I supposed to do? Conclude that the white powder in and around his nose was fucking *sweet n low?* Oh, gee, yeah, that would make sense. Did I mention Jack got a tattoo? He got the word LOSER tattooed across his stomach in gothic letters. It fucking rocks...however...uh...u reckin I should heed that warning?

Anyway, the show was *great.* We made some kick ass connections in Little Rock and have shows lined up there. It was weird driving such a short distance, playin', and then driving back. Little Rock has a great feel to it. I really like it there.

6.1.96

Saturday afternoon. I am off work and stuck in traffic by a stalled train. I talked to Natasha today about Jack and I told her the powder on his nose story and she laughed and said, "Hey dude, at least he's *advertising* that he's a loser." **No shit**. They think this whole thing is really funny. Tonight I am going put on my kick ass new outfit and go out with the fantasy rock star boyfriend...because that's what he is.

6.2.96

Went to 616 with Jack last night. I got all dressed up in my new outfit. I felt like a tittie dancer. I was wearing PANTY HOSE under my evil kineval-looking short shorts and a tight ass see thru shirt. When he got to my apartment, he just looked at me, stunned, and said "damn...you're wearing *that*?" I just giggled and told him fuck yeah I was wearing it. He wasn't the only one surprised. When we got to the club, Jesse and Ian *freaked* out on me, as did the macho rock-god types on the scene. It made me a little uncomfortable the way their eyes moved up and down my body. It's amazing how differently I was treated in that skimpy outfit. Men came out of the dark corners of the club all night, offering to buy me drinks, starting conversations. It was like I had fresh blood poured all over me and they were bears coming out of hibernation. Overall, it was fun being sexy for the night, but I'm much more comfortable in cut off overalls, my collection of T-shirts with various obscenities written on them, and my airwalks.

Jack and I put X-mas lights on my bed. They look so cool. The band is goin to St.Louis for a showcase next weekend. We are goin to try to go to Six Flags. That is gonna be so much fucking fun.

6.6.96

Sitting on the balcony of the hotel in St. Louis. I can see the arch from here and the city sprawls out busily underneath me. It's really cool out here. The headache my cappuccino removed earlier has returned.

I had a great time at the club with Jack the other night. I realize that my fear of *losing* him to a tittie dancer is probably what inspired me to dress like one for the night. That is just SO not me…it was fun for a night but the relationship just aint worth all this trouble. Plus he fuckin doesn't show up when he is says he will, which is just plain disrespectful. I have made a bazillion excuses for him and I like him so much, but I think I am starting to disrespect myself for *letting* him dis me.

6.7.96

Tonight at the club, I met a guy that said he is a Vampire. His *real* name is Vladimir. He showed me his driver's license to prove it. He was fine as hell and extremely charming. He tried to make me 'feel his power'. I didn't feel shit. We are at some dudes house we don't know. He has big silver shoes. I am outside on his porch. We had a freaking *ball* at six flags. It was *great* hangin out together and riding rides all day. I am so glad we got to do that. We rode batman like *six* times. I did not know that Ruger was afraid of heights—but I found out when we went on the Ferris wheel. He crouched way down and laughed at himself for being scared. We rode the water ride thing too…and got completely soaked. It was so fucking fun. As broke as we always are I am so glad that we got to do something so awesome together.

The show last night was *great*. We went back to the club tonight because Hack was playin'. The guys got *so fucking shitty*. I can't *remember* seeing them so shitty. Today we went to the arch and to the park beside it. I think that arch has a lot of energy about it. I feel like it really is a sort of gateway of sorts. It may just be that the architecture of it and its size are just overwhelming. Or maybe it really is energy.

6.8.96

Driving in the pouring rain. We just pulled over to let it die down because it is *really* pouring down hard as *hell*. We are almost home. We stopped at Roadie Jed's trailer in hickville Arkansas to drop off the trailer. We shot guns an shit. It was cool.

I slept in the van last night. The silver shoes guy had hardwood floors and he claimed his own bed, so the van looked like the best choice. It was actually cold in the van, but really comfortable. The trip to St. Louis just isn't long enough. I can't believe I just said that.

I guess I just don't have that *concluding* feeling that I get at the end of road trips. God, I am so glad to be alive, to be clean, and to be in this band. I love my boys. I am so glad to be a part of this. I am glad I gave up my old lifestyle to commit myself fully to this. I love them. I love what we are able to do together. I sent Cal a letter. I wonder if he got it. Graham's band is playin tonight in the Pinch. I am thinking about going. Maybe I will chill at home and just paint. Maybe I will take one of my baths with the jazz playin and just soak.

6.9.96

What a wonderful nite. Natasha and Wren and Fern came over and we drank coffee and did mad libs and cut up. It was *so* great. Natasha got her clit pierced. Demetri did it of course. Apparently, they are still messing around. I would like to get mine done, but damn I bet that hurt like a *mother fucker*. She said it didn't, but *damn*. That is like *the **most*** sensitive area.

Jack called me. I was pretty surprised. He asked who was over, cuz he could hear all the folks laughing in the background. He asked if they would be here late, and I said no, not too late. He said he would call back later, but of course, he didn't.

6.12.96

Sittin at work. I am trying to learn the difference between my thoughts and my feelings. I never knew they were two different things. I have always ran on whatever was in my head and heart—but never took the time to distinguish between the two. I have learned that thoughts are like "I wonder if Jack will call"…and then *feelings* are the knots in my gut that occur simultaneously with the thought…that knot would be sadness or fear. Hmmm. I am powerless over the way I *feel*, but not over the way I *act* as a result of the feeling. I don't have to worry incessantly…

6.14.96

It is *so* hot in my apartment. I can only imagine how much worse it would be if the big ass tree wasn't there protecting this old house. Savannah and I hung out. I went to her house yesterday and played on the Internet. She hangs out in chat rooms. All those people seem to have their own language. I felt like a goofy outsider. Graham came over the other night. I wanted to fuck him. Even if I wasn't 'tied' to Jack I would have hesitated. I don't know what part of me just wont let me relax and just have sex with people. I take sex so seriously. Why? The boys don't. I know other girls that don't. So why am *I* the prude? Jack is only the sixth guy I have ever slept with. I guess because with Graham part of me gets the feeling that he has a girlfriend…I guess it's because of his strange hours…and he never asks me to go do anything with him…he just shows up and starts seducing me.

6.18.96

I called Cal. I just woke up feeling him all in the house. I think my motive was some sick-ass kind of reassurance, which I did *not* get. **He has a new girlfriend.** It fucking *sucks*. Hell, I made my bed. I must lie in it. *I* am the one that let *him* go. I must deal with the consequences of my actions. I felt my blood starting to boil under my skin when he told me. I called him to feel better and after calling him, I feel worse. Hell. At least I am aware of this behavior. Maybe the next time I need to be reassured I will be more careful in who or what I choose to provide that. Wait a minute. Did I just write that? Wait a minute. I think that's why I used. I used to shut up the hostility in my mind and to feel better about myself. So, now that I don't have dope—am I using *people*?

6.19.96

I had a bizarre and disgusting dream. I was riding in a car with crazy ass Mitch from the bar. As I drove, he had sex with a four year old in the back seat. God it *disgusts* me. I am still really shaken by it.

We are goin on the road tomorrow. Playin in Kane tuck. Never played there before. Then were gonna head up north...Chicago, I think...and of course Champaign...the trip should be cool.

12

Truck Stop Showers, Tranquilizers, and Nasty Chicken Legs

6.21.96

It is *so* fucking hot in the van. Man. We haven't even played yet and it already smells like ass in here. The blue velour cushioned walls just really hold in the heat. It's like a dark, hot tomb. At least I'm getting a breeze in my spot…sitting behind Ian as he drives with his window down. The side windows just pop out at the bottom a few inches. I'm playin CHAOS A.D. on my jam box and the gritty anger of Sepultura's grooves seem to fit the greasy, sweaty atmosphere in the van. Nobody is saying much…it's too hot to talk…and I'm glad they are quiet…because if they were talking, they'd be complaining. It's hot enough in here without attitudes.

6.21.96 later

We just stopped at a gas station. The heat had gotten so intense for me that I went to the bathroom and took off all my clothes and stood there naked, splashing cold water all over myself. I didn't even care if anyone walked in! Then I stuck my whole head under the faucet. I changed into the clean t-shirt and shorts I brought to sleep in. It felt so good to have on dry clothes. The bad news is I started my fucking period. Yuck. In the fucking heat. I wont bleed too bad for a while, but I stuck a wad of toilet paper in my panties anyway. We've only been back on the road for twenty minutes and I can already feel a moat of sweat forming in the seam of my bra. Jesse is thumbing his acoustic…Ruger looks like he's dozing…seems like a good idea.

6.21.96. later

As I woke, I wondered if I was still sleeping…because out my window, in a sea of dark green grass, was a *castle*…a medieval fortress…made of stone so cold it cooled the air around it…and as it slipped out of sight I just sat there, rubbing my face…"Didja see that, Flo? Max said. "Didja see the castle?" I was perplexed. Where the hell were we? Max quickly caught me up to speed. I had slept for hours, and we are in Kane Tuck. Apparently, some rich horse racer-guy built that castle for his wife…or something like that. We are just a few from the gig. And we are on time, which was why Max is in such a good mood. My clothes are soaked, as I sit here writing. Yuck. I'd give anything for a shower before this gig…but that aint gonna happen.

6.21.96 later

We had to park the van down the street from the club. It's in the college district. We loaded in and set up and did a little sound check. Now were just waiting to play. I just walked down the strip and found a place to eat. I couldn't believe they weren't hungry. I'm sittin at a little place down the road. I feel *so* freakin dirty. I haven't used a sock to bleed on in a long time—but I'm glad I had one. I need to find a convenience store. I don't know where we are gonna crash tonight.

6.22.96

What a fucking evening. The guys said our gig sucked *major* ass...which prompted them to be assholes for the rest of the night. They said they were embarrassed to be hangin out in the damn club. I think what really made them be dicks was the fact that we did not remember that the time changed here—and we went on an hour later than we were supposed to. That has never happened to us before. It was odd how people kept looking at us and the club was packed...but we were just playin' pool and hangin out. Then the guitar player of the band we were opening for said, "What are you guys doin'?" Are ya'll gonna play?" We felt *so* stupid. So, the set was cut down and we played, apparently, like shit. I never hear the mix they do. I thought it was all right.

The real bomb struck *after* the gig, though. Max was hungry, so I took him to the little place I had found. We talked about Cal. **I** brought it up and asked if he had seen Cal. I should've fucking known better. I was not prepared for what he said. He told me that yeah, he'd seen Cal recently and met his girlfriend and that they partied together. Partied? The last I knew, from Cal's own mouth, was that he wasn't getting high. There was a sick grin on Max's face as he saw the color leave my skin. "You know he never really stopped, don't you?" It pissed me off—no actually, it really hurt. It hurt me that Cal was potentially using, and had been, but it hurt worse that Max would drive that stake in my heart joyfully. I felt immediately sick and I started shaking a little bit. I tried my hardest to act calm...and cool...like this was not the news to me that it was. I knew I could not trust Max with that weak part of myself...the vulnerable, scared side of me. I have felt a funny vibe from him for a long time now...he can be so kind...but also *such* a jerk. It sucks that I cannot trust him. It fucking sucks. I don't know if I fooled him. I was so flooded with fear and my thoughts just *raced*. We made it back to the club and I was a wreck. I felt sick—physically, from this conversation. The boys were all pretty drunk and the headliner was done playin'. I went to the pay phone and called Carey. She was asleep. I hated to call so late, but I was really scared of how powerful the emotions were that I was feeling. I was not in safe company. I needed to talk. She got right up. She could barely hear me over the AC DC blaring through the club. I told her everything. She calmly told me that I had *expectations* of Cal. That I put these expectations on him. Expectations of him sitting there, missing me, wanting me back, not getting high, not dating, being the person I wanted him to be. She said it was a form of controlling him and perhaps he had broken these ties when we broke up. I was amazed. I had no idea I was *controlling* him. He had *volunteered* to stop using, I told her. She said, "Yeah, but **news flash**—you aren't together anymore. He can make his own decisions and does not have your expectations on him anymore." I was devastated—but I knew she was telling me the ugly truth. I wanted Cal to sit there and be a good boy until I might want him back. That is so fucking unfair of me. It explains why I was so devastated when he told me he had a girlfriend. Because it was not part of my 'plan'. Yikes. I am a sick fuck. Talking to her calmed me down. Afterwards, I sat on the steps of the club, knowing I was stinkin', and just stared into the midnight blackness of Kentucky. People stumbled over me; the weird sweaty girl who isolated on the steps as they left the blaring club.

As I write, we are en route to Illinois. The horror of last night has been replaced with something I've never felt. I can remember feeling last night's fear and pain, but I am not feeling it now. As I look out my window and see the green plains, I have this strange sensation that I am going to be okay. That Cal is going to be and do exactly what his God wants him to be. *I* may not be in God's plan for Cal and I have to accept that. I have to let him go completely. It doesn't hurt—the thought of letting him go. It has always hurt before. I realize how wrongly I have treated him—even if it was only in my own head. I am seeing an image in my mind of a large hand…and Cal is comfortably sitting in it…surrounded by a pile of books…doing what he loves…and in another large hand is me…sitting here writing in my journal…I know who's hands they are…and they can worry and life manage and take care of everything so much better than I can. I want this strong and gentle hand around me…I give up fighting…because this feels so much better…because it will care for me and make decisions for me better than I can for myself. I will never understand God. I have to accept that. I cannot wrestle with that any longer. It is high time I quit freaking out and trust this power—that *could* restore me to sanity…if I am willing to believe that it can. I believe it can and I know really want it to. "God that I don't understand…can I **stay** in your hand…because it sure feels good…"

6.24.96

Man, this weekend was rough. I stayed with Sabrina to avoid the party at the Hammerhouse. She is so cool. She has the coolest house. She told me she has a friend from her work that she wants to set me up with. She says we are *perfect* for each other. His name is Roman. She has this Xeroxed copy of a picture of him and he is *beautiful*. I told her I was gonna chill on the dude thing for a while. She understood.

We *rolled* Friday night. It *stomped*. We played with a bunch of bands—it was some festival or something. Jack's band played up here too. He and Ruger have gotten to be pals and Ruger has gone to work with him a little bit. He was kind of a jerk to me until after we kicked so much ass. I think his whole band was surprised to see us pull in such a draw. We are sold out of the bad ass new shirts we got. It's weird having a t-shirt with my own face on it. It's easy to get caught up in the scene here and feel like a real rock star.

Saturday night we stayed in town and I had three entertainment choices. I could hang with the rock stars who were gonna dose and go to a laser light show, hang with the drunks at a new club in town, or hang with self. I really felt the urge to 'be a part of' Saturday, so I opted out of hangin with self and I went to the laser light show. It was on The Doors and everybody was dosing. I cannot explain the boredom and torture of sitting in a laser light show sober. I will never *ever* listen to the Doors again. We are getting ready to head out for home.

6.24.96 later

Man. We **broke down**! We are currently at a Super 8 motel that Max paid for. We broke down on the kind of stretch of highway that has absolutely NOTH-ING around it. The kind you hope to god you don't ever break down on. And of course, it was hot as hell outside. Max and Ian walked to find a phone while Ruger paced around the truck cursing. Adam was with us and he started poking around under the hood. Jessee got out his acoustic and strummed a bit. We actually rolled up onto an exit ramp before we stalled completely and it just so happened that on the spilling hill of the ramp, those purple flowers were everywhere. I always looked at them when we are driving and I have often longed to run through them or roll down the hill on them. Well, I took my chance. I sat in the middle of those purple flowers. I even rolled down the hill a little bit. What I discovered is that they appear to be a flowing sea of purple at 80 miles per hour, but when you are knee deep in them, they are scratchy and full of bugs. Not so fun. Ruger laughed at my bouquet of flowers and called them a "Flo-quet". Max came back two hours later via a tow truck, which towed us to the next town and to a dealership. They were just about to close for the day, so we had no choice but to leave it there and wait until the morning. It started to *pour down rain* as soon as we started walking to this hotel. I don't know why that was so funny to me, I guess because we were just *so cruised*, and I pushed play on the tape deck of my wet jam box and "County Boy Can Survive" was our theme song as we trudged down the road.

When we got here they all ate tranquilizers and passed out. I took a long hot bath and now I am watching the Discovery Channel and it's on Alaska. I called my boss and she was cool about me not being there tomorrow. I called Natasha and Carey and Hope just to chat with all of them. It was good to catch up. It's amazing that it takes a mild disaster in my schedule to give me the time to spend with friends. I guess I'm gonna curl up in between these stinky, snoring boys I love and crash.

6.25.96

Attitudes are not good this morning. Ruger wants to go home. Max bought everybody lunch at the Denny's inside the hotel and while we ate Ruger told us he was leaving. He said he is calling Sallie to come and get him. He pitched *such* a fit. He can't handle being inconvenienced. Poor fucking baby. He is *such* a fucking baby. I guess the rest of us aren't inconvenienced! Just him! What—does he have to get back to *work*? Hell fucking no. Whatever. I guess I just kind of thought we were in this together. I don't have to *like* the way he is acting to *accept* the way he is acting. And, hell, whoever said we were supposed to stick together through something like this? If he wants to leave, he can leave. It is my *expectations* of what everybody should do that fuck me up every time…and when you add my penchant for fairy tales and fantasy *that* is a lethal mix.

I am sitting inside the dealership now. Ruger and I have been coloring in a coloring book with the crayons on the little table and chairs in here. He would *die* if I told anybody he colored with me. Shit, I'm just glad he has calmed down. Apparently it is the timing chain that is messed up on the van. It's going to cost at least $600 to fix it. They say it should be ready by the time they close. I read the paper and tried to do the crossword. It's two o' clock in the afternoon and they've been working on the van *all day*. Adam and Jesse are outside with the U Haul. I guess I'm gonna see what they are up to.

6.25.96

Now *this* is **really** being cruised. We hung out by the trailer for the rest of the day until the truck was ready. We had a good time singin' songs and goofing off. We even played the Jerky Boys for the car salesmen and they *loved* it. Right at closing time, the mechanics said the truck was ready and they test-drove it down the block. We whoo-hooed and packed up for home. We made it about...oh...ten miles down the highway when the van started overheating again. The smoke started pouring out everywhere and it stunk *real* bad. We pulled off the interstate and let it cool off for an hour and then made it to the next exit where we put five quarts of oil in it. It just leaked right out. The guys were so fucking pissed off. The dealership that we had just left was closed for the day. So, we spotted a shitty, scary looking motel on the other side of the interstate where I am now. We drove the van as close as we could without it blowing up. With our equipment in the U-haul, we couldn't leave it at that gas station. We walked to this hotel and we were all hungry so Max walked back up the road to look for some food. All he found was a nasty bucket of chicken from a shitty gas station. We each ate a nasty chicken leg. The sun was just starting to set when we got here so I decided to spend some time alone outside. There is a sweet little nook of trees right outside the door and I took my jam box and my Enigma CD and my drum case with all my books and incense and candles in it outside. I did a circle right there, right outside the door. It was wonderful. I called the quarters and relaxed in the energy I raised. It was then when I realized that today is my nine-month birthday. I have been clean for nine months today! That's *so* amazing. It's like being born ya know, a nine-month gestation period before birth. I thought a lot about Cal when I was in that circle. I thought about the realization that I had had when we left Kentucky and about how God had him in his hand. I smiled at the thought and I asked the powers that be to protect Cal and I offered up some light for him, if it was in accordance with his God's will for him to receive it.

When it got dark, I came inside and the guys were almost asleep. Tranquilizers again. I took *another* long hot bath! I could get used to this! I am enjoying being off work. It's like an insane form of a vacation, because it's one I am *forced* to take. There is a cool looking documentary coming on HBO in a minute. It's called "Paradise Lost" and it's about those three little boys who were murdered across the river in West Memphis and about the three boys accused of the crime. I am so excited to get to watch this!

6.28.96

Man is it good to be home. We got home Wednesday night. I missed three days of work in all.

We called the dealership first thing the next morning and they sent a tow truck after us. They worked on it for a couple of hours and basically pronounced it dead. We called Adam's girlfriend and Jed from Arkansas and they hooked up a rescue road trip to come get us. They got there right before dark. Adam, Max and Ian rode with Adam's gal, and Ruger rode in the truck next to Jed, so that put me and the dog in the back of the truck. I didn't mind *at all*. It was *so* fucking awesome because the weather was so clear. I played my Tori Amos tape full blast while Jesse slept next to me and I just stared at the moon and thought for 6 hours. It is a pity that car's have roofs on them, because on the interstate, you can *really* see all the stars. As the road rolled on, I realized how much I have missed by being inside the covered van while we traveled at night. I haven't seen stars like that since Cal and I used to lay in the street in Walnut Grove. It was *awesome;* at least, until we got to Jed's in Arkansas, where the mosquitoes are so thick in the air you feel like you are being shot with a million b-b's from a bb gun. I buried myself under a blanket to survive their deadly attack. We dropped off the U Haul at Jed's and then they took me home.

7.1.96

Damn the months fly by so quickly. It's amazing. I spent most of yesterday by myself. It was nice. I cleaned up and put some pics in an album and took an amazing bath. I have been working a lot of magick lately. On the trip I did a circle, I did one here yesterday, and then last night in the bath. I went up to the coffee shop last night and hung out with everybody. That jukebox has the most bizarre collection on it. We always play Sir Mix A lot's "Baby Got Back" and mix it up with Johnny Cash.

Oh, I saw GEOFF Saturday night! No fucking lie! Geoff from Jackson…who I was so crazy about. Jesse threw a *huge* party at his house and I decided to go for a minute. When I walked in, he was the last person I expected to see. He is *still* a sexy mother fucker. He walked up to me and put his arms around me. Just smelling him and being that close to his body again reminded me of the time we spent together and how scared I was back then. I was so new in the band, in the town, and in that circle of friends and he had made me feel safe and comfortable, if only just for a while. He told me I looked great and we walked outside to talk. I could tell by the slurring of his words that he was pretty lit, yet I really wanted to believe him when he proceeded to tell me he really screwed up by letting me go back then. He looked right into my eyes and told me how good it was to see me. All my old feelings for him rose to the surface at that moment. He then pushed himself up close to me…and started to whisper to me about how much he missed me and how much he has thought of me…and could he come over to my apartment…because he just really, really missed me. He then proceeded to *beg* me to leave the party, at that moment, and take him to my house. My body really thought that was a great idea, but my head disagreed. I told him that if he really wanted to spend some real time with me, that he would call me the next day when he was sober. I knew he wouldn't call, and he hasn't.

I got home pretty early Saturday night. Graham came over. It was actually cool to hang out with him, but nothing happened. I talked to Savannah and she told me her AOL bill was $300.00. She is freaking the fuck out. I've been pretty obsessed with the Cal thing and we talked about it. I guess what I think I want is to know the truth. Did he fool around on me before we broke up? What would I do with this information if I had it? Use it to hurt myself with? Or let him go easier? I'm not sure if what I have been practicing is *acceptance* of the situation or if I'm just ignoring the situation. I must accept the fact that I will just never know, because even if I asked him outright, it's possible that I would debate the accuracy of whatever answer he gave me anyway, which would just lead to more mindfucking. I will just never know, and I need to accept that. I feel at this moment…that I can move on from this…thank you, God.

7.2.96

I went to a meeting last night and then to Chilli's with everybody after. I got the phone bill today and I can see that Cal is using the calling card that I pay for and he is staying at some chick's house and calling Mitch's a lot. Damn. Why does that bug me so much? Is this part of letting go?

I talked to Carey and we are gonna go camping together in September. I am really excited about it. I can't wait to go to Fall Creek sober for real! I told her about the phone bill and she was pretty upset about it. It appears I forgot to mention to her the agreement Cal and I made about me paying his probation in exchange for him letting me keep the phone in his name. She said that me paying his probation and the phone thing is really just a sneaky way of me keeping him bound to me and keeping him in my life. She demanded that I call him up and tell him the deal is off. I honestly cannot see myself saying this to him! I told her that he doesn't really live in reality, and she said that was not my problem. I told her that I didn't want to break the agreement I had made with him, and she said it was rooted in ulterior motives to begin with and it needed to be severed. She has an answer for *everything*. I called the phone company and I owe them $775 bucks. To get my own phone turned on in my own name I would have to pay that off.

Yikes.

7.4.96

We've been practicing a lot. We are writing some bad ass new shit, too. We got this new practice place way the fuck out in West Memphis. It's in this garage behind a lawnmower repair shop. Max's friend works there and his dad owns the place so he hooked it up for us. It's pretty cool so far; it's just a hell of a drive over there.

I had another weird dream. I dreamt of seeds the size of almonds…and they were in the palm of my right hand, and they were covered with menstrual blood. I recall opening them, revealing the insides of the shell, and looking at the real 'seed'. There were between six and nine of them. Then I recall thinking I could swallow all of them and maybe one of them would 'take'. I then remember flushing them down the toilet rather sadly. I did not recall the dream until I woke up to my period starting as I sat on the toilet to pee and blood gushed into the water. Cal was in the dream somehow. He knew about the seeds. My dream book says seeds represent reproduction and may indicate an idea that has been planted in my mind and is germinating new life experiences. Hmmmmm.

7.6.96

I bought a wood burner yesterday. Cal took ours and I have been missing having one. As soon as he tip of the burner hit the plank of cedar I was testing it on, I started to cry. I haven't smelled that since Cal was here. It's amazing the power of the sense of smell…and how attached it is to memories. I allowed myself to feel the pain of his loss, and then I moved on and started making something for Hope's baby. Speaking of babies, **Max** is about to be a father. He called me today and told me his girlfriend was pregnant. He is excited. I only pray that maybe this will motivate him to chill on partyin so hard.

7.9.96

I got a kitty! She is black and soft. I have two names for her and I cant decide on which one. Malkuth and Binah. Malkuth is the Sephiroth of Earth in the Jewish Kabbalah and Binah is the Sephiroth of understanding, with a female influence, so it will probably be Binah, but we'll see. I sure would like to cruise practice so I can play with my kitty, but I can't do that to them. Kitty will get used to the apartment by herself I guess.

KISS is going to be in town tomorrow night. It's their reunion tour, which is kind of frightening, because it makes me feel old. They are gonna be in full make up and everything. I never saw them live like that. It would rock, but I'm not paying a million dollars to see it.

7.10.96

Just got back from KISS! Michelle Waters, my high skool best friend came in the salon today for me to do her hair and we decided to go together. It was wild to go to a concert with her again, because in high skool that's all we ever did…camp out for concert tickets and go to shows. We would get to the parking lot at like 5:00 on Friday and read magazines an shit until it got dark and then we would drop acid so we could stay up all night and secure our spot on the list. All kinds of crazy shit used to happen at those camp outs. It was a blast. We even camped out if the opening acts were worth a shit…simply because it gave us something to do. KISS was pretty cool…it was something to say you did, and we didn't even stay the whole time.

Ruger and I had an interesting conversation this morning. He told me about all his money problems and then we talked about the band. He told me that Max told him he felt like he needed to do "something" because now he has a child on the way. I hope that doesn't mean quit.

7.11.96

The guys said on our last trip they know I am mad when I grab my notebook and start writing fast. Well hell, guess what? They are right! I am mad because I wanted to go home tonight and hang out with my new cat—and they call me at fucking five thirty and tell me I have to go to fucking *practice*. I guess we do have a big show coming up…and I should just shut the fuck up and quit whining. I should accept it even thought I don't like it. Fuck. That is so much easier said than done.

Natasha asked me to speak at her second birthday meeting. That is incredible. What the fuck am I gonna say? What the fuck kind of message do I have to offer? That I still get pissed as hell when I don't get my way? And I'm in a band full of drunks and dope heads, but that's okay, because we're gonna get signed and be famous?

13

Self-pity Parties and Stolen U Hauls

7.12.96

Those mother fuckers were LATE last nite. They did not get there till fucking ten o' clock. I used my time alone in the practice room wisely, though. I rearranged my kit so I have one rack tom now in the center and I dig the shit out of it! We made our set list for the show...seventeen songs...lets see....each song is roughly five minutes, and five times seventeen is eighty five...so we will play an hour and twenty five minutes...that's a long set...

7.13.96

Binah drove me *nuts* again last night. She is a demanding freakin cat. She wants *every bit* of my attention. I cannot brush my teeth without her whining to be in my arms. It's kinda cool though, that she likes me that much.

I've been thinking lately a lot about the band and wondering if maybe we really aren't gonna go anywhere. And what the hell am I gonna do then? I have had these crazy thoughts that they are considering kicking me out again. I haven't felt that in a long time. This time it's not because I am a girl, but because I am *sober*. That I really just don't fit in anymore with them. And *then* they come up with this idea out of nowhere to record next week and finish mixing all of our shit. It just seems like something is up. I guess I just feel really disconnected from them. And they are pissing me off with the fucking off practice thing.

7.17.96

Sitting at the coffee shop. I busted my ass, literally, the other night at practice. I was waiting them to show up and dude let me take his four-wheeler out around the block. It was fun as hell but when I tried to brake on the gravel it tipped over and I am really lucky I did not fuck myself up bad. I kind of dove away from it as it turned over and I landed on my hip. It fucking *hurt*. When everybody got there, we practiced our *asses* off. We did our seventeen-song set *twice*. It kicked our butts…well…it kicked mine. Things with them seem okay. I think I am paranoid. And, as everybody tells me, I *think* too fucking much. Mom got me some roller blades. I am excited! I bet I bust my ass really bad though.

    I dreamt about Cal last night. I wish I wouldn't dream about him, because I wake up feeling like I have spent time with him and then I miss him *really* bad. It's the waxing moon, so maybe I should do something to help the situation. Maybe I could take some action to put some closure on us. Because, as much as I hate to admit it, it is over for us, and he has moved on regardless if I have or not, so I need to move on, too.

7.18.96

At the train station waiting on Sabrina to arrive. She is gonna hang for the weekend. It's like six forty five in the morning and it's scary as shit down here. I have never even been here before. I did not realize that the train here goes straight up to Chi—town, and stops off in Champaign. I have so much I need to do before the gig. I need to get new heads for my drums…because I want them to be fuckin *poppin*! We have promoted the shit out of this deal. The commercial for the show has been on the radio…and Ruger is doin a live interview the day of the show. We have flyers all over town and everybody is talking about it. And we are ready as hell for this! I am really excited. I think that thundering sound must be the train…

7.21.96

Man…last night's show was fucking *awesome*. The place was so packed that you couldn't *move*. *Everybody* was there…including **Cal**. Max warned me that he was probably gonna be there. He couldn't ever go to my gigs when we were together! God *damn* it hurt to see Cal there with another girl…man…it fucking *killed* me. He ignored me as best as he could, and then I just walked the fuck right up to him and said hello. Without thinking, I told him he could come by today if he wanted to get some of his things. He said he might. What the hell was I thinking? I was trying to act all cool…like him being with that girl did not bother me. He promptly introduced me to her; more like her *smeared* her across my face. Then he brushed me off real quick. Damn. It fucked me up really good. But, I made my bed and I suppose I am lying in it. I beat the living hell out of my drums. Natasha, Carey, her fiancé Rickie, Demetri, all kinds of folks came out. It was really fucking cool of them. I'm glad Carey was there.

Oh, I just want to have a self-pity party. I am just still having a hard time dealing with this. I don't know where Sabrina is; she is probably with Max and them.

One really awesome thing that happened last night is that we got the opening spot on a bad ass show—we are opening for Cannibal Corpse and Anthrax August 10th. That is gonna fucking *smoke.* I can't believe it.

7.23.96

Ya know, now that I think about it, it was really *bogus* of him to barge up in my house Sunday with his girl and all those fucking people in tow. It was so hot that I couldn't ask them to stay outside. It was like *twenty* of them. I just fell apart as he raided the bookcase and the closets and the herbs. I started to cry and I ran and hid in my bedroom. One dude I didn't know who had come with them from the Grove came into my room and asked me for my autograph. I just lost it. It was *so* awkward. The whole thing was just *awkward.* Hell, once again, I opened my damn mouth, and told Cal he could come over like I was Ms. Cool and it wouldn't bother me, and it tore me apart. I told him he could do it, so I cant get mad at him. I did **not** expect twenty people, though. I didn't want an audience! I feel like such an ass for crying in front of all of them. I feel like an ass for lots of reasons. He said he'd pay his probation for now on and he said he'd keep the phone on for me as long as I kept paying the bill. And then, as he left, he looked at Binah, and he told me to take care of her. Through my tears, I told him I would. God it was just yucky.

7.26.96

Now every time I listen to the new Tori CD I am going to think about that awful day…because it was playin when he was here. It was a fucking divorce with an audience! Shit—I was already in the middle of a pity party! Now my sadness is turning into anger. I am considering calling him to tell him we are opening for Cannibal Corpse next month and he needs to come up that day and get the rest of his shit. God, could I really do that?

I must just try to accept everything that has happened. I cannot change it. All I can change is how I react to it and what comes out of my mouth as a response to it.

I am going to put our relationship in a box…literally. I have got to take some fucking action because this shit is taking over my life. I worked really hard to have this life and I'm not going to give it up.

7.27.96

My feelings are hurt because the guys all got together to watch the video of the show and they did not invite me! Geoff called to tell me about it but it was like eight thirty when he did and it had already been on for a while. Maybe my feelings of exclusion aren't just all in my head. I met Carey's ex boyfriend Cooper tonight. He looks a lot like Max. It's weird. She told me that it bothered her that day knowing that she was going to be seeing him. I was glad to hear that because sometimes it seems that her life is really easy and it's good to know she goes through shit too. Sometimes I think she couldn't possibly ever had a drug problem and she is just a counselor who spies on drug addicts for some crazy unknown reason.

I went to grab the book on stones, the one on runes, and the one on herbs for the rite I am planning and they were all gone.

7.30.96

Well, it's full moon. Today is the day. It's actually *blue* moon, the second full moon this month. I have bathed in herbs for the past two nights and I can feel them all over me. The incense is ready and so is the box. I have the sigils to draw on it and the right stones out and the right runes. I have done my research well. I am proud of myself. I have photos of us, the tools he made for me, the stones we freed from the earth together…things he made me…I am ready to let this go. I have to. It is killing me.

8.2.96

The Cannibal Corpse/Anthrax show is coming up and it's gonna *rock*. They are planning to have some *meet the band thing* at some bowling alley the night before. It sounds kind of stupid. Then we've got a little road trip later in the month and I am looking forward to it. We are still without wheels as the van is dead in bum-fuck Illinois. It is too dead to bother repairing but Ian's dad wants to tow it home anyway. We are trying to work out how we are gonna get up north. It has put some pressure on us, but not much, since the little label that has formed to sign us may be able to pay for a van for us to stay on the road. Now, that's RUGER's account of it, mind you, and I haven't heard shit from the label people themselves, so as always I will really believe it when I see it. We are still gonna lay low on shows and do one a month or so in Memphis. We are practicing for the rest of this month till we leave.

I did the rite to help me let Cal go. I don't have unrealistic expectations of it. What I needed was to take some action. To *do something* about it. To do something with my hands. I know time will heal my wounds, but I guess I just get ready for them to be gone *right now*. I am ready to move on. I feel better because I did something constructive, and stopped whining and having pity parties (listening to Sara McLaughlin in the dark with candles lit…by myself…and not answering the phone) I know the only way out is through, and if what I have been doing is *going through* then it's worth it to get to the other side, but it still sucks. The only men in my life today are the ones that I truly love, my boys…my band. This band thing is so much like a marriage. At least it is for me and I haven't even ever been in one for real. I guess the difference is in a marriage the common goal is to stay together and meet each others needs—and the band has the same goals, but even more of them. The band makes *music*…we participate in a mental, emotional, and very physical union that makes us *completely* dependent upon each other to achieve it. I wonder sometimes if they think my priorities are not in order, because of how much I value my sobriety. I wonder if they realize that I got sober so I could be the best I could be. I was about to walk away from all of it…just so I could stay stoned…and I'm so glad I didn't. At the same time, I wonder if that level of commitment exists for them. To make this work would they change if they had to? What would they be willing to change? How committed are they *really*? Am I wrong to look at unorganized bullshit in the band as a lack of commitment?

8.5.96

It is hot as *hell* outside. There is a window unit in the garage where we practice, thank freakin' GOD, or we would die. I'm taking much better care of myself. I am trying to call and chat with them to stay connected and I'm meditating every morning and then roller-blading before work. Ruger came up to the salon and took me to lunch today. It was nice. Last night they were late for practice again, and I had my skates in my truck, so I just skated the neighborhood till they got there. Skating is fun as shit. It doesn't feel like exercise at all. If it did I wouldn't fucking do it. One of my customers asked me out today and I told him no. And I have had a secret crush on him, too! I told him some lie about how it would not be professional, and he told me he would *go to another stylist*. That was very flattering, but I still know the last thing I need to do is run off all crazy in my head over a dude. Just like the whole Jack thing. I was *so* crazy about him…but trying to figure him out just took up too much time in my head. I don't want to have to *wonder* how somebody feels about me. I want to *know*. I mean, I don't want to spoil the excitement of getting to know someone, I guess I just don't want to play games. I also want to move through the thing with Cal a day at a time and really *feel* it. With another dude to deter me, I don't know if I could. Come to think of it, I haven't thought about Cal once all day until *now*. Wow!

8.7.96

Sitting at the coffee shop waiting on Natasha and her best friend, Fern. Everybody calls him Fern because one night on a highway in bumfuck Tennessee he stopped at a Podunk hotel to get a room. The lil old man at the counter asked him if he was 'one of em' *ferns*…" He was saying the word *foreigner*, but it came out sounding like *fern*. So the name stuck. People are playin cards and chess and games all around me. Lots of freaks in here. I love it. I guess I'm one of them. We are gonna do some mad libs and hang out.

Things are getting so much better for me. I don't know if it's the exercise…the meditation…or just a hint of peace on the wind. The only disturbing thoughts I have at all are about the future of the band…but instead of freaking about it, I just honor the thought and try to let it go. I don't know where we will wind up, but I do believe in right action. I just don't know if the actions we take are the right ones sometimes. It's not *my* band, it's *our* band and I have to consider everyone's ideas. Yet, sometimes I feel like its *Rugers* band…and I don't know if I would make the same decisions he does. Regardless, I am sticking through it all the way. I haven't come this far to give the fuck up. Opening for Cannibal Corpse and Anthrax isn't exactly the biggest claim to fame but it gives me hope that we are moving upward. I think I see Natasha.

8.10.96

We practiced last night and then went to the bowling alley thing. We took a hundred glossy photographs of the band and wound up having to autograph and hand out every single one of them. I could not *believe* it. I felt like such a rock star. So did Ruger. He ate it up, too. He said he thought Anthrax was pissed because we signed more shit and were approached by more people than they were. We just went to hang out; we didn't expect to be signing shit. We brought the photos at the request of the radio station and the bowling alley people. I didn't think we'd actually sign them.

We are currently at the Daisy. There are people everywhere—well, roadies anyway. This is gonna be a big ass show. There are buses out back and big 18-wheelers and everything. It's kind of a game of hurry up and wait. They let me leave work early to get down here, which was cool as shit. It doesn't look like we are going to get a sound check at all. Our gear will also sit on the stage in front of Anthrax's and Cannibal Corpse's stuff, so their wont be much room on stage at all for the guys to move around. Oh well. It's still gonna be fun.

8.12.96

That *mother fucker.* I picked up my phone earlier today and it was **dead**, so I went to the pay phone and called Bell South and they said Cal had disconnected it. I am *so* pissed. Could he have not called and warned me? Could he not have given me a chance to make arrangements? Why did he have to spring this shit on me like this? That is so uncool. I called Carey cuz I was so mad. She calmed me down and told me it was a bad arrangement in the first place, and that it was his phone and he could do whatever he wanted with it. *Damn* it. I know she is right, but it just pisses me the fuck off. I had *so* much shit to get done and not having a phone fucking *sucks.* I feel like I am in prison when I don't have a phone. This sucks. I called Mom and she said she might be able to help me pay my big ass seven million dollar phone bill so I can get one hooked up here, but it will be a few weeks. Fuck.

The Anthrax show was fucking *amazing,* even though it was still daylight when we took the stage. We pretty much played for the road crews of the other bands and our friends. It sucked having to be so cramped on stage, and they cut the power amps backs so we didn't have full volume, which is a trick every headliner plays. It was okay. We were just glad to get to do it. At least I was.

8.15.96

Headed up north. I'm riding in the SUBURBAN. Yay! I love this shitty ass old truck. All our gear is behind my head, in the lair of loss. We do not have the trailer anymore. It seems that it was *not* bought with the band fund as I was told, but it was, in fact, *stolen*. **No fucking shit.** We have been carrying our gear in a *stolen* trailer for over a year. It is a *miracle* that we still have our equipment because if we had been caught it would have been *impounded*. I felt like such a dumb ass when Jed told me that. I guess I feel like I should have known. It is *that kind* of crazy fucking bullshit that makes me think about the future of this band. I mean if we are willing to put our equipment on the line like that, where are our fucking priorities? They fucking *knew* better than to tell me the truth about that shit because I would have gone the fuck *off*. They fucking filed off the serial numbers on that mother fucker. What a bust. Hell, I guess *my* dumb ass used to ride with a quarter ounce in my panties and a fucking bong under my seat.

Max is renting a car to come up here and Ruger was *so* fucking pissed at him about it. He wanted Max to ride along with him in Adam's truck. He and Adam are following us because there just isn't room for six of us in here with all out gear. He was even *more* pissed at Max because he was still asleep when *we* were hitting the road. He is worried that Max won't make it in time for tonight's show. I'm not that worried. He did this a long time ago and it all worked out. I think Max will make it. We are playin in Chicago tonight and tomorrow night and then going down to Champaign Saturday to play a benefit concert on Sunday. We are crashing at Sabrina's. I talked to her on the phone last week for a long time. She said she would leave us a key because she may be at work when we get there Saturday. She also said she would make this huge crock-pot full of homemade chili for us. That is *so* cool. She is so good to us. She and I talked on the phone this week and she really wants me to meet her friend Roman. He sounds really interesting. She said he is an amateur actor in a local guild and he goes to college. She knows my situation and she respects it, but says it wont hurt me to just meet him. I told her I would. He is coming to the show Sunday night.

8.17.96

Sitting at Wes' in Chicago. I called Carey this morning and told her about the stolen trailer business. I told her it is shit like that that makes me think the band is on a sinking ship. She told me that until I am prepared to see them hit the big time without me that I don't even need to talk about quitting. I hate that she is right.

The show last night smoked, as did the one Thursday, which Max made it to in the *nick* of time. Ruger was pacing back and forth for an hour and I could practically see the smoke coming out of his ears while he walked. He was *so* pissed. I have been eyeing the bottles of liquor on the top of Wes' fridge remembering the days when I was here with no buds and I drank that shit straight. During the freakin *day*. I am so glad I aint got to do that shit today just to feel comfortable in my own skin. We are gonna go eat at Zorba's and then head out for Champaign. I love Chicago. It still overwhelms the shit out of me but I have grown very fond of it at the same time. Natasha used to live here. I wish she could tag along with me on a road trip sometime. Ruger is still talkin about us all moving up here. I just laugh at him now. It doesn't even freak me out anymore. I've been quite introspective this trip I think. I've just been enjoying the peace in my life and I have been so grateful for it. It makes me so grateful to God. I really have become a more comfortable version of myself, which is what Carey used to tell me would happen to me if I stayed clean and surrendered my life to God. I was *terrified* to do it, because I thought I'd like start wearing pink and pearls and going to church or some shit. Now I realize that it's *okay* to define God however you want, and that definition of God is okay, and will truly save your ass. I have spent years trying to *understand* God instead of *using* God. Today I have a God in my life that I *absolutely* do not understand, and it is working better for me than anything I ever did. Sometimes I feel like I should dedicate my life to the service of this God…and that my life now is all about service to *myself*…I feel sometimes that my life is so self centered…it's all about me being a rock star. I work with drug addicts who want to get clean, but my *main* priority is getting a record deal and doing this full time. Sometimes I wonder if that is being selfish.

14

Dead People Dancin'

8.17.96 later

At Sabrina's. Everybody is piled up in the floor watching TV. We are all going to some club tonight just to party. Jed and I both have cash and I have been talking about getting a steak for two days, so he took me to the restaurant Sabrina works at. I was hoping to meet Roman there, but it turns out he works with her at her *day* job, not the waiting table's job. Anyway, she said he is going to come over before the show tomorrow night. I've looked at his photograph about two thousand times and I must admit I am very curious about meeting him. Not that anything could really *happen* between us, since I live so far away, but I feel that tinge of excitement in the air I don't think can be too wrong. I think it reminds us that we are alive.

8.19.96

On the way home...It is the *most* beautiful day. I got in to Sabrina's house at six thirty this morning. I was a little embarrassed, because I have never stayed out all night with a boy that I just met before. I figured the boys would pick on me really bad or something. Max was up when I got in and he just said "Hey, Flo!" and I expected some jeers, but he did not realize I had just walked in the door. Then he said "Wait a minute...did you just *now* get here? I embarrassedly said yes, and he laughed at me and told me he was glad I *got some*. I told him I *didn't* get some…and he laughed and said I didn't have to lie to him.

Roman got to Sabrina's at about five thirty Saturday night. When he walked in the door, my heart started to thunder. He is soooo beautiful. His hair is blond and thick…and forms a curtain at his chin that divides to reveal his dazzling topaz blue eyes. He is taller than me, and was dressed *well-*in black leather…with these beautiful white crosses along his sleeves. The immediate connection was definitely mutual. His voice is electrifying…it's confident…clear…and has this bell tone quality that I have never heard before. It's like there is a cacophony of organ pipes in his throat…and they are gently struck as he enunciates his words. I could look at his face and listen to his soothing voice for hours. And I *did*…he and I *talked* from the time the show was over…until six thirty this morning when he dropped me off at Sabrina's.

We went to the show together. He stared at me from the pit and I tried to avoid his gaze so I could concentrate. The place was *packed*…a sea of bodies pressed into the stage…and fists in the air went back as far as I could see. There was a unique energy afoot.

After the show, he asked me if I wanted to hang out. Of course I did! I asked if we could go get some coffee. He said that was a great idea. He opened his van door for me and I got in and I looked at myself in the bitch mirror and started laughing at my reflection. I didn't realize I had make-up all the way to my chin and my pigtails were crusted sticks stuck to my head and throat. I grabbed for my backpack and started to clean up. He told me I looked great…and that I was bad ass…and that the sweaty drummer chick look was incredibly sexy. He asked me if I would mind stopping by his house, because he collected stones too, and he wanted to show them to me. I was nervous, because I was so enthralled by him, and I don't quite understand dating lingo, so I didn't know if agreeing to go to his place would mean I was gonna fuck him. I was relieved to find him a *complete* gentleman. His house is in the Hammer district, old and charming with a sprawling porch. Roman lives with four people, who are his siblings, sort of. He is best friends with their younger brother, so he is like one of their family. His room is *awesome*…it looks like my own apartment…CD's everywhere…posters, music equipment…candles everywhere…he lit some incense which smelled almost as good as he did. He sat on the bed next to me and pulled out a box of beautiful sparkling stones. We looked at every one of them together and I caught him staring more at me than the stones in the box. He asked me if I was hungry, and I was, so he ordered us pizza. When it got there, we went outside on the porch and he appeared from the kitchen with two wine glasses and a carton of chocolate milk. That was the sweetest sight to me. He smiled and said it was all they had to drink. We toasted our glasses of milk and ate pizza, and while we ate, this dude walked past the house with a funny guitar case in his hand. We called out hello, and he approached us, and pulled out his mandolin. He played for us, as we ate pizza, and tried not to stare at each other. After we ate, he asked me if I would like to go for a walk. We walked down the dimly lit street, past the charming houses...talking about everything. We talked about the band, witchcraft, drugs, dreams, religion...our favorite authors...In the spirit of the romance of the evening, I took his arm as we walked. I have never been treated with such reverence by a man. When we arrived back at his house, we kind of quit talking and looked at each other. He asked me what I would like to do *now*. It was four o' clock in the morning. I shyly asked him if we could go get coffee. He smiled at me, and I swear he looked relieved. We went to Perkins, where people can still drink coffee and smoke simultaneously. At the table, I must have been staring at his mouth...and thinking about kissing him...because he interrupted my day-dream to ask me what I was thinking about. I very bravely told him the truth. "I am thinking about leaning over this table and kissing you." I could not believe I had said it. But I *did*, and the next thing I knew he asked the waitress for the check and we walked out into the remainder of the night. As we strolled to the van, he stopped walking. I did too. He looked into my eyes, and slowly bent his face down, and placidly pressed his mouth onto mine. In my mind, I saw all the fireworks in Boomtown ignite in that moment. He and I smiled at each other...and he pulled me into him...and we held each other as the sky grew lighter and lighter. We then walked to the van, and he opened my door for me, and we began the drive back to Sabrina's.

He asked me *so* many questions on that drive. "Are we going to do this" I think was one of the first...I think I told him we were crazy if we didn't...and I meant it, because I have never met anyone like him...and I wasn't going to pass it up simply because of distance. He asked me if I had ever done it before...had a long distance thing...and I told him no...I had not and he said he had not either. When we got to Sabrina's we wrote down all of our information. I *really* fucking hated telling him that I did not have a phone! We then kissed each other passionately for a way to brief period of time. He said he would come see me in Memphis soon. I got out of the van, and ran around to his side and kissed him again. He drove off into the sunrise.

I am absolutely *enamored* with this man. "Mr. Roman Reicharts, what have you *done* to me?" Oh, man...as the road draws on before me he is all I can think about. I keep replaying the evening in my head and as I do I can *feel* the way I felt. After he left, I was so pumped that I could not sleep. I put on my roller blades and skated through Sabrina's neighborhood. There is a road off her street that goes through a cornfield. The sun rose as I skated and thought about how grateful I was for everything in my life. For the band…for the opportunity to be on the road…and meeting people…and for this wonderful new man in my life and the possibilities it could bring. I realized that I may never talk to him again, although I don't think that will happen, but I just tried to separate myself from outcomes and concentrate on how great I felt *at the moment*. I thanked God for the chance to be *this* fulfilled in life…for the part of my character that takes risks…for the ambition I have…for my drive…and for being sober to where I can take life by the reigns and fully *live*. Oh…we are about to stop and get some road grub.

8.20.96

I am in bed about to crash. I hung out at Natasha's tonight. She and Wren have been watching every episode of Twin Peaks in order and tonight was the final episode. I told her all about Roman, who I talked to twice today. He is so fucking cool. I cannot believe it. He is awesome.

I called Cal today. I called information and found his new number. I asked him why he cut the phone off and he said he needed it—that he and his girlfriend moved in together and they needed to hook the phone up. I asked him why he did not call me and let me know he was going to do it, and he said he didn't know. That bothered me a little bit. I told him he needed to come and get his shit.

8.21.96

Oh man did the shit hit the fan *today*. **Cal** showed up at my work this morning, with his girlfriend and his parents in tow, ready to get his stuff. Cal demanded the keys to the apartment. I felt like if I gave him the keys, he would take *every-*

thing, so my boss let me leave for the day. When we got here, it was a *nightmare*. He was so bitter and rude about everything. He started taking every book off the shelves and started piling them into boxes. I *demanded* he stop, saying that some of them were mine, and he said no, that *he* had bought them. We probably bought $400 worth of books while we were together, mostly with his money, but I'm the one that paid the rent, the phone bills, and the utility bills. I guess I just assumed that since *I* paid the bills and *he* bought the toys, that we would split them down the middle. He did not agree with this. I just gave up fighting and let him clean me out. I went in the bedroom while they were packing shit up and called Carey. She told me to calm down and she would come over, and it would be all be over soon. I told her how unfair he was being to take *everything*, and she said that I should have discussed this with him a long time ago. She said all I can do is take it as a lesson learned. I also called Roman. I knew he couldn't talk long because he was at work, but I knew just hearing his voice would sooth me and calm me down. He told me that the sound of my tears was the worst sound he had ever heard. When I got off the phone with him, I went into the barren living room. Cal was standing there with his staff. He said he was done and he was leaving, and he turned and left. As sad of a thing as it all was, I was kind of glad he was gone. It felt *immediately* different in the apartment. Not good or bad, just different. It felt like it was MY apartment, mine alone. Carey got there in time to watch them drive away. The apartment was a disaster, and she helped me clean up and put some semblance of order back into things. I put on a pot of coffee and we wound up laughing and talking on the couch. At about three thirty, there was a knock on the door. When I opened it, there was a man holding a bouquet of beautiful sunflowers, asking if he had the right address. I was *stunned*. I nodded that he had the right address, and I took the flowers and sat them on the empty coffee table. I pulled out the card, and held it, savoring a moment of not knowing what it said. The card contained three words…three words that still resonate in my mind. It said *"from your gentleman"*

8.26.96

So much has been happening. I haven't had a chance to stop and write. I am *crazy* about Roman. We talk everyday. The little old ladies that come into the salon all want me to sit with them while they are under the dryer and tell them all about him. One of them pointed out to me that I was singing as I swept the hair up and she asked me if I was in love. I told her I was. I think this is that love at first sight thing I've always wanted to believe in and never did. This is exactly what I wanted…to skip the bullshit and get right down to what is real. And that's exactly what we have done.

I got a new sponsee. Her name is Fiona. She is a rave kid and her pants are so big that people could hide in them. She is real cute and was real sprung. She lives with some DJ people and I'm not to sure how safe of an environment that is, but shit, if I can stay sober around the band, *anybody* can stay sober *anywhere*. I am glad to have her in my life, because it helps me to be responsible for my own recovery. It would be real easy for me to find my self-esteem in being a rock star…or to find it in this man. I know the hole within me is god—shaped…and no man or band or bong hit is going to work for the long haul. The crazy thing is I will *forget* all of this if I don't keep it fresh in my mind, and carrying this message to another person is the best way to do that.

We have a big ass show coming upon the seventh. Sabrina and Roman are gonna drive down for that weekend. I am *so* excited. I have already taken off work. I cannot wait to see his face again. He got a picture of me from Sabrina and he says he carries it with him all the time. She gave me the Xeroxed picture she had of him on her refrigerator and I carry *it* around with *me*! I am *sprung*.

Ruger, Max and Ian all came into the salon today and I did their hair. It was fun. We are all excited about the show on the seventh and we are talking about doing a *big* ass Halloween show in October…really busting our asses to promote it and doing radio spots and everything. We may try to get Hack and Joseph's new band to play. I don't know if I wrote about the Bone Squad break up. It fucking sucks. They were *so* **close**; they worked *so* hard. I guess shit just happens. We talked about the label and it all seems to be tied up in money issues. It all smells like bullshit to me. I feel like I never get the whole story. I'm glad I don't get my hopes up anymore. I like the layin low thing we are doing in Memphis. It keeps things fresh.

9.2.96

I sent Roman a care package today. I made it for him yesterday. I made him a box and put sachets in it and a tape of the band and some pictures and all kinds of little stuff. I put Portishead's "Wandering Star" on a tape for him, because it reminds me of him, and put it in the box, too. I also put a candle in it that I consecrated with runes and I put incense in the box and it smells *so* good. When I got back from the post office I checked the mail and he sent me a letter. He wrote it on this beautiful parchment paper with a quill pen. He is *so tasteful*. The envelope was sealed with *wax*. How classy can you get? And the letter itself is even better…His handwriting is an art into itself, real swirly and dramatic. It says, "You, my lady, have brought me to my knees". *Damn*. And then it says, "My feelings for you are a river along which I travel" *Man!* And *then* it says "The gaze in your eyes when they are beset upon me could carry no price" It goes *on and on* like this…and he talks about how he is looking so forward to making his memories of me real to him again…and he closes with this quote from W.B.Yeats that says… *"But I, being poor, have only my dreams. I have spread my dreams under your feet. Tread softly, for you tread on my dreams"*. That is so beautiful. I have waited for this man all my life. I have always longed to be so cherished…and I thought it was only in the movies that people really did things like this…and *said* such beautiful things…but right now in my life, this is REAL. This is really happening. And it is happening to *me*.

9.5.96

We have been practicing our asses off. Tonight we did the whole set for the show *twice*. We have written two new songs and they are fucking **awesome**. I feel like I am getting more experimental on my kit and willing to take more risks. It feels good. We have a commercial on the radio and word is the place is gonna be *packed*. I am *so* excited. Some of the crew from the salon are planning to come! Sabrina and Roman are heading down Friday when they get off work and should be here around one o' clock in the morning. I have finally had the chance to fix up my apartment some so it looks like **I** live here. The Hammer's got kicked out of their house and the last time we were in Champaign, they gave me that big ass black gothic candle holder that I always admired, and I have it up over the fireplace. I got some three-foot long burgundy taper candles on the mantle on either side of it and it looks cool. I have a swag of black fabric draped over the bamboo that Cornfed gave me that sits over the big bay window. My Hebrew letters line the sides of the main window and I have a black sheet over the ugly ass Al Bundy couch. I have the big ass square of glass that we all drew on with china markers as my coffee table, and it actually looks cool as shit. It has my stone collection all over it...and they twinkle in the sun as it streams through the window. It looks like me in here *finally*.

Roman got his care package today. I talked to him earlier and he was so excited about it. He *loves* the song...the Portishead song. We talked about our weekend together and talked about the fact that he was going to be *sleeping* here and we talked about *sex*. It was so cool to get it out in the open, because we both have obviously been thinking about it. We agreed that it would take the pressure off if we just decided that this weekend was not the one for *that*. I felt relieved. I think he did too. This way we can just hang.

I am feeling overwhelmed. I have so much to do. The apartment is a mess and I have put off cleaning till tomorrow night due to practice this week. I need to do my nails, clean the house, do laundry, get groceries...oh god...I don't even want to make a list...

9.6.96

Man. I am *exhausted!* But my anxiety and excitement is keeping me awake. It's a little past midnight and Roman and Sabrina should be here any minute! I got off work, went to the grocery store, and came straight home. I cleaned the *hell* out of this apartment. I mean, I scrubbed the bathroom...I dusted the candlesticks, I cleaned out the refrigerator...I washed the sheets and pillowcases and cleaned out from under my bed...I changed the kitty litter and swept and mopped the whole apartment. I am wiped out. I *finally* got done cleaning and took a shower. I changed clothes *three* times. I don't want to look like a slob when I see Roman, but I don't want to look too fixed up either. So, I just decided to wear something I would wear to bed, so I am wearing my Redneck Vampires T-shirt and some black satin boxer shorts with little ants on them. They are cute. And my black glitter socks. I know I probably look like a dork, but he might as well know the real me. I have my Portishead CD playin, candles lit, some incense burning...and a pot of coffee on. What an excitingly peaceful moment. The candles flicker as air from the window unit moves through them...and even though the air conditioner is loud and the music is playin, there is a stillness in here that is just blissful. I am so grateful to have this apartment. I remember when Cal and I moved here. We were living with that nasty psycho girl in the flea circus. And before that with Mitch, and then Lana, and then the cabin. And then I have lived on Jesse's couch, and Kathy's couch, and Rita and Sadie's place, and just anywhere I could. And not to mention Sabrina's, Wes', the Hammerhouse, and countless other couches. I am *so* glad to finally have my own home. I hope I never lose this feeling.

9.9.96

I don't even know where to begin with this weekend. It was *wonderful*. It was beautiful. It warmed my heart to see Roman…and tore it out to see him leave. We had an absolutely *fabulous* weekend together. He is so fantastic. He is so perfect. There has got to be a flaw somewhere. I am not comfortable being this happy which is really a shame. I keep waiting for the bomb to drop.

The show was a *huge* success. Waiting a month or so between shows has been a really good idea, because the crowd draw seems to double. We played our two newest songs and they went over really well. A lot of my sober friends showed up. They were all down front in the pit, and Carey wore her Redneck Vampires shirt. It is really good to have her there, because she and I talk about the band all the time. I am always talking about whether or not I am on a sinking ship.

Fiona called me the night of the show and said she was having a hard time at the Rave party kid house where she lives, so I told her she could go with us if she wanted to. We picked her up on the way downtown. She knew I played in a band but I don't think she knew what *kind* of band, and from what she said to me afterward she was totally blown away by us. She told me she could not *believe* the person playin drums and the person who is her sponsor were the same people. She said that I am such a gentle person, and that the girl on stage was so angry, and gritty and beat the *shit* out of the drums. I told her it's why I *can* be so gentle…because I have the drums to assault with my anger!

It was a huge comfort to have Carey there, especially when Ruger pulled a bogus fucking stunt. I do not know why the hell he did it…or what kind of problem he has with Roman, because for some reason in the middle of our set between songs he said into the microphone, "Hey, lets all get together after the show and help Flo find a *real* man." I could not believe he said that. I was mortified, and even more so for Roman who was backstage, and I felt so bad. I was so pissed. I glared at Carey, saying with my body "can you fucking believe that?" Her mouth was still wide open that he had even said it. After the next song, I *had* to redeem myself *and* my man. Knowing our next tune was the one that specifically directs a person to go fuck themselves, I got up off my throne and stepped down off the drum riser, which I have never done, and walked right up to Max and asked for his microphone. He just about toppled over; he was so shocked to see me standing there. What surprised me the most was when people started to *cheer* for *me*. I wanted them to shut up so I could curse Ruger out in front of the whole place, but I found satisfaction in simply saying, "This next song…is for *Ruger*"

Luckily, as it turned out, Roman must not have even *heard* Ruger, because he never said a word about it…to me or to Sabrina. After the show, I made sure Fiona had a way home, and Sabrina then took Roman and I back to my apartment. I was *so* sweaty and nasty from the gig. I took a shower and then he got in after me while I made coffee. We spent the next two hours intertwined on the couch whispering in each other's ears and kissing passionately. We wound up in my bed, and *didn't* stick to our agreement about sex. We made love for the next two hours…and it was flawless…

Earlier on Saturday, Sabrina and I and Roman went to Elmwood cemetery. It is so old and it looks like it is right out of a horror movie. It is a registered historic place; full of really old graves all clustered together…some of them are like twenty ft tall. The weather was *perfect*. We hung around in midtown and went to Maggie's Pharm and got some incense and had a late lunch. We had a good time.

Sunday at about five o' clock in the morning Roman and I went to Perkins and had breakfast. He said I fell asleep at the table! We made it back to my apartment and crashed. They left Sunday at about two in the afternoon. He left me a tape to listen to. Dead People Dancin'…or something like that. It is the strangest…most ethereal music I have ever heard. It is hallowedly beautiful. I am listening to it now and wearing his leather jacket. He left it here on purpose.

I am going to go up to see him next. I am going to take the train up there. It's only like a hundred bucks or something like that. My truck probably would not make it, so that's not even an option.

9.10.96

Man. I haven't ever written about my birthday that's coming up! I almost have a whole *year* clean. I cannot fucking *believe* it. I cannot believe I have not gotten fucked up in a whole fucking year. I never dreamed I would make it this far. I mean I knew *other* people did this kind of shit, but I really didn't think *I* would. I guess I just took it one day at a time. I really kind of had too. I guess there have been times when I took it a fucking *hour* at a time, even *five minutes* at a time. Speaking of which, Fiona is doing okay. She is inching along like I was in the beginning. Carey and I are going camping together at the end of the month to do my fifth step. I am looking forward to it.

I got my train ticket booked yesterday. I am going to see Roman Saturday the 21st. The train leaves that night about 10:00pm and I will get there around 6:00 am. Then I get back on the train Monday night and get home Tuesday morning. It's not long, but it's better than nothing. We talk on the phone everyday, sometimes two and three times a day. I am crazy about him. I can tell him anything. He is so gentle and really wants to hear what's going on in my world. He calls me "*love*" and his "*fair lady*". He is amazing.

9.11.96

Sitting at work. Get *this* shit. I was on the phone with Roman this morning. He and I are talking about last weekend about the fact that we had sex, against our agreement. I had absolutely *no* idea that this bothered him at the time, but apparently, it did. He tells me that he was nervous. I told him I couldn't tell he was nervous! *Then* the next thing out of his mouth fucking *threw* me big time. He says "Well, I *am* an actor! **Oh my god**! What the fuck! I think this is the big ass freakin bomb I was waiting for. I knew he was too good to be true. When he said that to me I was like, "Wait a minute...if you *acted* your way through that, then how much of the other stuff that has been said and done is all an act too? He was lost for words...he said that was not what he meant...but I told him I needed to think about this and we got off the phone. Sabrina called me about fifteen minutes later and said he was freakin out. I told her my side of the situation and she agreed that if she were in my shoes she would feel the same way. She explained to me that Roman is absolutely captivated by me, and she can personally vouch that his feelings for me are *not* an act at all. She told me that time would surely prove all. This just sucks. I was just about to reconsider the Cinderella story.

9.11.96 later

Oh my god...I cannot *believe* it...I was at my station doing hair in the salon...and this lady walks in with these long white boxes...and she goes up to the desk, and they direct her to *me*...and she is delivering something for me...and I open the boxes...and Roman has sent me **THREE DOZEN** long stemmed red roses. The lady that delivered them was the owner of the shop, and she said she wanted to *personally* deliver them because she wanted to see the woman that was receiving *three-dozen roses*. She said she had *never* in twenty years of business had that request. The card said, "*I hope you can find it in your heart...to give me another chance...Your Gentleman*" **Holy freakin shit**! All the little old ladies in the salon are freakin out and telling me he is a *keeper*...and they are telling me all their love stories and how glad they are they gave their husbands second chances. The stylists, on the other hand, call them *guilt* roses. If I walk away from him now I will always wonder if it was the worst mistake of my life. Oh god, they are so beautiful...*he* is so beautiful...call me a sucker but *damn*...three dozen roses? I am gonna call him.

9.12.96

I talked to Roman again last night when I got home from practice. He is so wonderful. He was so apologetic and I listened intently to him explain. He said he never meant to bring the fear into me that he did. He told me that he talked to Sabrina for a long time and she explained to him how chicks are always afraid of getting played, and that the way he treats me is so unusual that it seems like it's all an act. He told me I *deserved* to be treated like a princess...and that he wasn't going to stop. He apologized over and over for what happened, explaining the way it was taken was not what he meant at all. I told him it was cool…and it is. All I can do is give him a second chance. It just still sucks to me because I was already slightly suspicious of him and this just kinda proved my fears.

To add even more flavor to this mix, he told me about his ex girlfriend from a long time ago who he is still friends with. He explained to me that he and Samantha are just friends, and that she had called and will be coming down from Chicago Friday night to spend the weekend. She asked him if she could crash at his place. Apparently, Samantha is this ultra Goth chick who he was *really* infatuated with for a long time. Now that she has heard through the grapevine that has a girlfriend, she wants his idolatry back and has conveniently arranged a visit. **Damn**. I wish I could go up there unannounced this weekend! I am not gonna tell Roman that she cant stay in his house, because I don't want to be all like that. I have to find a way to *be* there without really being there. Hmmmmm

9.14.96

Well. Leave it to me to find a way. Last night I called in the troops, and for three hours I posed **NAKED** with his leather jacket on and three dozen roses all over me. The pictures are currently being developed via one hour processing at the camera place, and then I will tuck them into the black velvet and chrome album I found and drop them at the post office to be FED EXED to his house. They will arrive at his house before noon tomorrow morning, when Goths are groggily slurping their first cup of coffee and trying to avoid the light of day. Oh Ms. Samantha. You are fucking with the wrong woman's man.

9.14.96

Ahhhhh. The sweet savor of revenge. Roman just called me here at the salon. He said a mysterious package just arrived at the house as he and Samantha were having coffee. Am I good or what? He just kept telling me over and over that I was *beautiful* and that I was bad ass for doing that and Samantha was suddenly in a big hurry to get on the road. HA! The girls at work cant *believe* I did this. Shit, I can't believe it either. I have never posed nude for a photograph in my life. The stylists *really* can't believe it because the guys at the photo place get there hair cut in here. They keep saying I'm gonna have some new customers now. Ha!

We are supposed to practice tonight but Joseph from Bone Squad's new band is playin in the Pinch and I bet they are going to fuck it off to go up there. We will see. We are playin' the 20th at the Addict with a couple other bands. Ruger says we aren't even really gonna promote it. We are just gonna play and save the promo shit for the big ass Halloween show next month. I love Halloween. Roman is going to definitely try to be here for that.

9.17.96

Fiona just left. She is a sweet kid. Her car died a week ago and she is taking the freakin MATA bus to work everyday. That is some damn determination. Fuck. She works at Domino's, which has *got* to suck. I did the pizza job in high school and it sucked for me. I can't imagine doing anything but hair. I have been doin it for years now, except when we were on the road for so long. When I look back on that now, I think not working was more about being stoned more often than it was about being free to be on the road. I think being on the road was a good excuse not to work. Oh hell. I do recall some month long stretches we were gone. Damn, we had fun, too. It's so easy to romanticize those days. It's easy to think getting stoned twenty-four hours a day was *the shit*, and now I am missing out. What is more difficult to remember is how awful it was to have to ration out enough to last me for the duration we were gone. And the yucky feelings of running out and not having any more and having like a week to go. Just that empty, shitty feeling of wondering how I was gonna get high. Fuck. I had forgotten all about that. When we broke down for five days I would have gone out of my fucking mind if I had been using back then. It would have *sucked*. There are people who can smoke dope some days and go a week without it and have no problem with that. More power to them. I wish I was one of those people. God, I do. I fucking *love* pot. *Pot* isn't a bad thing. But when a person like me smokes it might as well be crack. One hit is too many and a thousand hits would never be enough to sustain me. It's not the drug itself that is dangerous, it's the way I abuse myself *with* it that is the problem. The way I lie to myself when I smoke it...telling myself everything is all right…avoiding dealing with reality and real feel-ings…hiding in that false sense of security and ignorance. I am so grateful for the truth. Even though it is surely the narrower path.

Roman sent me a letter. It is so beautiful. I love getting letters and cards from him. This one, as all of them, is written on lovely parchment with his quill pen. It says,

> *I still cannot believe I have done something to cause a compromise of your trust and faith in me. Explanations are no use, as trust is something that must be gained through actions. It is through actions that I plan to gain your trust back. To quote the song my dear,* you *are the sweetest perfection I have ever known. I so anticipate touching your lips with my own that I can almost taste them now. You are the most brilliant star in all of the heavens. I cannot wait to be surrounded by your miraculous presence."*

Damn! I swear it sounds like something from a book, but *he* really *is* that creative and thoughtful and intelligent and original and inventive. It is so lovely to still get letters from him. I like the fact that he writes letters. Especially because he never mentions that he is sending me anything, and when I check the mail, my heart is just warmed even more. I am so excited and nervous about going to see him. I leave this Saturday. He says he has lots of cool shit planned. He says it's all a secret though.

Carey and I are excited about our camping trip. God I have so much going on. We are playin Friday at the Addict, and then I work Saturday, and then my train leaves Saturday night, and then I get back Tuesday and work all week and Carey and I leave Friday to go camping, and then Monday I will celebrate my first year and pick up my medallion at the meeting. Holy freakin shit. Whose life is this?

15

To Thine Own Self Be True

9.23.96

He met me at the train station early Sunday morning. He appeared out of the freezing cold air and fog in his long black coat holding a bouquet of lilies…with a big smile on his face. He held me for a long, long time…We went to his place and sifted through the bodies of the partygoers who were crashed out from the bash the night before, and made it to the kitchen, where he had brewed a pot of coffee for me. It was piping hot and perfect. We retired to his room, after saying hello to the roommates who said they had heard volumes about me and were thrilled to meet me. They were all so nice. When he opened the door to his room, I was astonished to see it totally changed. He had painted it black, and covered the windows with black mat board to look like the windows of a cathedral. He had taken shades of blue tissue paper and cut them out arranged them onto the glass to look like it was stained blue. The room had a delicate blue glow as the light of day peeked in. Candles were lit everywhere and incense was burning that smelled just like my lilies. He had put a Redneck Vampires flyer up and had pictures of us together all around it. It was like being in a sanctuary. He proposed a toast with his coffee to us, and to our weekend. We drank our coffee as we sat Indian style from each other across the bed, re remembering what it was like to *hear* the voice and *see* the person at the same time. He scooped me into his arms and held me across his lap kissing me slowly…and then…he *took* me. I can't think of another word to call it. We fell asleep for a few hours, and then got up and he said we had a big day planned. He took me to meet his *parents*. They were *so* wonderful. We had coffee and looked at old embarrassing pictures. I was *so* honored to meet his folks. You know it's some real shit when you meet the parents. When we left there, we went to a shopping mall, where we went inside and he led us to a gourmet food market. He proceeds to purchase homemade potato salad, fresh mozzarella and Brie, crackers, grapes, and a big bottle of fresh apple juice. He was talking me on a picnic! And we went to *Allerton*. That place is so amazing. It's full of secret sculptures hidden way back in the woods and I swear it has a very masculine sexual energy lurking in its shadows. When we got there, he drove to the part of it where this 50 ft sculpture of a God is, with a well-mani-cured lawn all around it. He got out of the car and went to the trunk, where he got out blankets and his CD player. We had the *loveliest* afternoon...sitting together on that blanket...under the gaze of that big marble God...listening to Bach's cello pieces and feeding each other cheese...I felt like a queen.

That night Sabrina wanted to cook us dinner, so we went back to his place and showered and then went to her new apartment. It was so great hanging out with her and she made the *best* dinner. After that, we went back to his house and went for a walk...the same walk we had taken the night we met. He told me on that walk that he did not see his future without me in it...and he wanted to know how I felt about that. **My God!** I told him, as we stood in that dimly lit street, that I could not have ever dreamed I would get everything I wanted in another person...and that I didn't even know what I wanted until I got it. The man's *eyes* teared up when I said that to him. We went back to his house...and curled up next to each other...and professed our love for each other...knowing it sounded crazy...but doing it anyway. On Monday, he got up and had to go to work, and I slept the whole day. I was woken up by kisses on my cheeks...and he ordered us pizza from the same place we had had it before, and he bought out the chocolate milk, and the wine glasses. It was so sweet. Then, sadly, I packed up, and he took me to the train station. As the train pulled in, it sounded like it was *mourning*. He held me close to him...and said he'd see me soon. After I boarded, he waited on the platform until the train was out of sight. And here I sit, in the smoking car on the train headed home, as the cigarette smoke of strangers curls around me like his very arms.

9.25.96

Today is the day! Carey came up to work and took me out to lunch for my birth-day. I cannot *believe* it was a year ago today that I went to a meeting and cried my eyes out. My intention was really not at all to join this way of life, but just to fig-ure out how to calm the fuck down with using *so* much. I just wanted the *conse-quences* to stop. The dependency. The daily habit. The self-hate. The negative self talk. Hell, if I could stop all those consequences of using still *today*, and still get to be fucked up sometimes and enjoy the shit out of it, I would, but it just doesn't work that way.

Roman sent a package to me at the salon. He told me not to open it until I could get him on the phone. When I finally reached him, he told me to go open it. Inside was a beautiful, rosewood-handled athame, sharp as shit, with roses on the hilt. It is so exquisite. I almost cried when I saw it. It made him happy that it made me so happy. He wrote me a beautiful card that said he was so proud of me, and he fully supports anything that I am a part of, especially if it makes me happy. He is so fucking cool. He going to a wedding in California the first Saturday in October, and he really wanted me to go, but I don't think I can get off work and practice. He is going to have his return flight come here and then leave out that Tuesday night. I have to think of something amazing for us to do.

I called to check in with the boys. It's weird having seen or heard from them really since the show, which *rocked*. I don't even care what they think about our performances anymore—or if they act like dicks. When the crowd is that pumped, we *must* be doing *something* right. The place managed to be packed, even though we did no promotion whatsoever, and that put everybody in a really good mood. When the crowd is thick like that there is this energy exchange of some kind…and they just seem to feed us with their energy…and then the music we make feeds them back…and this exchange goes on all night. I still like playin at the Daisy best of all, though. Rumor is the Addict is gonna close down. It's gonna be a shame, because even though love playin the Daisy more, the Attic has been a rock club for a *long* time and Memphis needs a seedy ass place like that. It gives the scene flavor. We are practicing tonight and tomorrow night, and then Friday, Saturday and Sunday I will be with Carey in the woods, spilling my guts to her. I am not really nervous about it. I respect the steps, or I wouldn't be doing them, and I respect that they have worked for countless people, so I don't see what the big freakin deal is. She has heard most of this shit anyway. I totally trust her. We talked over lunch about the band. She asked me if they knew I had a year sober. I hadn't even thought about it. I think the last time I mentioned my sobriety in dates to them was when I told Max when I had twenty days clean. Telling them had not even crossed my mind. I don't want to make anyone uncomfortable, and if the tables were turned and somebody in my band got all clean and I wasn't it would make me uncomfortable as fuck. I don't even think they think about it. She asked me what my latest thoughts were on my future with the band. I told her I had made pros and cons lists out the ass, and thought about it endlessly, and that I just felt stuck. I told her how I felt damned if I do and damned if I don't. If I quit, it could be the worst mistake of my life. If I don't quit, that could be the worst mistake of my life, too.

10.1.96

I am waiting on the guys to get here for practice. Man. My weekend with Carey was *so* awesome. It was so great to just get away and Fall Creek is so freakin beautiful. I feel so connected there. I could have done without all the damn Grateful Dead music on the way though. She loves that shit. She used to follow them and support her habit selling balloons full of nitrous oxide at the shows. I still just cannot picture that. She was a stoner like me.

Most of my fifth step was full of shit that I am *jealous* about and I did not even realize it. I did not realize a *resentment* is an event that makes you angry *every time you replay it in your mind.* That's the shit that makes finding peace so difficult, when you can replay that kind of shit over and over in your head like it's on a tape. I have plenty of those, and we talked about each one and I saw my own part of it. I saw how my expectations of others get in my way and make me angry. How I write scripts for people and get mad when they don't read them. How I lie to myself and I don't accept people for who and what they are. I am moving on to the next step now, where I look at the defects of my character and get ready to have them removed…and replaced with assets in my character. They aren't removed by magic. Carey says when we align our will with God's we quit re-acting out of anger and jealousy and start acting on life out of love and acceptance. Wow. She says you do that via the seventh step prayer, which is just asking God to take away the bad and add the good in you. She has her own version of the prayer. She asks God to help her be the best she can be. I think that is fucking awesome.

I had a care package from Roman waiting on me when I got home. It was full of pictures of us from his parent's house and from Sabrina's and a lovely letter. He is a *gem*. I am *so* lucky to have such a wonderful man in my life. I can't wait to see him this weekend! I am going to color my hair. I have been wanting a change…the blond just aint cutting it anymore. I have been thinking about this color called Bright Ass Fucking Yellow. I think it would be awesome.

10.14.96

Today is my birthday! I am twenty-six. I have not written in *forever*. I have been so busy working and practicing and hitting meetings when I can and I have even found time to paint. I did this one based on this dream I had. It's me, viewed from the back, and I am facing three doors. One is multicolored, and represents the unknown, one is black and green, the adopted colors of the band, and the other is red, yellow and blue, my representation of an education. In the center of my back is a fourth door, in gold, and I am oblivious to the door inside of myself because I am to busy looking at the doors in front of me. It's not a good painting by any means, but I like it for what it's about and I like that I can let myself paint and it doesn't have to be amazing looking.

I dyed my hair bright ass yellow. It is fucking *awesome*. It is so bright that it hurts to look at it. Roman *loves* it. I also dyed another part of me *purple*! Fiona came by when I was in the middle of this process, and I was wearing Roman's blue flannel housecoat and walking around really funny, so I just confessed what I was up to. She laughed her ass off. She might as well know the crazy ass real me!

Roman and I had an *amazing* time together last week. It literally just gets better and better. I picked him up from the airport and we headed downtown and went on a carriage ride. It was so lovely. When we got to back to my apartment, I had covered the stairs with rose petals that led into the hall and then into the living room and all the way to the bathtub. We lounged in the tub surrounded by candles…listening to the dead people dance…it was *incredible*. Sunday morning we went outside and had our coffee on the front porch as people were walking from their cars to go to church. We wound up *doing it,* standing up on the porch, right as they were walking by. God it was so awesome. He is so fucking wonderful. He cooked me dinner…homemade spaghetti…and it was *so* good. He is coming back up for our Halloween show. His birthday is in November and I already have his gift. It's a cigarette case, beautiful shiny silver, and I had the inside of it engraved. It's a line from a U2 song, which he said is his favorite quote, and the lady at the engraving place said she make an exception on their policy of no profanity when I asked her to put "I *fucking* love you" after the quote. It is *so* bad ass. He is going to *love* it.

10.31.96

Tonight will be fun. The radio station has been promoting the shit out of it. The whole band is dressing up and wearing crazy make up. I'm gonna wear my black wig and put it into pigtails. I'm gonna do my eyes really heavy and black out one tooth. I have this ridiculous old denim overalls/baby doll skirt thing and I sewed a rebel flag onto the front pocket of it, and I am going to put a fake bloody tampon on my dog collar! HA! Tonight I truly *will* be a redneck vampire!

I have this funny feeling it could be my last show. I am going to think about that the whole time I am up there and really try to see if I could walk away from all of it. I just don't know. I feel like sometimes I am on a sinking ship and other times I feel like we are the *shit* and I must be *crazy* to think about leaving. One of the mottos of the clean and sober lifestyle is "to thine own self be true". I think about that a lot. Am I being true to myself by being in this band? By being a musician? I think so. But at the same time, how much of me have I not yet allowed myself to discover because I have been focused on just *one* facet? It's been three long years…the best of my life. This band and all of our experiences have taught me what it means to *be alive*. To *fully live*. To completely, wholly, embrace every moment; not knowing or worrying about what would come after. We have taken life by the reigns and pushed our humanity…blindly…into the unknown. Maybe this is what music is all about-to understand our humanness…and expand its limits. I guess I just think I might want to experience living in some other modality—to push limits in another area. I think about going to college sometimes. No, I think about going to college *a lot of the time*. I hoped to stick this out long enough to at least really record a real album, and go on the road. But when I look at that in another light, we *have* recorded an album, and we *have* toured, just maybe not in the way I thought we *should*. I just don't know if I could really walk away from all of this or not. I don't want to fuck them or myself.

11.5.96

I guess sometimes all things must come to an end. What I didn't expect was for it to feel like a death. I didn't expect to *grieve* so much. I didn't expect to *cry* this hard. I didn't expect any of this. I have thought about quitting every minute since out last show. I just had to get to the place where I knew I would be okay with watching them succeed without me. I had to be able to walk into a new facet of life with no regrets. I think I decided to do this a long time ago; I was just waiting for the right time to actually *do* it. As I sat there today on the couch, thinking about it **again**, I just picked up the phone and I did it. I called Ruger. I told him I was out. I just told him. The words came out of my mouth and listened to myself say them as if I was in another place. I'm know I'm not just walking away from **them**, I'm walking away from *the whole thing*. I don't know why I must be so black and white, but I know if I was going to do this it was going to be with *them* or it was going to be with no one. He was shocked but then he just said "okay" and we got off the phone and I just sat there with it in my hand. It took me a while to hang it up. As I did, I felt a huge weight lift off of me and I saw a door open up and I saw light. Then the tears came. I cried for the teenage girl who wanted this so bad. I cried out of anger that it did not work out the way I wanted it to. I cried for the dream that I was letting die. I cried because I was letting them down. I cried for the knowledge that I was walking away from the biggest and best thing I had ever done. I cried because I feared I was making the biggest mistake of my life by quitting, and for the fear of making the biggest mistake of my life if I didn't.

Natasha and Fern and Carey all just got here. It's like somebody died and they are all coming to help me while I grieve. I am numb all over and I can't cry anymore. I don't feel like I am even in my body. I think I am checking out. I am terrified of the way I feel.

11.6.96

Max just left my apartment. He called me and asked if he could come over. I told him sure. He has never even been here before. He brought the video from the Halloween show with him. He told me he wasn't going to say *anything*, he just wanted me to watch the video all the way through. It was a *bad ass* show, with a bad ass crowd. He and Ruger were *hittin'* that night, as we all were. Yet all I could think about the whole time I watched it was about how many endless nights I spent in the van wondering if I would turn thirty in the back of it...*still* tryin to make it. I thought not about how *great* we are, but how *unorganized* and bratty we can be. How we sell drugs on the road and haul our gear in stolen trailers. How life is a gamble and I don't know if this is the slot machine for me anymore. How if I *kept* pushing I would not go to college, or have any chance to do anything else in life while I was still young.

When it was over, Max quietly turned it off and sat down. He told me he knew how much I enjoyed being the center of attention and that I would miss the hell out of the band. I told him he was right. I didn't know what else to say. It was so awkward. He left with his head kind of down and I just curled up on the couch and cried.

11.11.96

I haven't written in a while. The past few days have been very difficult, but in a strange way, I feel like a weight has been lifted. I did not know I could grieve and feel better at the same time. I bet this is kind of what a divorce is like, except this one is with *four* husbands, and I feel the loss in my heart of each one of them, not to mention the band as a whole. My phone rings…and I kind of brace myself. I am afraid that one of them may have the magic words that will make me change my mind. Natasha, Wren, Fern and Fiona are all real supportive. I haven't heard from *one soul* from the music scene, though. Roman said he'd get the next flight down just to hold me if I wanted him to. I told him no. I wanted to face this one alone. I got myself here, and I wanted to get myself out. I am so grateful I had the chance to have done as much as I did musically, and now I want to take the rest of my youth and see what the rest of the world has to offer. I am thinking about going to college in the spring. I wonder if you can major in *everything*.

11.20.96

Ruger called. They have tried to work in their new guy in time for their show but it's not working out, and he asked me if I would play this *one last gig* with them. I told him I would. I don't want to let them down anymore than I already have.

It's on the 27th. I told him I would practice with them, but he said not to worry about it. I feel so awkward, but I am glad I can help them out. Oh, *god*. I can't imagine getting the fuck back up there.

11.28.96

I am sitting in my apartment…surrounded by my drum kit. They look so strange in here…they look black in the candlelight. I did it. I played that show. I got the fuck up there and played my *heart* out, *knowing* it would be my last time. As my heart beat in synchronicity with my feet, I played for Ruger and for Max and for Jesse and Ian…thinking of how I loved each of them as I watched at them from my drum throne. In the powerful energy of my final moments with them, I made *wishes*…wishes that all their dreams would come true. I played for every moment I had ever spent in front of a stage as a teenager…dreaming to be up there…I played for all the times I thought I could never do it…I played for *Flo*…for the little girl that was scared she wasn't good enough…and for the woman that discovered she *was*.

The author can be contacted through the publishing company or by sending an email to:
diaryofaredneckvampire@yahoo.com

About the Author

Flo received her Bachelors Degree in Fine Art and is currently working on a Masters Degree in Religious Symbolism. She can be found chain smoking in seedy diners in Memphis, Tennessee and frequents Glastonbury, England, where she is pretending to work on her thesis. She still keeps a diary.

0-595-29554-1